Vol. VIII

W9-CIC-689

No. 1

Bible Expositor and Illuminator

Large-Print Edition

WINTER QUARTER   December 2016, January, February 2017

Creation and Salvation

UNIT I: The Saviour Is Born

UNIT II: All Creation Praises God

UNIT III: The Church Is Born

Edited and published quarterly by
THE INCORPORATED TRUSTEES OF THE
GOSPEL WORKER SOCIETY
UNION GOSPEL PRESS DIVISION

Rev. W. B. Musselman, Founder

Price: $5.50 per quarter*
$22.00 per year*
*shipping and handling extra

ISBN 978-1-59843-437-8

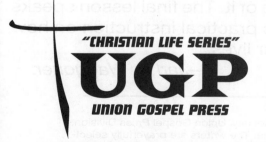

"CHRISTIAN LIFE SERIES"
UGP
UNION GOSPEL PRESS

Lessons based on International Sunday School Lessons; the International Bible Lessons for Christian Teaching
© 2013 by the Committee on the Uniform Series and used with permission. Edited and published quarterly by The
ed Trustees of the Gospel Worker Society, Union Gospel Press Division, 2000 Brookpark Road, Cleveland, Oh;
Mailing address: P.O. Box 6059, Cleveland, Ohio 44101-1059. www.uniongospelpress.com

LOOKING AHEAD

Our lessons this quarter touch on the broad and crucial themes of creation and salvation. Salvation, as Scripture tells us, is found in Christ alone (cf. Acts 4:12). The historical account of His arrival in this world is most fully presented in Luke's Gospel.

Lesson 1 tells us of the angelic announcement to Mary that she would bear the Messiah. The Lord chose a humble young woman from an insignificant village to fulfill His plan for Christ's birth. The second lesson relates Mary's visit with her older relative Elisabeth and the divine testimony both women gave to the promised Saviour carried in Mary's womb.

Lesson 3 backtracks a bit to give us some background on how Elisabeth's husband received a message from the Angel Gabriel that they would be the parents of John, the forerunner of Christ. The fourth lesson takes us to the familiar passage in Luke 2, which describes the birth of Jesus and the witnesses God provided to that event.

The second unit of lessons takes us to the Psalms and focuses on the Creator and the creation. Psalm 33 invites us to praise the Creator for His glorious attributes and His mighty work of Creation. Psalm 96 calls us to praise God for His greatness and glory and even looks forward to Christ's second coming.

Our lesson in Psalm 65 stresses God's provision for all His creation, including us. Psalm 104 reveals God's greatness and wisdom through His creation. Psalm 148 is a beautiful poem that calls on heaven and earth and all that is in them to praise God. Our studies in this unit should enrich our worship as we contemplate the many reasons we have for praising God.

Four lessons in Galatians complete our quarter and give us valuable truths regarding our salvation in Christ. Lesson 10 reminds us that we are children of God by faith alone. Lesson 11 describes the spiritual bondage from which Christ has delivered us and warns against enslaving ourselves again to works rather than resting in God's grace.

In lesson 12 Paul described the freedom we have in Christ, the need to stand strong in that freedom, and the proper use of it. The final lesson speaks of the fruit the Holy Spirit works in us and offers practical instruction on how those character qualities are to be upheld in our lives.

—*Jarl K. Waggoner.*

Israel and the Church

FRANK PASS

The first eleven chapters of Genesis describe four key events: 1. God's creation of a perfect universe in six days, crowned by His creation of man to rule over that universe (chaps. 1—2); 2. man's act of rebellion against God, which plunged the entire creation under the curse of sin (chap. 3); 3. God's judgment on man's continual and increasing wickedness through a worldwide flood that destroyed every living creature except Noah, his family, and the animals on the ark (chaps. 6—9); 4. a second judgment through the confusion of tongues at the Tower of Babel, scattering man over the face of the earth and foiling his plan to make his own name great (chap. 11). It must be noted that events 2, 3, and 4 all include God's judgments on man's rebellion against Him. The enmity between God and man requires redemption.

These four events set the stage for the outworking of God's plan of redemption contained in the rest of Scripture. In Genesis 12 God initiated that plan by choosing Abraham and making a threefold promise: 1. God would multiply Abraham's descendants and make of him a great nation (vs. 2); 2. God would give to Abraham a particular piece of real estate in which that nation would dwell (vs.1); 3. God would bless Abraham and through him bless all the other nations of the earth (vs. 3). God would later confirm this promise to Abraham through a covenant (chap. 15), the first of several covenants that would govern the relationship between God and Abraham's descendants.

God's covenant with Abraham begins to unfold throughout the rest of Scripture. God multiplied Abraham's descendants, and they became the nation of Israel. God redeemed His people from Egyptian bondage and entered into another covenant with them at Mount Sinai (Exod. 20—23). The purpose of this covenant was to set Israel apart from the other nations of the world so that she might be to God "a kingdom of priests, and an holy nation" (19:6). The covenant's overarching requirement was that Israel love the Lord her God— and Him only—with all her heart, soul, and might (Deut. 6:5).

Israel's obedience to the covenant stipulations would bring blessings, while disobedience would bring curses (Deut. 28). The ultimate curse would be loss of residence in the Promised Land (chap. 30).

Israel's history confirms God's faithfulness to His word. Her idolatry and disobedience first divided the covenanted Davidic kingdom (cf. I Kings 11:31-35), then took both Judah and Israel into exile (II Kings 17—18; 24—25). While she was out of her land, God sent prophets to call Israel to repentance and assure her of His love. The prophets declared a future day when Israel would be restored to her land and become the witness nation to the world that God originally intended her to be. They also spoke of a future Davidic king who would rule Israel according to God's righteous requirements.

Jesus Christ came as that King in fulfillment of Old Testament prophecy. Upon proclaiming the nearness of the

(Continued on page 186)

Scripture Lesson Text

LUKE 1:26 And in the sixth month the angel Ga′bri-el was sent from God unto a city of Gal′i-lee, named Naz′a-reth,

27 To a virgin espoused to a man whose name was Jo′seph, of the house of Da′vid; and the virgin's name *was* **Ma′ry.**

28 And the angel came in unto her, and said, Hail, *thou that art* highly favoured, the Lord *is* with thee: blessed *art* thou among women.

29 And when she saw *him,* **she was troubled at his saying, and cast in her mind what manner of salutation this should be.**

30 And the angel said unto her, Fear not, Ma′ry: for thou hast found favour with God.

31 And, behold, thou shalt conceive in thy womb, and bring forth a son, and shalt call his name JE′SUS.

32 He shall be great, and shall be called the Son of the Highest: and the Lord God shall give unto him the throne of his father Da′vid:

33 And he shall reign over the house of Ja′cob for ever; and of his kingdom there shall be no end.

34 Then said Ma′ry unto the angel, How shall this be, seeing I know not a man?

35 And the angel answered and said unto her, The Ho′ly Ghost shall come upon thee, and the power of the Highest shall overshadow thee: therefore also that holy thing which shall be born of thee shall be called the Son of God.

36 And, behold, thy cousin E-lis′-a-beth, she hath also conceived a son in her old age: and this is the sixth month with her, who was called barren.

37 For with God nothing shall be impossible.

38 And Ma′ry said, Behold the handmaid of the Lord; be it unto me according to thy word. And the angel departed from her.

NOTES

The Promise of a Saviour

Lesson: Luke 1:26-38

Read: Luke 1:26-38

TIME: 7 or 6 B.C.   PLACE: Nazareth

GOLDEN TEXT—"Behold, thou shalt conceive in thy womb, and bring forth a son, and shalt call his name JESUS" (Luke 1:31).

Introduction

Even before God created heaven and the earth, His plan of salvation was in place. In eternity past, that plan was established and sure—so much so that in Revelation the Apostle John described Jesus as the "Lamb slain from the foundation of the world" (13:8), and the Apostle Paul could speak of believers being chosen in Christ "before the foundation of the world" (Eph. 1:4).

God's plan to redeem His fallen creatures, however, was worked out in human history, beginning immediately after the sin of Adam and Eve with the promise that One would come to crush the serpent's head (Gen. 3:15). From God's covenant promises to Abraham (12:2-3) to the detailed offerings and sacrifices of the law to the prophecies of God's servants, the Israelite nation looked forward to the Deliverer who would bring to fruition God's plan.

Sadly, when the Promised One arrived, the nation rejected and despised Him. Their hopes of a glorious deliverance from political oppression by a conquering king blinded them to the One who had to first save them from their sins. Perhaps part of that blindness was due also to the humble circumstances of the Saviour's birth.

LESSON OUTLINE

I. AN ANGELIC APPEARANCE—
Luke 1:26-30

II. A DIVINE MESSAGE—
Luke 1:31-37

III. A HUMBLE RESPONSE—
Luke 1:38

Exposition: Verse by Verse

AN ANGELIC APPEARANCE

LUKE 1:26 And in the sixth month the angel Gabriel was sent from God unto a city of Galilee, named Nazareth,

27 To a virgin espoused to a man whose name was Joseph, of the house of David; and the virgin's name was Mary.

28 And the angel came in unto her, and said, Hail, thou that art highly favoured, the Lord is with thee: blessed art thou among women.

29 And when she saw him, she was troubled at his saying, and cast in her mind what manner of salutation this should be.

30 And the angel said unto her, Fear not, Mary: for thou hast found favour with God.

The angel's objective (Luke 1:26-27). Luke's Gospel is addressed to Theophilus, a man who apparently was a Greek and thus a Gentile. Luke's goal was to set forth in orderly detail the facts about the earthly life of Jesus Christ in order to encourage and strengthen the faith of Theophilus and his other readers (vss. 3-4). He began with events leading up to the birth of Christ, specifically the miraculous conception of Elisabeth, who would be the mother of John the Baptist (vss. 5-25).

Mary, the mother of Jesus, is introduced in the sixth month of Elisabeth's pregnancy. At that time an angel was sent from God to Mary's hometown, Nazareth of Galilee (Luke 1:26). The angel was Gabriel, the same angel who had previously appeared to Elisabeth's husband, Zacharias, in Jerusalem, announcing the coming birth of John the Baptist (vss. 13-19). Now, six months later, Gabriel had a similar task in Galilee, about seventy miles to the north.

Nazareth was a small village on a hilltop about eighteen miles west of the southern tip of the Sea of Galilee. The town apparently was of little significance, as it is not mentioned in the Old Testament. Furthermore, Nathanael's comment in John 1:46 suggests Nazareth did not have a good reputation.

God, however, had chosen a special person in that village, and He had an important message for her—one important enough to be delivered by an angel. That person was Mary, a virgin, who was "espoused to a man whose name was Joseph" (Luke 1:27).

Espousal is somewhat akin to our engagement, but it was much more binding. It was a formal marital agreement that continued for about a year before the official marriage took place. However, "the parties during this [espousal] period were considered husband and wife" (Stein, *Luke,* B&H).

Joseph and Mary clearly had not yet "[come] together" (Matt. 1:18), and Mary was still a virgin. Joseph was a descendant of David (Luke 1:27), but he was a common man who would pass on to Jesus the carpenter's trade (cf. Matt. 13:55). Mary, who was probably still a teenager at this point, apparently did not enjoy great status, either (cf. Luke 1:48), and we know from the couple's later offerings in the temple that they were poor (Luke 2:24; cf. Lev. 12:6-8).

The angel's greeting (Luke 1:28-29). Gabriel's appearance to Mary was accompanied by comforting and reassuring words. He declared her "highly favoured," or graced by God, indicating that she was the special object of God's grace and that the Lord was with her. While Mary is consistently presented in Scripture as a godly young woman, the Lord's special presence with her was an act of grace.

Mary's immediate response was not fear, as we often see in the Bible when people encountered angels (cf. Luke 1:12; 2:9). Gabriel's reassuring words may have allayed any fears she naturally might have had at the angel's appearance, but they also perplexed her. Luke 1:29 says Mary was "troubled at his saying" and wondered about this greeting. "Evidently in her modesty she did not understand why a heavenly visitant should greet her in such exalted terms" (Morris, *Luke,* InterVarsity).

If there was any fear in Mary, it came not from the angel's appearance but from his words. Why would this heavenly messenger come to such a lowly young woman in such an obscure village with such words of blessing?

The angel's encouragement (Luke 1:30). While Mary did not respond verbally, Gabriel saw her uneasiness and told her not to fear. He then reassured her that she had in fact "found favour with God." The emphasis here is again on the Lord's favor, or grace, not on Mary or her righteousness. Knowing she rested in God's grace meant there was nothing about which she needed to be anxious.

We too would do well to heed the words of the angel. If we have experienced God's grace in salvation through faith in Christ, any time we spend worrying about what might or might not be is wasted time. His grace is sufficient for whatever we might experience in this life (cf. II Cor. 12:9).

A DIVINE MESSAGE

31 And, behold, thou shalt conceive in thy womb, and bring forth a son, and shalt call his name JESUS.

32 He shall be great, and shall be called the Son of the Highest: and the Lord God shall give unto him the throne of his father David:

33 And he shall reign over the house of Jacob for ever; and of his kingdom there shall be no end.

34 Then said Mary unto the angel, How shall this be, seeing I know not a man?

35 And the angel answered and said unto her, The Holy Ghost shall come upon thee, and the power of the Highest shall overshadow thee: therefore also that holy thing which shall be born of thee shall be called the Son of God.

36 And, behold, thy cousin Elisabeth, she hath also conceived a son in her old age: and this is the sixth month with her, who was called barren.

37 For with God nothing shall be impossible.

A son promised (Luke 1:31). The grace of God would be especially revealed in Mary's life through the birth of a son. The angel's message was simple and direct: Mary would conceive, she would bear a son, and her son's name was to be Jesus. While it took only seconds for Gabriel to speak the words, they must have taken Mary aback and caused her mind to race with the implications.

That her son was to be named Jesus also must have raised questions. "Jesus" is the Greek equivalent of the Hebrew name Joshua. The name was not unique, but it was uniquely given, and this must have been a hint to Mary of the special nature of her son.

Joseph also was told later that Mary's son was to be named Jesus, which means "the Lord saves," but he was told the significance of the name: "He shall save his people from their sins" (Matt. 1:21). Mary was not told the significance. Perhaps there was too much other information for her to absorb at this time.

The son described (Luke 1:32-33). Gabriel continued without interruption to describe Mary's son. Just as Gabriel had announced that John the Baptist would be "great" (vs. 15), so he also declared that Jesus would be great. Jesus, however, would be far greater than even John. His greatness speaks particularly of His "being and nature" (Stein), which the angel went on to describe.

Gabriel added that Jesus would be called the "Son of the Highest," that is, the Son of God, and that the Lord would give Him the "throne of his father David" (Luke 1:32). As the Son of God, Jesus would be equal with God the Father (cf. John 5:18). This means Jesus is God.

Whether Mary fully grasped the idea of Jesus' deity at that point is not entirely clear, but she surely understood the significance of inheriting the throne of King David and reigning forever over the house of Jacob (Luke 1:32-33). These words could only mean that Gabriel was describing Jesus as Israel's promised Messiah (Christ), or Anointed

One (cf. II Sam. 7:12-17; Ps. 89:20, 29).

The Jewish people of Mary's day knew of Daniel's prophecy (Dan. 9:24-27), and from that prophetic timetable, they knew that the Messiah's coming was near. There was great expectation as they looked forward to the arrival of their Deliverer and His mighty reign (cf. Isa. 9:7).

What the people failed to understand, however, was the spiritual nature of Christ's work. They would first need to accept their Messiah and be delivered from their sins. Only then could they dwell with Him in His unending kingdom. As they would learn, the reign of Christ over David's kingdom awaits His second coming (cf. Rev. 19:11—20:6).

The birth explained (Luke 1:34-35). Mary's first words are interesting. Given the angel's amazing, almost unbelievable, promise, we might have expected words of doubt, as was the case with Zacharias (vss. 18-20). Instead, she fully believed what the angel told her. Still, there was one matter that troubled her. "How shall this be, seeing I know not a man?" (vs. 34), she asked. Gabriel had mentioned neither Joseph nor her impending marriage, and Mary had correctly understood that he was saying that her son would not be conceived by the normal means. She believed the Lord's promise given to her by the angel, but she could not see how this possibly could be.

The Angel Gabriel did not offer a biological explanation; indeed, there was no natural explanation for a supernatural miracle. He simply said that the Holy Spirit would come upon her and she would be overshadowed by the power of God. This was, in fact, the only explanation for what Mary would soon experience. Although a virgin, she would conceive through a mysterious, divine work, ensuring that the child she conceived would be the holy Son of God.

We usually refer to the miraculous virgin birth of Jesus. Aside from the surrounding circumstances, however, Jesus' physical birth was quite natural and no doubt followed the course of childbirth with which we are familiar. It was the virgin *conception* that was the real miracle and for which there is no natural explanation.

Scripture clearly sets forth the virgin conception and birth of Jesus Christ. The great prophecy of Isaiah 7:14 looks forward to it, and the united testimony of the Gospel writers declares its fulfillment. Mary was Jesus' mother, but God, not Joseph or any other human man, was the true father of Jesus. This truth is foundational and necessary to the Christian faith.

While we cannot explain the mechanics of the conception of Christ beyond acknowledging that it was a supernatural work, we can understand the necessity of it. A human mother guaranteed that Jesus was fully human. Yet as the Son of God, He remained also fully God. This divine work in Mary's womb also, in some way, preserved Jesus from inheriting the sinful human nature. "If he were born of two human parents, it is very difficult to conceive how he could have been exempt from the guilt of Adam's sin" (Elwell, ed., *Evangelical Dictionary of Theology,* Baker). These important doctrinal truths, while perhaps not fully explained by the virgin conception of Jesus, certainly require it.

The promise confirmed (Luke 1:36-37). The Angel Gabriel did not simply tell Mary that she would conceive supernaturally; he also gave her confirmation of the work God would do. This was a gracious gift to Mary. She did not express any doubts about God's plan, though she may still have been perplexed by the details. However, the Lord gave her a sign that would be a source of encouragement to her in the days ahead. That sign was that her "cousin Elisabeth" had "conceived a son in her old age."

In accord with the angelic message to her husband, Zacharias (Luke 1:13), Elisabeth had conceived, despite her old age and years of barrenness (vs. 7). While the word translated "cousin" (vs. 36) can simply mean "relative," it is clear that Mary knew her, however distant a relation she may have been. But with Elisabeth in seclusion for five months (vs. 24) and living a considerable distance away in the hill country of Judea (vs. 39), Mary knew nothing about her pregnancy. This exciting news that God had worked miraculously in her relative's life would confirm to Mary the angel's message to her, for it proved that "with God nothing shall be impossible" (vs. 37).

Mary clearly was a woman of great faith. However, as a human being, she was, like all of us, quite capable of becoming discouraged and falling prey to doubt. God's work in Elisabeth's life would be a source of encouragement to remind Mary that He can do anything and that He is faithful to His promises.

God's Word has many wonderful promises for us. We need to review them often to remind ourselves that He loves us, that He hears our prayers, that He is present with us, and that He will never forsake us. His promises are often repeated because we are weak and we need reassurance. He also graciously gives us examples of people like ourselves who lived by faith in spite of great hardships.

A HUMBLE RESPONSE

38 And Mary said, Behold the handmaid of the Lord; be it unto me according to thy word. And the angel departed from her.

Mary asked only one question of the angel, and it concerned how God was going to accomplish what He promised (Luke 1:34). The only other words she spoke were words of humble submission to God's will. She called herself the Lord's "handmaid" (vs. 38), or slave girl, a term that "expresses complete obedience" (Morris). She gladly submitted to God's plan, asking that everything be done according to the angel's word.

The divine plan of salvation required a young woman who was willing to submit to God's will despite the hardships it would entail and despite the inability to fully understand everything God had in store. Mary did not know everything, but she did know God, and she knew He was worthy of her trust and complete commitment.

Do we know God in such a way that we will trust Him even when we do not understand what He is doing or where He is leading us? He is a gracious God who is worthy of our complete faith.
—Jarl K. Waggoner.

QUESTIONS

1. At what particular time was the Angel Gabriel sent to Mary?
2. What indicates the lowly status of both Nazareth and Mary?
3. What was Mary's relationship to Joseph at this time?
4. How did the angel greet Mary, and how did she respond? Why did she respond this way?
5. Was Mary's godly character the key to God's choosing her? Explain.
6. What is meant by the title "Son of the Highest" (Luke 1:32)?
7. What in Gabriel's message proved to Mary that her son would be the Messiah?
8. What were Mary's first words in response to the angel's announcement? What was her concern?
9. Why is the virginal conception of Jesus necessary doctrinally?
10. What news did the angel give Mary to confirm the promise?
—Jarl K. Waggoner.

Preparing to Teach the Lesson

Prophecy and its fulfillment are God's hallmark of authenticity. The promises of the coming Saviour are some of the most striking examples of this. God makes prophecies come to pass because He is in control. His plans are set, and He has the power to make events happen, no matter how impossible it seems from our viewpoint. In teaching this lesson, make a strong point that God never fails to keep His promises. He has promised to save us by His grace apart from our works. We can rely on His promises.

TODAY'S AIM

Facts: to see that God makes and fulfills His promises and to realize how completely trustworthy they are.

Principle: to trust every word from God even when we do not understand how or when it will be fulfilled.

Application: to rest confidently in God's promises as the basis of our security in life.

INTRODUCING THE LESSON

We are constantly beset by people who say, "Trust me!" This can include everyone from used-car salesmen to our national leaders. (Be sure to modify this if you have a used-car salesman in your class!) Even well-meaning people who make promises to us are often unable to carry them through. Times change, people change, and the circumstances of life make it nearly impossible to say what will happen next.

When Isaiah prophesied about seven hundred years before the birth of Jesus that a virgin would conceive, give birth to a son, and call Him Immanuel, it may well be that no one believed it at that time. Those who read the prophecy over the intervening seven hundred years may have doubted it

would happen or questioned how it could possibly be done. Only God could make all three of these elements of prophecy happen at the same time.

DEVELOPING THE LESSON

1. God's promise to Mary through the Angel Gabriel (Luke 1:26-33). We are so used to this story that we may fail to see the wonder and impossibility of the promise to Mary. Still a virgin, she was engaged to Joseph and could not conceive without a man and losing her virginity. Furthermore, in ancient times, one could not know what the sex of the unborn child would be, so there was only a fifty-fifty chance of having a boy.

The angel said that the child would be called the "Son of the Highest (Luke 1:32)." The religious Jews were fiercely monotheistic. In their culture the son of anyone was viewed as being virtually the same as his father. So this could only mean that the child would be God come in the flesh. Since He was to reign over the house of David forever, He would be eternal. He would not die as humans do.

2. Mary's response to God's promise (Luke 1:34). The enormity and eternal implications of this complex promise of the coming Saviour would bowl over the staunchest of hearts. However, Mary asked only about how she could conceive, since without that, the whole promise could not be fulfilled. This was not a question of unbelief but rather a desire to understand and get the answers she needed for the situation. We can learn from this the principle that if God promises something, He already has the plan and power in place to bring it to fulfillment.

3. God's statement of how this promise was to be fulfilled (Luke 1:35-37). The angel's answer was not a simple "God will do it." The following details were given to Mary: the Holy Spirit would come upon her and the power of the Highest would overshadow her. This would bring about God's unique plan of sending His only begotten Son into the world, the Saviour of mankind. "Therefore also that holy thing which shall be born of thee shall be called the Son of God." This miraculous event had been foretold by the Prophet Isaiah (Isa. 7:14).

Actually, the answer given to Mary is as overwhelming as the miracle of the promise itself. We have no idea how any of this could have been done. The Scripture does not give any more details how or when this happened. We only know that Mary became pregnant with the Lord Jesus. We never need to know how God is going to do anything. God may not explain to us how He will fulfill His promises. How He saves us and cleanses us from sin will forever be a mystery to us. We do not have the capacity to understand this mystery.

4. Mary's faithful answer (Luke 1:38). Mary's faith is seen in this verse. She was obviously satisfied with the angel's answer and was perfectly willing to be used in God's plan.

ILLUSTRATING THE LESSON

We can trust God's promises as accomplished fact.

ALL THINGS ARE POSSIBLE

GOD'S PROMISE

MARY'S FAITH

MANKIND'S BLESSING

CONCLUDING THE LESSON

God is under no obligation to tell us what will happen in the future. He does not have to make us any personal promises; however, He has given us many great and precious promises in His Word. We can rely on them in the face of events and threats that may seem to contradict the very promises of God.

We can look at missions as an example. Missionaries have undoubtedly relied on God's protective presence with them in hostile situations, only to suffer martyrdom at the hands of those they are sent to serve. Does this mean that God has failed to keep His promise that He would be with them and protect them as they carried out His Great Commission? Not at all!

First of all, missionaries are protected eternally. They have gone to heaven, which is far better than being in this world. Also, we have often heard that the lives, and even deaths, of missionaries have been the very catalyst that brought whole people groups to faith in Christ. What looks like a tragedy to us may be God at work fulfilling His greater purposes.

Remind your students that we have neither the authority nor the power to hold God to His promises. (People usually do this to try to get God to handle their personal situations in ways of their own choosing.) We need not "remind" God of His promises. We need to remind ourselves of His promises, and there is no better way to do that than to study His Word. We have no idea how God plans to carry out His promises!

ANTICIPATING THE NEXT LESSON

In our next lesson, we will look at Mary's song of praise to God and discover applications for our lives.

—Brian D. Doud.

PRACTICAL POINTS

1. God does not burden us with unmanageable tasks (Luke 1:26-27; cf. I Cor. 10:13).
2. Understand that you are part of God's royal family (Luke 1:28).
3. Trust a true word from God (Luke 1:29; Heb. 4:12).
4. As children of an esteemed and exalted Parent, we are privileged (Luke 1:30-33; cf. John 1:12).
5. Respect the order and timing of God (Luke 1:34).
6. The Holy Spirit's power makes Christians overcomers (vs. 35).
7. Obedience resurrects dreams (vss. 36-38).

—Lendell Sims.

RESEARCH AND DISCUSSION

1. Why is it sometimes easier to accept words from people rather than the promises of God? How can we strengthen our relationship with God and increase our confidence in Him (Luke 1:29; cf. Matt. 8:8; Col. 1:10)?
2. Why is it important for us to understand and accept that Jesus came as the Second Adam (Luke 1:31; cf. I Cor. 15:45)?
3. Many generations passed after God promised to send David's heir. What should believers do while waiting for God to fulfill His promises (cf. Isa. 9:6-7; Rom. 15:8; Heb. 6:12)?
4. Why is it hard for us to keep our promises?
5. What was Mary's reaction to the angel's announcement?

—Lendell Sims.

ILLUSTRATED HIGH POINTS

What manner of salutation

In contrast to the angel's lavish declarations of God's favor toward Mary, a more typical biblical salutation consisted of humbly asking God to bestow His favor (cf. Num. 6:25). Unaccustomed to being noticed, it is no wonder that Mary felt fearful at being showered with such seemingly immodest accolades.

Mira is a star that has been studied by astronomers for four hundred years. Yet only recently has NASA discovered that it has an exceptionally long, comet-like tail. This came to light (literally) when, for the first time, a space telescope scanned it with ultraviolet light, thus revealing its previously unnoticed splendor.

God sees us in a different light than people do. Like Mary, may we all leave a legacy of light.

How shall this be?

As Nicodemus was mystified by rebirth, Mary struggled to understand the concept of incarnation. Although the mysteries of God are beyond our natural understanding, we can learn much by observing our physical world (cf. Job 12:8; Rom. 1:20).

Einstein's theory of special relativity, $E = mc^2$, states that "every mass has an energy equivalent and vice versa" (www.wikipedia.com). In other words, they are different expressions of the same essence.

Scripture teaches that in His preincarnate form Jesus was a noncorporeal person called the Word. As the Word, Jesus was the creative force that brought all things into existence (cf. John 1:1-3).

Miraculously, when the Holy Spirit came upon Mary, the Word was placed into a tiny human embryo who was small yet every bit equivalent to His earlier form. The formula is: the Word = the Man, Jesus!

—Therese Greenberg.

Golden Text Illuminated

"Behold, thou shalt conceive in thy womb, and bring forth a son, and shalt call his name JESUS" (Luke 1:31).

In biblical times the name given to a child was very important. Names were often laden with significance. Today's parents are likely to name a child based on personal preference, sometimes just because they find it superficially appealing. There may be some family meaning perhaps, or some other intended significance, but the import does not run as deep.

In Bible days the name spoke of character and sometimes even had prophetic significance. This was certainly the case when the Lord Jesus was given His name—a name that, as the song says, is the "sweetest name on earth" ("Oh, How I Love Jesus," Whitfield). This week's golden text brings this home to us.

In the prophecy of the visiting angel, the promise of the birth of the long-expected Saviour came to Mary. The context here is both miraculous and amazing. It is hard to fathom the profundity of the virgin birth of our Lord. There were astonishing prophecies made in conjunction with the Lord's birth, an example of which is Luke 1:32-33. Christ's greatness, uniqueness, deity, sovereignty, and Lordship are all conveyed. Clearly no other such person has ever been or ever will be born.

The glory of the Lord Jesus is seen in the name He was given, which is at the heart of this week's text. Interestingly, His parents did not choose the name; rather, the Angel Gabriel announced what it would be. It most certainly came from God Himself. Mary learned from the angel that she would conceive and bring forth a son, but she did not get to pick His name.

The name of the Messiah had its roots in the Old Testament. The original Hebrew term is a term that refers to God being deliverance or salvation. The term is used often in the Old Testament. The Lord Jesus' name announces that He brings the promise of salvation to mankind. Jesus was meant to be a deliverer, a rescuer, a savior. That is why He was given this name. Every man, woman, boy, and girl across the earth must turn to this one Saviour in order to receive the gift of eternal life.

We should realize that the Lord's name in the Hebrew language was the name Joshua. It was a common name at the time of the Lord's birth. But in the New Testament, the Lord is always distinguished from any other Joshua. He is Jesus, the unique and only Son of God, the Saviour of the world.

We see Jesus' name in Scripture associated with titles like Christ and Messiah. He was the Lord Jesus, the Anointed One prophesied for centuries. He is the only hope of the world.

It is important to remember that the deliverance the Lord Jesus brings is primarily a spiritual deliverance. Matthew 1:21 makes clear that the Lord came so that sinners could be forgiven before God. Christmas is about Jesus. Jesus provides the forgiveness of sins. The peace, love, joy, and hope of Christmas are found in Him, the unique and only Son of God. He is the one who saves us.

—*Jeff VanGoethem.*

Heart of the Lesson

The word "promise" is defined as "a statement telling someone that you will definitely do something or that something will definitely happen in the future" (www.merriam-webster.com). Nothing warms the heart like a promise fulfilled. Too often we are surprised when people keep their promises to us; however, we should be expectant when God makes a promise to us. We never have to fear that He will go back on His word, for His words are true.

1. An unlikely visitor (Luke 1:26-28). We often base the validity of a promise on the character or authority of the one who made it or the relationship we have with that person. For instance, if we had faithful parents, we could trust them when they made a promise to us. If our boss makes a promise to us, we expect him or her to fulfill the promise based upon the authority of his or her position in the company.

The Angel Gabriel did not just randomly visit Mary. The Bible tells us that he was sent by God. While we are always surrounded by angels, they do not make a habit of revealing themselves to humans unless our Heavenly Father advises them to do so. Therefore, it is imperative for us to understand that Gabriel was sent by God to give Mary not just a message but a promise.

2. The promise (Luke 1:29-33). What was the promise that Mary received from the angel? The promise was twofold. First, Mary had found favor with God. The dictionary defines the word "favor" as "friendly regard shown toward another especially by a superior." Because God approved of Mary, she was given this second and much more important promise: "Thou shalt conceive in thy womb, and bring forth a son, and shalt call his name JESUS."

And there was more! Mary was not going to give birth to an ordinary child. No, this child was destined to be great. He would be King, sit on David's throne, and His kingdom would have no end.

3. The promise confirmed (Luke 1:34-38). A promise is communicated either through the spoken word or the written word; however, how the promise comes to pass is often more involved. Mary was perplexed. She asked the angel, "How shall this be, seeing I know not a man?" Gabriel told her that the Holy Spirit would come upon her and God's power would overshadow her.

Mary must have been overwhelmed. At some point perhaps she wanted to pinch herself to make sure she was truly experiencing this angelic visitation.

God is gracious. He always knows how much we can handle and how much we are mentally capable of processing. God always confirms His promises; He did so with Mary. God, through Gabriel, told Mary a secret that she could not have known other than by Him. Her relative Elisabeth was six months' pregnant even though she was thought to be barren! The knowledge of Elisabeth's pregnancy would prove to Mary that the words she heard were true. The angel said, "For with God nothing shall be impossible" (Luke 1:37).

God gave Mary the promise of a son who would be the Saviour of the world. The birth of Jesus Christ shows that God kept His promise. God still makes promises. His Word is full of them. What is even more exciting is that God still keeps His promises.

—Kristin Reeg.

World Missions

God takes promises seriously. Every promise He has ever made is true and indisputable (II Cor. 1:20). In God's eyes, we do better to make no vows at all than to make one and break it. The integrity of God is so stellar that we can stake our eternal lives on the flawless accuracy of His message. A young virgin named Mary recognized the veracity of God's word that came to her through the Angel Gabriel. She embraced its truth immediately and received the greatest blessing anyone could receive.

At nineteen years old, Jeremiah believed an inner message that God wanted to use him to bless the people of Haiti. He had visited the island annually on church mission trips from age fourteen and had participated in feeding and teaching the children there. He watched as the church he attended built a school and an orphanage in a particular village. By age nineteen, Jeremiah knew what God had called him to do. His desire was to raise enough money to pay the bills of every patient on the pediatric floor of a hospital the group regularly visited.

Starting with his church, Jeremiah began to solicit funding and volunteers to join him. His group went to family, friends, classmates, coworkers, businesses, foundations, and public agencies seeking finances to help Jeremiah's dream materialize.

Jeremiah made a promise to his group that he would not stop until he had the money to pay the bills for the entire floor of the Haitian hospital. It appeared to be a nearly impossible task, especially for this small team of teenagers and financially struggling young adults. But Jeremiah persevered, serving as an example and encourager for the others. He knew he had received the promise of God that he could do all things through Christ. The effort, which was initiated in the early spring, concluded that same autumn. Jeremiah indeed reached his goal of $9,000 to take to Haiti. He was able to pay every medical bill on the entire pediatric floor of the hospital!

Both the Virgin Mary and Jeremiah believed these words from God: "For with God nothing shall be impossible" (Luke 1:37). Though young, both teenagers understood the integrity of God and committed their futures to the truth of His words. By acting on the promise of God, Jeremiah succeeded in completing a grand missionary effort. Mary believed and gave birth to Jesus, the greatest missionary, who would change the eternal destiny of all mankind.

Thank God for His promises. Thank God for our Saviour, Jesus Christ. Thank God for sending His missionaries throughout the world with the gospel. It takes compassion, sacrifice, and great love to go beyond the perimeter of our own areas of comfort to take the love of Jesus to others. Our Saviour left heaven to come to earth to save us. Mary abandoned merely human thinking and safety to embrace the plan of God for her life. Jeremiah forsook the comforts of home to help suffering, needy people in Haiti.

Not all of us may travel far or experience extreme, hazardous conditions, but we each have promises from God. He vows to help us fulfill His plans for our lives. God's plans may at times seem difficult, challenging, or even unreasonable. But as we carry out our assigned missions, we can remember that all things are possible with God.

—*Beverly Medley Jones.*

The Jewish Aspect

Luke was the right man to cover today's theme, "The Promise of a Saviour," which focuses on the conception of the Messiah Jesus. During Paul's two-year confinement in prison in Caesarea (Acts 24:27), Luke probably treated his number-one patient. This allowed plenty of time for him to interview eyewitnesses to the essential details of the birth of the Lord Jesus (cf. Luke 1:1-3).

Luke related the visit of the Angel Gabriel with an amazing message for a young virgin of Nazareth named Mary. She was a descendant of King David, the royal household to which the Messiah must be born (cf. Luke 3:23-31). Mary was espoused to a man named Joseph. Joseph also was of the house and lineage of David (1:27; 2:4).

The fact that the couple was espoused (Luke 1:27) places us in the heart of Jewish teaching on marriage. Marriages were family affairs, and the uniting of two people required an engagement contract that was as binding as marriage itself. The document, *erusin,* spelled out the biblically based promises that the young couple were bound to until the *ketubah,* the final marriage contract (Jacobs, *The Jewish Religion,* Oxford University Press).

An important element in Gabriel's explanation of God's plan to Mary is the mention that Elisabeth, her relative, had "also conceived a son in her old age," though she had been "called barren" (Luke 1:36). An earlier note in this chapter states that Elisabeth and her husband, Zacharias, "had no child," and "both were now well stricken in years" (vs. 7). We are to understand that the conception of John the Baptist, Elisabeth's only son, was a miracle of God.

God's governance over childbirth is emphasized throughout the Old Testament. This may have been because childbirth would be the avenue by which salvation would come to man (Gen. 3:15-16).

Hannah is a clear illustration of God's sovereignty over human procreation (I Sam. 1:2). Elkanah had two wives. One was very fertile, producing sons and daughters. The other, Hannah, had no children. Twice we are told that God had closed her womb (vss. 5-6). No reason is given for God's sovereign act, but it clearly was not the right time for the birth of Hannah's son, Samuel, who would play a commanding role in the transition to a monarchy in Israel.

There are other examples of the Lord "closing the womb." Abraham passed off his wife Sarah as his sister to the people of Gerar, for he feared the people might kill him in order to take her. God intervened, and for a period of time, every womb in the king's family was closed by God (Gen. 20:18).

Jacob worked to obtain a wife and received two. Leah was a good wife and had many children. However, her sister Rachel was Jacob's great love. Rachel was barren for some time until God "opened her womb" (Gen. 30:22).

Michal, Saul's daughter and David's wife, saw her husband leading the procession to restore the ark of the covenant to Jerusalem. David was "dancing before the Lord" (II Sam. 6:16). Later, Michal upbraided David for his disgraceful performance before the women of the city, and God rendered her barren for life (vs. 23).

Luke beautifully relates the planned conception of Mary with the words "Therefore also that holy thing which shall be born of thee shall be called the Son of God" (Luke 1:35).

This is a good time to reflect on how Christ came into the world as Saviour.

—Lyle P. Murphy.

Guiding the Superintendent

In 1848, James W. Marshall discovered large quantities of gold at Sutter's Mill in Coloma, California. The news of this discovery traveled throughout the United States and the world. It encouraged people across the world to leave their homes. They came to California with the hopes of becoming wealthy. Unfortunately, only a few people became wealthy, while many others became impoverished. The promise of wealth did not come true. No doubt many people were disappointed at the outcome.

In this week's lesson, we learn about God's promise of a Saviour to lost humanity.

DEVOTIONAL OUTLINE

1. Gabriel's appearance (Luke 1:26-28). Mary's relative Elisabeth was six months pregnant with John the Baptist (Luke 1:24). The Lord commissioned the Angel Gabriel to go to Nazareth.

Gabriel's assignment was to visit Mary. Mary was a young virgin who was espoused to Joseph. This meant Mary and Joseph were engaged to be married. Joseph's ancestors could be traced back to David. Gabriel appeared to Mary and greeted her with a salutation. Gabriel indicated that the Lord was with her and that she was highly blessed among women. She met with God's favor.

2. Gabriel's announcement (Luke 1:29-33). Gabriel's appearance startled Mary. She was perplexed by his salutation. Gabriel reported that Mary was greatly blessed. Indeed, Mary had found favor with God; God was pleased with her life. Gabriel conveyed to Mary that God had given her a distinct honor—she would be the mother of the Messiah!

Gabriel indicated to her the significance of the Messiah's birth. He would be referred to as the "Son of the Highest" (Luke 1:32). Gabriel told Mary of this Son's future supremacy. God would give David's throne to Him. He would reign over Jacob's house. This meant that He would rule over Israel. His kingdom would be perpetual.

3. Gabriel's assurance (Luke 1:34-38). Mary was a virgin. Without sexual relations, she wondered how pregnancy could occur. Therefore, she questioned Gabriel about his comments.

Gabriel assured Mary that the pregnancy would occur. It would not be a normal one. The Holy Spirit would take control, and God would perform the miraculous. Although naturally impossible, God demonstrated His supernatural power. He would do something beyond explanation or reason. Upon hearing Gabriel's assurance, Mary stated her willingness to be the vessel to bring Jesus into the world, and then Gabriel left Mary.

AGE-GROUP EMPHASES

Children: It is never too early to expose children to God's promises. They need to know that their Heavenly Father cares about them. Help your children understand that God's promises are indicators of His love and purpose for them.

Youths: This lesson directs young people toward a holy lifestyle. Help them understand that Jesus' birth occurred through someone young like them. Help them see that God may bless young believers with lives of great purpose. They will then experience in a richer way the promises and rewards that result from holy living.

Adults: Due to challenging situations, adults sometimes forget or even doubt God's promises. Remind them that they should always maintain hope. God's promises are always yea and amen (II Cor. 1:20).

—Tyrone Keith Carroll, Sr.

Scripture Lesson Text

LUKE 1:39 And Ma'ry arose in those days, and went into the hill country with haste, into a city of Ju'da;

40 And entered into the house of Zach-a-ri'as, and saluted E-lis'a-beth.

41 And it came to pass, that, when E-lis'a-beth heard the salutation of Ma'ry, the babe leaped in her womb; and E-lis'a-beth was filled with the Ho'ly Ghost:

42 And she spake out with a loud voice, and said, Blessed *art* thou among women, and blessed *is* the fruit of thy womb.

43 And whence *is* this to me, that the mother of my Lord should come to me?

44 For, lo, as soon as the voice of thy salutation sounded in mine ears, the babe leaped in my womb for joy.

45 And blessed *is* she that believed: for there shall be a performance of those things which were told her from the Lord.

46 And Ma'ry said, My soul doth magnify the Lord,

47 And my spirit hath rejoiced in God my Saviour.

48 For he hath regarded the low estate of his handmaiden: for, behold, from henceforth all generations shall call me blessed.

49 For he that is mighty hath done to me great things; and holy *is* his name.

50 And his mercy *is* on them that fear him from generation to generation.

51 He hath shewed strength with his arm; he hath scattered the proud in the imagination of their hearts.

52 He hath put down the mighty from *their* seats, and exalted them of low degree.

53 He hath filled the hungry with good things; and the rich he hath sent empty away.

54 He hath holpen his servant Is'ra-el, in remembrance of *his* mercy;

55 As he spake to our fathers, to A'bra-ham, and to his seed for ever.

56 And Ma'ry abode with her about three months, and returned to her own house.

NOTES

The Promise Affirmed

Lesson: Luke 1:39-56

Read: Luke 1:39-56

TIME: 7 or 6 B.C.　　　　　　　　　　　　　　　PLACE: hill country of Judea

GOLDEN TEXT—"Mary said, My soul doth magnify the Lord, and my spirit hath rejoiced in God my Saviour" (Luke 1:46-47).

Introduction

Mary, the mother of Jesus, was a remarkable woman. Like all human beings, Mary was a sinner, and God's choice of her to bear His Son was an act of divine grace. However, the young woman God chose for this crucial role in the eternal plan of salvation possessed great faith, and she humbly and faithfully followed the Lord.

This is all the more impressive when we realize two things. First, Mary was probably a mere teenager when the Angel Gabriel visited her and told her she would bear Jesus, the Messiah.

Second, Mary undoubtedly was well aware of societal expectations. To become pregnant during the betrothal period was sinful, shameful, and unacceptable. It was grounds for ending the marriage agreement (cf. Matt. 1:18-19).

The shame and accompanying ridicule would follow her. Moreover, to publicly claim (she never did) that she had conceived by the Holy Spirit would have marked her as mad, if not blasphemous.

Mary surely knew what she would likely face in the years ahead, but she was more concerned about pleasing God than appeasing people. Mary was a remarkable woman because she knew and followed a remarkable God.

LESSON OUTLINE

I. **MARY'S VISIT**—Luke 1:39-40

II. **ELISABETH'S BLESSING**—Luke 1:41-45

III. **MARY'S PRAISE**—Luke 1:46-55

IV. **MARY'S RETURN**—Luke 1:56

Exposition: Verse by Verse

MARY'S VISIT

LUKE 1:39 And Mary arose in those days, and went into the hill country with haste, into a city of Juda;

40 And entered into the house of Zacharias, and saluted Elisabeth.

Mary responded to the divine message delivered by the Angel Gabriel by fully submitting to God's plan for her

(Luke 1:38). We are not told exactly when the divine overshadowing and conception took place, but apparently it immediately followed her words, "Be it unto me according to thy word" or soon thereafter.

After the departure of the angel, Mary hurried off "into the hill country . . . into a city of Juda" (Luke 1:39). "Juda" refers to Judea, the Roman province to the south, which included Jerusalem and the hill country surrounding it. The specific village is not named, but it was the home of Zacharias and Elisabeth.

As a confirming sign of God's promise to her, Gabriel had told Mary about Elisabeth's pregnancy (Luke 1:36-37). Whether or not Mary took this as an implied command to visit her relative Elisabeth, she seemed anxious to do so. Not only would it be an encouragement to her, but the news she would bring Elisabeth would encourage her older relative as well. There is no suggestion in the Bible that Mary left her hometown to hide her pregnancy.

When Mary arrived at the home, she greeted Elisabeth, who no doubt was overjoyed to see her.

ELISABETH'S BLESSING

41 And it came to pass, that, when Elisabeth heard the salutation of Mary, the babe leaped in her womb; and Elisabeth was filled with the Holy Ghost:

42 And she spake out with a loud voice, and said, Blessed art thou among women, and blessed is the fruit of thy womb.

43 And whence is this to me, that the mother of my Lord should come to me?

44 For, lo, as soon as the voice of thy salutation sounded in mine ears, the babe leaped in my womb for joy.

45 And blessed is she that believed: for there shall be a performance of those things which were told her from the Lord.

For Mary and her son (Luke 1:41-42). Mary's arrival at the home of Elisabeth was not just a reunion of the two relatives. It also represented the first meeting between Jesus and John the Baptist. "At this point the two miraculously conceived children encounter each other" (Stein, *Luke,* B&H).

It was the presence of the two children still in the womb that brought about Elisabeth's words of blessing. Upon hearing Mary's voice, the child within Elisabeth jumped, and Elisabeth was filled with the Holy Spirit. Mary had not yet said anything about her encounter with the angel, but Elisabeth's filling with the Holy Spirit, and the movement of her child, communicated to her that the Messiah was present.

The filling of the Spirit and His communication to Elisabeth explains why she was able to speak with understanding about Mary and her son without any prior knowledge of Mary's conception. She proceeded to bless both Mary and her son (Luke 1:42). In declaring Mary blessed "among women," she was saying that Mary was blessed by God beyond any other woman. The child she carried also was blessed. Following an Old Testament pattern, the first blessing (of Mary) "stands logically in subordination to the second. Mary's blessedness was based on the blessedness of the child she would bear" (Stein).

For Mary's presence (Luke 1:43-44). Under the influence of the Holy Spirit, Elisabeth also recognized how honored she was to be visited by the mother of her Lord. While the term "Lord" often refers to God, and Jesus was certainly God, Elisabeth was probably expressing her recognition here that Mary's child was the Messiah.

This was a joyous affirmation to Mary, who still had not spoken a word beyond her greeting. The promise of God was affirmed by one who herself had experienced God's gracious and miraculous work in her life.

Elisabeth went on to explain that when she heard Mary's voice, the child inside her (John the Baptist) had leaped for joy. The movement inside Elisabeth somehow conveyed her child's joy at the presence of Mary's child and revealed to Elisabeth His identity.

For Mary's faith (Luke 1:45). Elisabeth's affirmation, "Blessed is she that believed," employs a different Greek word for "blessed" from the one used twice in verse 42. There is no significant difference, though here she seems to be emphasizing the happiness Mary experienced because of her faith in God that He would indeed bring about what He had promised.

Elisabeth's words are important. They not only encouraged Mary, but they also offered unsolicited testimony that the Messiah's birth was imminent and that He would be born to a virgin girl.

MARY'S PRAISE

46 And Mary said, My soul doth magnify the Lord,

47 And my spirit hath rejoiced in God my Saviour.

48 For he hath regarded the low estate of his handmaiden: for, behold, from henceforth all generations shall call me blessed.

49 For he that is mighty hath done to me great things; and holy is his name.

50 And his mercy is on them that fear him from generation to generation.

51 He hath shewed strength with his arm; he hath scattered the proud in the imagination of their hearts.

52 He hath put down the mighty from their seats, and exalted them of low degree.

53 He hath filled the hungry with good things; and the rich he hath sent empty away.

54 He hath holpen his servant Israel, in remembrance of his mercy;

55 As he spake to our fathers, to Abraham, and to his seed for ever.

For her Saviour (Luke 1:46-47). Mary's wonderful words of praise in verses 46-55 form what has come to be called the Magnificat, after the first word in the Latin translation. Upon hearing Elisabeth's inspired words concerning her son, Mary began to praise God. Her words reveal great depth in biblical understanding. Although she was still very young, she clearly had a thorough knowledge of the Old Testament Scriptures. Indeed, her words reflect the form of Old Testament poetry and almost wholly quote or allude to the Jewish Scriptures.

She began by exalting the Lord and rejoicing in the Saviour. Luke 1:46-47 are parallel, with verse 47 repeating the thought of the previous verse. Thus, her "soul" and "spirit" speak of her entire inner being. It was with all her being that she magnified, or declared God's greatness, and rejoiced in "God [her] Saviour." "Lord" in verse 46 is parallel to "God" in verse 47. That Elisabeth had just referred to Mary's child as "Lord" (vs. 43) points to the deity of Jesus Christ. The One who is Lord is also God and Saviour.

By referring to God as her Saviour, Mary was confessing her personal need of salvation. Although she had a special role in bringing the Messiah into the world, she was still a sinner and in need of His saving work. While Mary is worthy of honor as a woman of great faith, she must not be elevated to a place of worship as some have done. It was, in fact, her humble attitude before God in recognizing her sinful condition that opened the door for God to use her in such a significant way.

For God's grace (Luke 1:48-49a). Mary could rejoice in the Lord because of the grace He had bestowed on her. She was of "low estate," or humble position in society, but God had lifted up

His servant to the point that "all generations" would call her blessed. As the mother of the Messiah, she would forever be counted as blessed (cf. vs. 42).

Mary declared that the Lord in His might had done great things for her. She was undoubtedly speaking of her miraculous conception, which ultimately elevated her beyond anything she possibly could have imagined. By God's grace she was given more than she or anyone else deserved.

We too should often pause to thank God for His grace in our lives. Every good thing we have and enjoy is by His grace, for there is nothing in us that merits His blessing.

For God's holiness (Luke 1:49b). "Name" refers to one's reputation or character. In saying "holy is his name," Mary was affirming that God is morally perfect, both in His character and in all His actions. In His goodness toward Mary, He revealed His holiness.

For God's mercy (Luke 1:50). Mary saw God's mercy revealed in His sending the Messiah Jesus into the world. Mercy is kindness or compassion toward those in misery. Mary understood that in every generation those who fear God receive His mercy.

Christ's coming was the ultimate expression of God's mercy, for through His substitutionary death, poor, helpless sinners are freed from the misery of sin and eternal death. God's grace, or unmerited favor, works together with His mercy to meet our great spiritual need.

For God's power (Luke 1:51). While the verbs here and in the following verses appear to describe past events, they may actually be describing "the future work of God's Son with the certainty of a past event" (Stein). Mary praised God for the strength shown in scattering the proud. God's "arm" symbolizes great strength (cf. Ps. 89:10).

God demonstrates His strength by humbling the proud. Those who are proud in their hearts will in the end be brought low—scattered like a defeated and fleeing army—while those who humbly put their trust in the Lord will, like Mary, be exalted (cf. Matt. 23:12). This is an inviolable principle guaranteed by God's very character.

For God's justice (Luke 1:52-53). God's power assures us that in His eternal plan, His justice will be rendered. He puts down "the mighty from their seats" of power and exalts those "of low degree." The "mighty" here are people who reject God and seek power and acclaim for themselves at the expense of others. Such people will not escape the justice of God. He will see to it that they are brought low and that the lowly, humble followers of the Lord are lifted up.

The subsequent statement presents a similar thought. God fills the hungry and brings the rich to emptiness. This is not a condemnation of all the rich or a commendation of all who are poor. Rather, this is a recognition that God in His justice can reverse the human situation, and He will do so in order to satisfy His own justice.

It is possible that Mary was thinking of specific events in the past that demonstrated these principles; but the character of God is unchanging, and wrongs done in the past still demand ultimate justice. We may not see justice in our world today. In fact, we often see the very opposite. But the character of God guarantees that our humble faith and obedience will be rewarded in God's time, and the judgment of the wicked will come through Christ (cf. John 5:21-29).

For God's faithfulness (Luke 1:54-55). Mary also praised God for His faithfulness to Israel. The birth of her son would bring very real and tangible help to her people in particular. It is clear that Mary believed the angel's assurance that Jesus would be Israel's promised Messiah.

Mary saw what so many of the Jewish people would fail to see in the days ahead. Her son was the fulfillment of the promises given to Abraham and his descendants forever. Jesus would be the proof that God had in fact remembered His covenant with Israel and was acting in mercy toward them in sending them the Promised One.

Centuries earlier, God had promised Abraham that his descendants through his son Isaac and grandson Jacob would have a land of their own. They would be a great nation, blessed by God, and they would be a blessing to all the nations of the world (Gen. 12:1-3; 26:2-5; 28:13-15). The birth of Mary's son Jesus would prove the faithfulness of God to His promises to Israel. In Christ the promised blessing for Israel and the world would come.

Mary's words of praise reveal the heart of a woman who not only knew about God but also knew Him. Are we, like Mary, quick to praise Him for His holiness, grace, and mercy? Do we thank Him for His faithfulness, mercy, and strength? How often are our thoughts, words, and even prayers focused on ourselves rather than on the One who deserves all praise and glory? Only when we understand that we are lowly servants who deserve none of God's goodness will we give Him the honor He is due.

MARY'S RETURN

56 And Mary abode with her about three months, and returned to her own house.

While Mary remained with Elisabeth for about three months, nothing more is said about their interactions. We can assume, however, that their time together was mutually encouraging and prepared them for what lay ahead.

It appears that Mary returned home to Nazareth just a short time before or after Elisabeth gave birth to John. She returned knowing that one person understood her situation fully. This would help sustain her in the months ahead when her pregnancy would become known and her faith would be tested. She returned home not knowing how Joseph would respond or whether she would have to bear her son alone in a hostile world.

However, Mary would also return home with what she had left home with—an unwavering faith in God. In His grace, God had chosen her to bear the Son of God. She knew God's plan, and she knew something of what that meant for her, and it would not be easy. But her faith would sustain her through whatever came.

—Jarl K. Waggoner.

QUESTIONS

1. Why did Mary go to visit her relative Elisabeth?
2. How did Elisabeth know that Mary was carrying within her the Messiah?
3. On what was Mary's blessedness based?
4. Why is Elisabeth's blessing important to the biblical narrative?
5. What do Mary's words of praise reveal about her?
6. What in Mary's words point to Jesus' deity?
7. What proves that Mary, though a godly person, was not sinless?
8. How does God demonstrate His great strength?
9. In what terms did Mary picture God's justice?
10. How did Jesus' coming relate to the promise God made to Abraham and his descendants?

—Jarl K. Waggoner.

Preparing to Teach the Lesson

God is always at work and deeply involved in the lives of His people. Perhaps we rarely notice this in our personal lives and the lives of His people around us. But our lesson text this week clearly shows that He is. Before you teach this lesson, look for ways in your own life that show that God is at work.

Luke 1:39-56 was included in the gospel narrative for our instruction. The passage shows us how God affirmed His words to Mary through her relative Elisabeth. It also shows us how He was deeply involved in every detail of the Lord Jesus coming to earth and becoming our Saviour.

TODAY'S AIM

Facts: to observe God's miraculous workings in the lives of Elisabeth and Mary.

Principle: to recognize that the details of our lives are very important in our walk with the Lord and in our being effective witnesses.

Application: to develop a mind-set of looking for the hand of God at work in our daily experiences.

INTRODUCING THE LESSON

Human experience is not necessarily a revealer of God's plans for or involvement in the lives of His people. We must be careful of our interpretation of our own experiences or the experiences of others. We must believe the clear statements of Scripture, not old sayings or clichés. We may even have heard someone quote a secular poem or song to support their spiritual opinion! Worldly sayings can never replace the clear truth of God's Word. Two or three Scriptures on a particular subject at hand may suffice to show the Lord's teaching.

Our lesson this week looks into the lives of two of God's servants and teaches us some spiritual concepts important to our daily walk with the Lord. Both women showed humility and obedience to the Lord. Neither of them believed that she deserved anything special from the Lord but praised Him and rejoiced in Him when blessed.

1. The promise affirmed by Elisabeth (Luke 1:39-45). Have you ever felt as if you were all alone in your walk with the Lord? Sometimes even our spouses may not seem to be "with us" spiritually. We may need confirmation that God is at work in our lives. It is a great blessing when someone we love sees the hand of God upon us.

Mary had just been told that she was going to conceive miraculously by the power of God and the covering of the Holy Spirit. God's long-standing promise that He would send a Messiah to save His people from their sins was about to be fulfilled through her! Although Mary's response to the announcement in Luke 1:38 seems rather calm and obedient, it must have been an overwhelming encounter for her. A common human response could have been to wonder whether she had mistaken what God had told her. For confirmation, she went to see her relative Elisabeth, who also had been greatly blessed by God.

God had also miraculously intervened in Elisabeth's life to enable her to conceive when she and her husband, Zacharias, were both well past childbearing age. Mary traveled to the hill country to see her relative and hear about God's hand on her life. What Mary got in response to her search was probably more than she had expected.

God's responses to our asking, seeking, and knocking are often way beyond anything we would ask or think. Our lesson text reveals that Elisabeth's baby leaped for joy in his mother's womb and that she was filled with the Holy Spirit. This may be the only time that an expectant mother knew for sure why her baby leaped. Through a direct word from God, Elisabeth also knew that Mary was to be the mother of her Lord. She knew that God had blessed Mary because Mary had believed what God had told her. Just as Abraham believed God and it was accounted to him as righteousness, so also Mary believed and was blessed.

2. Mary's song of praise (Luke 1:46-56). This great honor was not bestowed on Mary because of her qualification for a miracle or because of her merits. God's choices of whom He acts through are based on His sovereignty and grace, not on human merit. None of us deserve anything. It is only by God's grace that we are saved or that anything good ever happens in our lives. Notice that Mary's song of praise is mainly about what God has done, not what she had done or would do.

This is in sharp contrast with the songs and views we hear from the unsaved or even from some Christians who might in the end be found to be exalting their own experience. An all-about-me attitude should not have any place in believers' thinking. Rather, we must acknowledge that God has blessed us by doing for us what we could not do for ourselves. He has saved us and is changing us to be more like His Son, the Lord Jesus.

Mary's song of praise dwells first on what God had done for her. God had specifically taken notice of her. It was a great blessing and an honor to be included in the outworking of God's eternal plan of redemption. Likewise, we should see that it is a supreme honor and blessing for each one of us to be part of God's family and to be used in His service in whatever way He chooses. Your testimony of God's grace in saving you can be part of the outworking of God's plan to save someone else and may be a source of encouragement to others.

Mary then recalled the great things God had done for His people Israel down through the ages. God has helped the humble and helpless and disciplined the proud and powerful. God has kept His promises and His covenant with Abraham and his descendants. We are all blessed by the faithfulness of God.

ILLUSTRATING THE LESSON

God sometimes confirms His Word to us through the lives of other believers.

HUMBLE BEFORE GOD

BLESSINGS

YES, LORD!

CONCLUDING THE LESSON

Whatever else we may do with our lives, let us remember to use the two marvelous qualities of humility and obedience. We already have them through the Holy Spirit's indwelling. It is always possible to resist the promptings of the Holy Spirit, but it is tragic and rebellious to do so. We can rejoice when God uses our common human experiences to reveal Himself to others. Humility can become our way of thinking when we remember who we are and who God is.

ANTICIPATING THE NEXT LESSON

In our next lesson, we look at Zacharias and Elisabeth and the conception of John the Baptist, the forerunner of Christ.

—Brian D. Doud.

PRACTICAL POINTS

1. We should acknowledge both great and small things the Lord does for us (Luke 1:39-44).
2. God will act in response to a small measure of faith (Luke 1:45-47; cf. II Thess. 3:3).
3. God's power transforms us into world changers. His power shames the prideful (Luke 1:48-51; cf. John 1:12; I Cor. 1:20).
4. God's plans make the sinner stumble and elevate the true believer (Luke 1:51).
5. God puts down and raises up those of His choosing according to His sovereign will (Luke 1:52-56; cf. I Sam. 2:7).

—Lendell Sims.

RESEARCH AND DISCUSSION

1. How is it possible that Elisabeth was filled with the Holy Spirit before Pentecost? What was the result of her being filled?
2. What does Elisabeth's question in Luke 1:43 tell us about her understanding of the nature of the Messiah?
3. Do you think that Mary had the same understanding as Elisabeth about the Messiah she was carrying?
4. What Old Testament woman had earlier praised God in similar fashion to Mary?
5. What indication is there in the text that Mary stayed until the birth of John?
6. Why would it have been wise for Mary to return to Nazareth after staying with Elisabeth for three months?

—Lendell Sims.

ILLUSTRATED HIGH POINTS

The babe leaped in her womb

Typically, John the Baptist responded to Jesus with joy and prophetic utterance. When Jesus arrived at Jordan's banks, John proclaimed, "Behold the Lamb of God, which taketh away the sin of the world" (John 1:29). Even during Mary's visit to Elisabeth, while yet unborn, John jumped for joy in the presence of his Saviour.

In Bergisches Land (a region of Germany), the community rallied to help some cows that were destined for slaughter. The cows' owner, a neighbor, had suffered financial reverses and lost his farm. His herd of twenty-four animals was placed into cramped quarters awaiting their end. Some neighbors, calling themselves "Kuhrettung Rhein-Berg" (Cow Rescue Rhein-Berg), created a pasture where the cows could live. The cows actually jumped for joy upon their newfound freedom.

When we come into the presence of our Saviour, do our hearts leap for joy?

Put down the mighty from their seats

Historically and universally, seats have represented power and privilege. Jesus noted men's habits of seeking the best seats (cf. Luke 14:8).

The world's elite often are portrayed as seated at the head of the table, on thrones, on expensive leather chairs behind big desks, or comfortably flying first class. The less privileged are relegated to waiting in standing room only.

Jesus, however, rules from a throne characterized by His mercy and grace (cf. Heb. 4:16; Rev. 5:6, 13). When the mighty have fallen, the church will be seated at the place of real privilege—by the Redeemer's side (cf. Rev. 22:3-5).

—Therese Greenberg.

Golden Text Illuminated

"Mary said, My soul doth magnify the Lord, and my spirit hath rejoiced in God my Saviour" (Luke 1:46-47).

This text began what many have called Mary's "Magnificat." The term "Magnificat" comes from the Latin term for "magnify." It is Mary's most powerful response to the news that God's promise of the long-expected Redeemer would be fulfilled through her. This was an astonishing and awesome privilege. It elicited a beautiful hymn of praise.

Our golden text focuses on two aspects of Mary's prayerful outburst. The first aspect is praise, as Mary anticipated the birth of the Saviour. To magnify the Lord as Mary did was to cite God's power, glory, mercy, and grace as He broke into history to fulfill His promise of salvation through His Son, the Redeemer.

Mary's song is filled with allusions to Old Testament passages of praise. It is likely that Mary meditated on these passages as she traveled to meet with her relative Elisabeth. Like most pious Jews of that day, she knew the Old Testament messianic prophecies, and she grasped what the angel had said to her about her role in fulfilling them. She realized that God was sending a Redeemer and that she would be the mother of the Child. Her meditation on what God was doing and what had been promised in His Word led to this great song of praise to God.

At its most basic level, the celebration of Christmas must be praise. The more we are steeped in the Scriptures, understanding all that God has done for the world and for us in Christ, the more we will give praise to Him. We, like Mary, should be ready to break forth in unbridled praise.

The second aspect of our golden text is Mary's joy. As she pondered God's promise and plan in sending His only Son to save sinners, including herself, her spirit soared to rapturous heights. She was rejoicing. The world was getting a Saviour. Mary saw God as her own Saviour. She was saved by divine mercy! What joy!

This joy came to her despite the fact that she would be a young, unwed woman with a child on the way—without a very believable explanation to give for this condition. The people around her were highly religious and often narrow-minded. She would appear to them as a young woman in trouble. Yet her joy overpowered these circumstances. The salvation of souls—the salvation of the world—was more important to her than the difficulties of her circumstances. What a spirit to emulate!

Are we caught up in the joy of what God has done and is doing for souls? Is our focus on the indispensable truth of salvation? Is this more important to us than seeking happiness in our lives? Are we in touch with what God has done in fulfilling His promise of salvation?

We can see the mind-set of Mary as she pondered the great promise she had received from the visiting angel. She was filled with praise for a powerful and merciful God, and she was filled with joy over the reality of the coming One who would bring salvation to the world. She set an excellent example for us. Our response in this Christmas season should be the same. Let us praise and worship our God and rejoice in our Saviour.

—*Jeff VanGoethem.*

Heart of the Lesson

Many people around this time of year make a Christmas wish list. Oftentimes we view this list not as a wish list but as a promise list. We promise to search and obtain every item on our friends' and family's lists. Why? Because we love them, of course!

Since I tend to be the more radical one in my family, the top three to five items on *my* list were always things only God could fulfill—like the perfect occupation or a dreamy soul mate. Regardless of what is on our lists, we are always overjoyed when we untie the bow and remove the wrapping paper to find the very thing we wrote on the list. Thus the gifts someone promised to give us became a manifest reality.

1. Confirmation of the promise (Luke 1:39-45). Very soon after Mary was visited by the Angel Gabriel, she went to surprise her relative Elisabeth. As soon as she entered Zacharias's house and greeted Elisabeth, the baby in Elisabeth's womb jumped! Elisabeth confirmed the promise that God gave to Mary in two ways. First, when Mary arrived, Elisabeth was indeed six months pregnant. Second, when Elisabeth became filled with the Holy Spirit, she confirmed that Mary was pregnant with the Messiah, saying, "Whence is this to me, that the mother of my Lord should come to me?"

2. God does great things (Luke 1:46-50). Can you imagine the scene at Zacharias's house? As if the joy the two women experienced just being in each other's presence after a great deal of time apart were not enough, they were both pregnant! Mary was so overcome with joy that she broke out into song. Mary was not singing the latest praise song she had heard at the synagogue; rather, she sang a spontaneous tribute of praise to God.

3. God is faithful (Luke 1:51-56). God will always reveal Himself to those who are looking for Him. He shows His strength to those who are weak. He exalts the humble. He satisfies those who are hungry. He keeps His promises from generation to generation. Mary recalled what God had done for her people in the past, believing that He would fulfill all the promises He made to Abraham. Mary's song of praise is really a testimony of the faithfulness of our God.

Sometimes the wait for a promise to be met seems never ending; however, can you imagine God's pleasure if, at the onset of a promise being fulfilled in our lives, we would erupt in praise? What if we would sing along with Mary, "He that is mighty hath done to me great things; and holy is his name" (Luke 1:49)?

Do our souls magnify the Lord? Do our hearts rejoice in God, our Saviour? Or have we become so consumed with our wish lists and wrapping paper that we forget why we have a holiday to celebrate at all? Let us not forget that God made a promise to Abraham, to David, and to His people that He would send a Saviour.

Sometimes a promise's fulfillment does not come in the packaging that we are expecting. In our haste and preconceived ideas of what a promise looks like, we reject the very thing our heart has been longing for because it does not meet our expectations. We have to trust that God knows our wish lists. He knows the promises that He has made to us. And when God fulfills a promise to us, it always exceeds our expectations!

—*Kristin Reeg.*

World Missions

"I am a creature of God, and he has an undoubted right to do with me, as seems good in his sight." This statement is a portion of the journal entry of twenty-year-old Ann Hasseltine, who wrote these words in 1810. Ann penned this passage shortly after a young missionary named Adoniram Judson asked her to become his bride.

Ann realized that her future husband was called into foreign missions. As she would soon discover, he would become one of the first American missionaries to travel overseas. She was facing the decision to accept a totally different lifestyle than she had planned from her New England home. Though she acknowledged the uncertainty of the future she was invited to embrace, Ann accepted the challenge as God's will for her life. Much like Mary, the mother of Jesus, Ann joyfully agreed to devote herself to the plan of God for her life.

Ann Hasseltine was raised in a Christian home in Bradford, Massachusetts. Her father was Deacon John Hasseltine, who was active in supporting missionary efforts. The family attended the church that hosted the American Board of Commissioners for Foreign Missions. It is believed that Ann met her future husband through her family's associations with this organization. Ann accepted Adoniram's proposal, and they were married in 1812. Two weeks after the wedding, the couple left for their first missionary trip to India. The following year they moved to Burma.

Ann was faithful to her call to the Burmese people. She learned several languages so that she could communicate the gospel. A long-time teacher, Ann began instructing the women and children throughout the region. She wrote several study books, and she translated the books of Daniel and Jonah into Burmese. She was also among the first to produce Scriptures in the Thai language when she translated the Gospel of Matthew in 1819.

In 1824, the Anglo-Burmese War broke out. Ann's husband was arrested and imprisoned under the suspicion of being a spy. In an effort to be closer to her husband, Ann moved into a shack outside the prison gates. She sent food and sleeping mats to her husband's fellow prisoners in an effort to help relieve their suffering. During her husband's seventeen-month imprisonment, Ann kept the missionary efforts alive and thriving. She wrote stories about her experiences and the struggles she faced.

The stories and letters Ann wrote were published in several periodicals and devotionals. She was very instrumental in informing Americans about the importance of missionary wives to the work of the gospel.

Ann Hasseltine Judson died in Burma at the age of thirty-six. During her short life, she left a legacy that has lasted nearly two centuries. She is known as the "First Lady of Foreign Missions."

Jesus' mother, Mary, rejoiced in God her Saviour. Although she did not understand all that would happen to her, she fearlessly trusted the word of the Lord for her life. Ann Hasseltine Judson, in the same spirit of trust, responded with a faith-filled affirmation. Both women pleased God and left personal legacies that are recorded in heaven and remembered on earth. May we all so embrace the will of God for our lives that we can each leave a testimony of faithfulness to Him.

—Beverly Medley Jones.

The Jewish Aspect

The Virgin Mary of Nazareth may have been as young as thirteen. Some suggest she was up to seventeen years old. Mary rushed off to the hill country to share her miraculous story with her relative Elisabeth. At the point of meeting, Elisabeth experienced her unborn child leaping for joy at Mary's greeting (Luke 1:41). This was a moment to cherish forever. The unborn Jesus, the Messiah of Israel, and His forerunner, John, were in a sense together for the first time.

Luke's Gospel has a special emphasis on the Holy Spirit. Luke carefully noted those who were filled by the Holy Spirit. Elisabeth's son, John, the angel prophesied, would be "filled with the Holy Ghost, even from his mother's womb" (1:15). Elisabeth was "filled with the Holy Ghost" (vs. 41) as her babe leaped in her womb. Later, Zacharias, Elisabeth's husband, also would be filled with the Spirit (vs. 67).

Years later, Jesus explained to the crowd at the Feast of Tabernacles that the Holy Spirit would be the common experience of the righteous of Israel. John wrote, "But this spake he of the Spirit, which they that believe on him should receive: for the Holy Ghost was not yet given; because that Jesus was not yet glorified" (John 7:39). The fillings of the Spirit Luke reported in our text for this week were unusual for the time.

Dr. J. Barton Payne pointed out that the most frequent mention of the Spirit's work in the Old Testament period is of His "infilling the leaders of God's people for their special protection or guidance" (*The Theology of the Older Testament,* Zondervan). Payne went on to say this filling was periodic rather than permanent. David feared the loss of the Spirit and said, "Take not thy holy spirit from me" (Ps. 51:11).

The passage we know as the Magnificat (Luke 1:46-55) is filled with signs of the kingdom reign of the Messiah. Gabriel set the scene for that teaching in Luke 1:32, saying of Mary's child, "The Lord God shall give unto him the throne of his father David." Mary's message is filled with the social implications of the glorious thousand-year reign of the Messiah. The reader will be blessed to read Genesis 17:19, the Lord's promise to Abraham concerning Isaac: "I will establish my covenant with him for an everlasting covenant, and with his seed after him."

Dr. Emil Schurer, in his very careful study of the Jews of Jesus' day, provided a wealth of material on the subject of the Messiah and His kingdom. Every believer of the church age will have a part in the Messiah's kingdom reign (*A History of The Jewish People in the Time of Jesus Christ,* Hendrickson).

Schurer spoke of two periods in Jewish kingdom teaching. In the first, the kingdom was seen as primarily for Israel. A later view extended it to a future world and, interestingly enough, to the individual believer (Schurer).

There have always been a wide variety of eschatological views in Judaism. But they seem united in looking for a return to the original peace and joy that prevailed in the Garden of Eden before Adam's sin rather than looking to abide forever in heaven.

In the second century after Christ, a startling passage in the rabbinical Talmud said of the Messiah, "And the Lord hath laid on him the iniquity of us all" (Isa. 53:6; Sanhedrin 98b). That was saving truth—truth rarely seen in the writings of the Talmud or rabbinic preaching.

—*Lyle P. Murphy.*

Guiding the Superintendent

Few things can be more comforting than someone delivering on their promises. This week's lesson demonstrates God's commitment to His people.

DEVOTIONAL OUTLINE

1. Elisabeth affirmed God's promise (Luke 1:39-45). After Mary's encounter with the Angel Gabriel, she went to Judea. She went to Zacharias's house. Zacharias, the husband of her relative Elisabeth, had been told by Gabriel that Elisabeth would bear a child (vss. 11-13). The child to be born was John the Baptist. He would be responsible for paving the way for the Saviour, Jesus.

When Mary and Elisabeth greeted each other, the baby inside Elisabeth leaped for joy. Elisabeth was filled with the Holy Spirit. She offered comforting words to Mary. She informed Mary that she was blessed among women. Mary had the distinct honor of carrying the Saviour in her womb.

Elisabeth felt honored that the future Saviour's mother visited her. Elisabeth understood the significance of the encounter. She expressed to Mary that the baby inside her had leaped for joy. Elisabeth remembered her husband's disbelief when told she would bear a child. As a result, Gabriel had told Zacharias that he would not be able to talk until John was born (Luke 1:18-22). Elisabeth commended Mary for embracing the promised birth and believing God.

2. Mary praised God (Luke 1:46-49). After hearing Elisabeth's encouraging words, Mary expressed her heartfelt praise in song. She magnified the Lord. Mary esteemed God highly and extolled Him.

Mary was grateful that God had selected her to be Jesus' mother. Mary realized her limitations, and she knew this was an unprecedented honor. She realized the magnitude of God choosing her. She was permanently linked to the Saviour of the world. Mary knew that future generations would refer to her as blessed, and she realized this was because of the power of God.

3. Mary testified of God's faithfulness (Luke 1:50-56). Mary then began to testify about God's faithfulness. She expressed how God had upheld the previous generations of Jews that revered Him.

Mary testified that the Lord had demonstrated His strength. He scattered the proud. He removed the arrogant leaders from their thrones. God exalted the humble. He provided for His people.

Mary reflected on God's promise to send a Saviour to Israel. She realized that God was merciful to Israel despite their times of disobedience. God fulfilled His promise to Abraham and future generations. Mary expressed her joy and thanksgiving for God's help. She stayed with Elisabeth three months and then journeyed back home to prepare for the Messiah's birth.

AGE-GROUP EMPHASES

Children: Point children toward trusting God. Even at their age, they are not too young to believe God, read His Word, petition Him, and expect Him to fulfill His promises.

Youths: Today's teens need to know the certainty of God's promises. Inform them that humans will often fail them. Help them understand that God, however, always delivers on His promises.

Adults: Adults have experienced the pain of broken promises. This can lead them to become cynical or distrustful. Use this lesson to remind them of the constant faithfulness of God.

—Tyrone Keith Carroll, Sr.

Scripture Lesson Text

LUKE 1:8 And it came to pass, that while he executed the priest's office before God in the order of his course,

9 According to the custom of the priest's office, his lot was to burn incense when he went into the temple of the Lord.

10 And the whole multitude of the people were praying without at the time of incense.

11 And there appeared unto him an angel of the Lord standing on the right side of the altar of incense.

12 And when Zach-a-ri′as saw *him*, he was troubled, and fear fell upon him.

13 But the angel said unto him, Fear not, Zach-a-ri′as: for thy prayer is heard; and thy wife E-lis′a-beth shall bear thee a son, and thou shalt call his name John.

14 And thou shalt have joy and gladness; and many shall rejoice at his birth.

15 For he shall be great in the sight of the Lord, and shall drink neither wine nor strong drink; and **he shall be filled with the Ho′ly Ghost, even from his mother's womb.**

16 And many of the children of Is′-ra-el shall he turn to the Lord their God.

17 And he shall go before him in the spirit and power of E-li′as, to turn the hearts of the fathers to the children, and the disobedient to the wisdom of the just; to make ready a people prepared for the Lord.

18 And Zach-a-ri′as said unto the angel, Whereby shall I know this? for I am an old man, and my wife well stricken in years.

19 And the angel answering said unto him, I am Ga′bri-el, that stand in the presence of God; and am sent to speak unto thee, and to shew thee these glad tidings.

20 And, behold, thou shalt be dumb, and not able to speak, until the day that these things shall be performed, because thou believest not my words, which shall be fulfilled in their season.

NOTES

The Forerunner of the Saviour

Lesson: Luke 1:8-20

Read: Luke 1:1-23, 57-66

TIME: 7 or 6 B.C.   PLACE: Jerusalem

GOLDEN TEXT—"Thy wife Elisabeth shall bear thee a son, and thou shalt call his name John. And thou shalt have joy and gladness; and many shall rejoice at his birth" (Luke 1:13-14).

Introduction

The faith of even the most godly people can sometimes falter. Elijah experienced a great spiritual victory on Mount Carmel (I Kings 18:17-46), but soon after he fell into despair when Queen Jezebel sought his life (19:1-4). Peter drew his sword, ready to defend Jesus to the death in the garden (John 18:10), but only hours later he denied knowing the Lord (vss. 17-18, 25-27).

Such experiences are all too common among believers. But why? No doubt, at least part of the reason is that we are all affected by the world in which we live. When we do not see any earthly way out of a difficult situation, we assume there is no way out. We believe in God and acknowledge that He is all-powerful, but His work is not always readily visible to our eyes. As a result, we often become discouraged.

Zacharias the priest is an interesting case study. He knew God, but when he was given a promise that seemed impossible of fulfillment, his faith failed him. The good news for both him and us is that one person's failure does not thwart the purpose and plan of God.

LESSON OUTLINE

I. **THE PRIEST AND THE PEOPLE**—Luke 1:8-10

II. **THE ANGEL AND THE MESSAGE**—Luke 1:11-17

III. **THE RESPONSE AND THE REPERCUSSIONS**—Luke 1:18-20

Exposition: Verse by Verse

THE PRIEST AND THE PEOPLE

LUKE 1:8 And it came to pass, that while he executed the priest's office before God in the order of his course,

9 According to the custom of the priest's office, his lot was to burn incense when he went into the temple of the Lord.

10 And the whole multitude of the

people were praying without at the time of incense.

Zacharias's ministry (Luke 1:8-9). After his introduction to his Gospel (vss. 1-4), Luke began his account of Jesus Christ. But he led off not with the birth of Christ but with the birth of the Saviour's forerunner, John the Baptist. Actually, the account begins more than nine months before John's birth.

Luke 1:5 introduces us to the Jewish priest Zacharias and his wife, Elisabeth. Both are described as "righteous before God" (vs. 6). They diligently obeyed His commands. By this time both were advanced in age, and they had never been able to have children (vs. 7).

The story begins with Zacharias executing his priestly service in the temple according to the set rotation. There were many priests in Israel—too many, in fact, to keep them all occupied in temple service. Therefore, the priests had been organized into twenty-four groups, or courses (cf. I Chron. 23—24; Luke 1:5). Twice a year, each course would serve in the temple for one week, with specific duties being assigned by lot.

On this occasion Zacharias had been chosen to burn incense inside the temple. This was a great privilege and a once-in-a-lifetime opportunity, since according to historical records, "a priest could not offer incense more than once in his entire lifetime" (Morris, *Luke,* InterVarsity). Thus, it was at the pinnacle of his priestly career that Zacharias received both the greatest promise to him personally and the greatest challenge to his faith.

The people's anticipation (Luke 1:10). Only Israel's high priest could enter the most holy place, or Holy of Holies, in the temple, and he did so only once a year on the Day of Atonement. Separated from the Holy of Holies by a tall, heavy curtain, or veil (cf. 23:45), was the holy place.

It was into the holy place that Zachar-ias entered to offer incense on the golden altar. This offering, symbolic of prayer, was presented both in the morning and in the evening each day. We do not know whether this was the morning or evening offering, but a large crowd of faithful Jews were gathered outside in the temple courtyard, praying and anticipating the reappearance of the priest when his duties were concluded.

THE ANGEL AND THE MESSAGE

11 And there appeared unto him an angel of the Lord standing on the right side of the altar of incense.

12 And when Zacharias saw him, he was troubled, and fear fell upon him.

13 But the angel said unto him, Fear not, Zacharias: for thy prayer is heard; and thy wife Elisabeth shall bear thee a son, and thou shalt call his name John.

14 And thou shalt have joy and gladness; and many shall rejoice at his birth.

15 For he shall be great in the sight of the Lord, and shall drink neither wine nor strong drink; and he shall be filled with the Holy Ghost, even from his mother's womb.

16 And many of the children of Israel shall he turn to the Lord their God.

17 And he shall go before him in the spirit and power of Elias, to turn the hearts of the fathers to the children, and the disobedient to the wisdom of the just; to make ready a people prepared for the Lord.

Fear of the angel (Luke 1:11-12). As Zacharias stood in the holy place, an angel appeared before him, standing beside the altar. This angel would later identify himself as Gabriel (vs. 19), the same angel who would appear to Mary in Nazareth six months later (vs. 26). The priest's initial response was similar to Mary's: "he was troubled, and fear fell upon him" (vs. 12). With his holy moment of divine service interrupted by this sudden appearance, it was only natural for Zacharias to be agitated and fearful, not knowing what the angel's presence meant.

Promise of a son (Luke 1:13-14). The angel quickly assured Zacharias that his presence meant only good news for the priest. There was no reason to fear, for the angel was there to announce the answer to Zacharias's prayer: his wife, Elisabeth, would bear a son.

There is no prior mention of the two praying for a child or specifically a son, but this had surely been their prayer for many years. Yet it is also quite possible that this request had not been voiced for some time; the hope of being parents might have given way to hopelessness now that they both were getting well on in years (Luke 1:7).

Their desire and prayer for a child, however, was now about to be fulfilled in an even greater way than they could have imagined. Moreover, Gabriel even told Zacharias what the child was to be named: John (Luke 1:13). "John" was not a family name, as we learn later (vss. 59-63), but its significance apparently was in its meaning. This child, miraculously given to a previously barren mother now beyond normal childbearing age, would be named John, which means "the Lord is gracious."

The angel's words in Luke 1:14 seem rather obvious and could apply to most any parents who welcome the birth of a child: "Thou shalt have joy and gladness." Yet the joy that John would bring to his parents would extend far beyond them. Not only would family and friends rejoice with them at his birth, but so also would many others who understood or would come to understand the role he would play in God's plan of salvation.

Prophecy concerning the son (Luke 1:15-17). The son who would be born to Zacharias and Elisabeth would bring joy to many people, and he would be "great in the sight of the Lord." No higher praise could be given to a person than this, and years later Jesus essentially repeated it, saying, "Among them that are born of women there hath not risen a greater than John the Baptist" (Matt. 11:11).

In the description that follows, John's greatness is presented in terms of his character and his role in preparing the way for the Messiah's coming.

First, the angel said that John would drink "neither wine nor strong drink" (Luke 1:15). While this was a requirement for a Nazarite—a person specially set apart to God's service by a vow (Num. 6:2-6)—it does not appear that John was one since other requirements for a Nazarite are not mentioned. It does, however, suggest a special mission for John (cf. Luke 7:33).

That unique mission also would be indicated by the work of the Holy Spirit in his life even before birth. John would be filled with the Spirit "from his mother's womb" (Luke 1:15). This expression, which is applied to no one else in the New Testament, "emphasizes the fact that God chose him and equipped him from the very beginning" (Morris).

To be filled with the Spirit is to be controlled and empowered by God the Holy Spirit. John experienced this from the very beginning of His existence. Luke described Jesus Himself as "full of the Holy Ghost" (Luke 4:1). All others Luke described as being filled with the Spirit publicly proclaimed Jesus as Saviour, Lord, and Messiah (1:41-43, 67-75; cf. 2:25-32). And so it would be for John.

John's future ministry, Gabriel said, would involve turning many people in Israel to "the Lord their God" (Luke 1:16). The Greek word for "turn" here is a word commonly used in the New Testament for spiritual conversion, or salvation (cf. Acts 9:35; 11:21; II Cor. 3:16; I Thess. 1:9). The Jewish people were privileged to have God's revelation in the Old Testament Scriptures, but the

New Testament clearly indicates that the majority of them were blind to the revelation of God in Jesus Christ. Still, there were some—even many—of his fellow Jews whom John would turn back to the true God.

The angel then spoke words to Zacharias that were certainly familiar to this godly priest. He invoked the prophecy of Malachi 4:5-6, applying it to John. John would go before the Lord—that is, Jesus the Messiah—in the spirit and power of Elijah. Like Elijah, John would be empowered by the Spirit of God. While—unlike Elijah—John performed no miracles, "there was clearly present in his ministry and preaching the power of the Spirit" (Stein, *Luke*, B&H).

The Spirit's power would be plainly evident in John's ministry, for his preaching would turn "the hearts of the fathers to the children, and the disobedient to the wisdom of the just" (Luke 1:17; cf. Mal. 4:6). What seems to be in view here are the results of people turning to the Lord, with family relationships being restored and the formerly wicked, or "disobedient," humbly submitting to the wisdom that characterizes the righteous.

Interestingly, the prophecy in Malachi that Gabriel applied to John in Luke 1:17 is originally presented as referring to Elijah. This is why the Jewish people expected Elijah to return before the Messiah's arrival (cf. Matt. 17:10). John denied that he was Elijah (John 1:19-21), yet Jesus later identified John as Elijah (Matt. 11:12-14).

This mystery deepens in Matthew 17, where Jesus said that Elijah *will* yet "come, and restore all things" (vs. 11), but He also said that Elijah had already come and been rejected (vs. 12). The disciples understood this last comment to be a reference to John the Baptist. Apparently, Jesus was saying that in some way, *"John could have been Elijah if Israel had accepted his message"* (Whitcomb, *The Rapture and Beyond*, Kainos). However, because John's message was rejected, Elijah will yet come at a later time just before Christ's return.

The result of John's future ministry would be a people who were ready for the Lord's arrival. His primary work would be calling people to repentance so that they would be prepared to recognize and receive Israel's Messiah and Saviour, whom John would precede and introduce (cf. Matt. 3:1-12; Luke 3:1-18). John would be the one crying in the wilderness, preparing the way of the Lord (Luke 3:4-6; cf. Isa. 40:3-5).

THE RESPONSE AND THE REPERCUSSIONS

18 And Zacharias said unto the angel, Whereby shall I know this? for I am an old man, and my wife well stricken in years.

19 And the angel answering said unto him, I am Gabriel, that stand in the presence of God; and am sent to speak unto thee, and to shew thee these glad tidings.

20 And, behold, thou shalt be dumb, and not able to speak, until the day that these things shall be performed, because thou believest not my words, which shall be fulfilled in their season.

Answer of unbelief (Luke 1:18). We might think a message delivered by an angel of God would surely be believed immediately, but Zacharias could not escape the physical reality that both he and his barren wife were now old, and having a son at this stage of their lives seemed impossible. He wanted to believe the angel's words, but he wanted a sign that would assure him that the joyous message was true.

Because we too are human, we can fully understand Zacharias's doubts; but the demand for a sign revealed a fundamental lack of faith that was inexcusable for a seasoned follower of the Lord. To demand a sign from God that His promises are true is to suggest that His word is not enough.

The realities of this life often challenge our faith. But when things seem impossible and hopeless and we are tempted to give up, we can still trust God and His Word. Even in the bleakest times, we can boldly and thankfully let our requests be known to God and be certain that "the peace of God, which passeth all understanding, shall keep [our] hearts and minds through Christ Jesus" (Phil. 4:7).

Consequence of unbelief (Luke 1:19-20). At this point the angel identified himself as Gabriel, one who stands "in the presence of God." Gabriel had been sent from God's very presence to bring this good news to Zacharias. Such "glad tidings" deserved a better response than Zacharias's doubt.

Zacharias would have immediately recognized the name Gabriel from Daniel 8:16 and 9:21, and any doubt about the genuineness of his message certainly must have dissolved. Still, there was a price to pay for the initial expression of unbelief.

Zacharias had requested a sign that the angel's words would be fulfilled. Now he was given a unique sign: he would be unable to speak until the day came that the things declared to him were accomplished. This indeed would be a sign, but it would also be a punishment, or chastisement, for his failure to believe the divine message, which certainly would be fulfilled at the proper time. That time came a little over nine months later when the newborn son of Zacharias and Elisabeth was to be named (Luke 1:59-64).

Hendriksen noted that God's justice was "tempered with mercy" (*Exposition of the Gospel According to Luke,* Baker). Because he did not believe the Lord's words given by Gabriel, Zacharias would suffer the judgment of muteness, but it would be only for a time. Like David and others who suffered for their sins, he was not abandoned by the God he loved and served.

This portion of Luke's Gospel sets the stage for the presentation of Christ's birth, as well as the beginning of His ministry, which was introduced by the divinely prepared forerunner. It gives us a glimpse of how God's eternal plan was carefully laid out and His instruments were chosen and prepared in accordance with what had already been prophesied. Nothing happens by chance in the world God sovereignly rules.

These verses also provide a gracious reminder that God's plan involves faithful but flawed people. We are all flawed, but let us be sure we always remain faithful followers of the Lord.

—Jarl K. Waggoner.

QUESTIONS

1. What made burning incense in the temple the pinnacle of Zacharias's priestly work?
2. How did Zacharias react to the angel's appearance?
3. What prayer did the angel say had been heard?
4. What does the name John mean?
5. How did the angel express John's greatness? How did Jesus later reaffirm this?
6. What evidence would point to the unique ministry of John in God's plan?
7. What would John's ministry entail?
8. To what Old Testament prophet did the angel liken John? Why?
9. What would result from John's ministry?
10. How did Zacharias respond to Gabriel's message?

—Jarl K. Waggoner.

Preparing to Teach the Lesson

This may be one of the most important and practical lessons of your teaching career. It bears on believing God and His truth in the face of impossibility. It may be that one of your students will come to faith in the Word of God through what you teach and the way you teach it. This is a great opportunity for you as a teacher and facilitator of God's Word. This lesson can really make a difference in your students' lives.

It may well be that all of us struggle with believing God. After all, much of what He tells us in His Word is counter to our culture's teaching and our own experience. Just the reading or reciting of spiritual truth can be used by God to bring people to immediate faith. Sometimes, as in the lesson we study this week, it takes a little extra explanation. This is where teaching becomes exciting.

TODAY'S AIM

Facts: to see God at work in Zacharias's life in bringing him to faith in the angel's message.

Principle: to realize that God will work in much the same way to help us understand and receive His Word.

Application: to learn to respond to God's Word in faith quickly and consistently.

INTRODUCING THE LESSON

The Bible is the story of God and of humanity's relationship to God. We can learn a lot by seeing the dynamics of this relationship and its outcomes.

Much of the Bible is prophecy. In fact, God repeatedly says that prophecy and its fulfillment are the hallmark of the authenticity of His Word. No one else can foretell an event and cause perfect and complete fulfillment every time. God could have simply carried out His plan to have John the Baptist born to this couple, but He chose instead to give them this prophecy, let them anticipate the birth, and live through the events that fulfilled the prophecy.

DEVELOPING THE LESSON

1. God's hand in ordinary circumstances (Luke 1:8-10). Someone might argue that Zacharias and Elisabeth were not ordinary people like you and me. Zacharias was a priest, and he and Elisabeth were an exceptionally godly couple. They were older and past childbearing age, so Zacharias must have been functioning as a priest for a long time. It is thought that Zacharias had never handled the duty of offering the daily incense offering in the temple. Our text says he was chosen by lot to do it on this particular day.

Proverbs 16:33 says, "The lot is cast into the lap; but the whole disposing thereof is of the Lord." The Lord determined the outcome of the "lot," or in modern terms, the "coin toss." So what looked like a daily event was really a divine appointment. We also read that all our days were written in His book before we were born: "In thy book all my members were written . . . when as yet there was none of them" (Ps. 139:16). There is no such thing as a random happening. Our average day may be just the time for God to break through to us with a divine encounter of great significance and personal growth.

2. God's message at the perfect time (Luke 1:11-17). Zacharias was stunned and shaken by the appearance of an angel. He was rightly afraid. Have you ever noticed that the first words out of an angel's mouth tend to be along the lines of, "Do not be afraid"? The angel said that Zacharias's prayer had been heard. We have no scriptural mention of it, but it is probable that the godly couple had prayed for a child for years. We know they had prayed at least once, and it had been heard. Now was God's sovereign time to answer the prayer and send the forerunner of the Lord Jesus into this godly home. The answer was to be far bigger than the prayer!

We must keep praying. Which prayer is answered and how it will be answered is not up to us. Our job is to pray. What a shame it would be to miss this golden opportunity!

3. God's proof to help the doubtful believe (Luke 1:18-20). Zacharias's answer to the angel was not total skepticism but a cry for understanding. He could not see how this could happen. God does not mind helping us with believing. What the angel foretold seemed impossible from a human viewpoint (Zacharias and Elisabeth were beyond childbearing age), so Zacharias wanted to know how it could be so.

Furthermore, the angel had foretold that they would have a son and gave his name. He had also given instructions and an indication of John's ministry and purpose in being born as a forerunner of the Messiah.

The angel said his name was Gabriel. (He and Michael are the only two angels whose names are given in Scripture. They both are archangels of the highest rank.) Gabriel told Zacharias that he stood in the presence of God. In other words, Gabriel's normal position was beside the throne of God. His name, rank, and position meant he had to be speaking the truth.

Gabriel gave Zacharias a miraculous sign of the truth of the message. Zacharias would not be able to speak until he had given his newborn son the name "John." Every word of the angel's prophecy came true at the proper time.

ILLUSTRATING THE LESSON

God's messages to us can be communicated through life's daily circumstances.

GOD ANSWERS PRAYER

CONCLUDING THE LESSON

We should remember that the Scriptures were given to us for our instruction and training (II Tim. 3:16). This lesson has shown us once again that the ordinary, seemingly random happenings of life can suddenly become part of a divine encounter. In His infinite wisdom and power, God may choose to bring about something special and life-changing. It may result in a spiritual rebirth. We should always be open to His leading. A great way to do this is to make a daily habit of reading Scripture and praying. We can open ourselves to hearing a verse in a way that we have not previously done. We can yield ourselves to God in a fuller way. We can obey Him with a completeness we have not yet experienced. We do not need a new revelation or new doctrine. Every word from God must meet the test of compliance with the written Word of God and a clear conscience before the Holy Spirit.

ANTICIPATING THE NEXT LESSON

In our next lesson, we take a new look at the Saviour's birth.

—Brian D. Doud.

PRACTICAL POINTS

1. Dependability pleases God; He rewards faithfulness (Luke 1:8-10; cf. Matt. 25:23).
2. We must keep an attitude of hospitality, always welcoming God (Luke 1:11).
3. Fear and anxiety blind us to the fact that God's timing is perfect. He is a good Father (Luke 1:12-13; cf. Isa. 65:24).
4. We should make sure our motivation is to please God (Luke 1:14-16).
5. We cannot serve the Lord without prepared hearts (vs. 17).
6. We do not please God when we ignore the facts, avoiding the truth before us (Luke 1:18-20; cf. Matt. 16:4; 17:17).

—Lendell Sims.

RESEARCH AND DISCUSSION

1. According to custom, Zacharias was chosen to burn incense in the temple. How did God use tradition and custom to foster His work? Can tradition and custom stifle His work?
2. Contrast the appearances of the Angel Gabriel to Zacharias and Mary. How are the two appearances similar? How are they different?
3. What is the significance of Elijah being the point of reference in Luke 1:17?
4. Who in the Old Testament questioned a pronouncement from God? Does such questioning necessarily indicate a failure of faith on the person's part?
5. Does the penalty given Zacharias seem unduly harsh?

—Lendell Sims.

ILLUSTRATED HIGH POINTS

Stand in the presence of God

Gabriel's purpose is to stand in the presence of God, as well as to speak to whom he is sent. This is much like the duties of a simple page. For years the page program in Congress used young men and women who assisted on the House floor or ran errands for the delegates.

In the United Kingdom, a "Page of Honour" has the duty of carrying Queen Elizabeth's eighteen-foot train for the State Opening of Parliament. He then drapes her long train down the steps below her golden throne and takes his place standing beside her.

Like the angels, we were created with a simple purpose—to stand in God's presence (cf. Rev. 7:9-12) and speak to whom we are sent. Unlike the United Kingdom pages, the train we carry is not made of mere cloth but of the glory of God (cf. Isa. 6:1; John 12:41).

Because thou believest not my words

Like the angels, priests were called to enter into God's presence (in the holy place) and then go out to minister.

On Tuesday, April 22, 2013, the Dow Jones Industrial Average took an alarming dive, falling 134 points in seconds. What had happened? A moment before, a tweet seemingly by the Associated Press read that there were two explosions in the White House and that the president was injured. The Associated Press computers had been hacked.

God could not allow the false report that would likely flow from Zacharias's unbelieving heart. False, unbelieving reports had repeatedly crippled the progress of Israel (cf. Num. 13:32, 14:36). How tiny yet world altering is the human tongue (cf. Jas. 3:5)!

—Therese Greenberg.

Golden Text Illuminated

"Thy wife Elisabeth shall bear thee a son, and thou shalt call his name John. And thou shalt have joy and gladness; and many shall rejoice at his birth" (Luke 1:13-14).

This text concerns the birth of John the Baptist, who was another important part of God's messianic plan. God determined that the Saviour would benefit from a forerunner who would prepare the world for His entry. Our text points to two mighty effects of John's ministry—first in the lives of his family and then in the lives of the wider world, since many would rejoice over his birth.

Obviously, John's parents, Zacharias and Elisabeth, were greatly blessed to have a role in the fulfillment of God's promise to send the Saviour. Joy and gladness came to them; this was personal. We cannot look at these Bible characters merely as passive instruments in the hand of a sovereign God. They were real people, and they personally received the grace of God in their lives. Let us always take the grace of God to heart in our lives so that it might instruct us in God's love and hold us strong in His mercy.

But the wider concern here is the joy and rejoicing that John's birth would bring to the many. His birth would have a widespread impact. His whole life and ministry would have a powerful role in preparing the way for the Lord Jesus. John's ministry exalted Christ, and the blessing of God's salvation came to many in those days.

John preached Christ, always making a clear distinction between himself and Jesus. He pointed others to the Lord, saying that he was not worthy to untie the sandal of the One who would come after him. In his day there was no greater preacher in the land than John, but his only intent was to point to the greater One.

John served Christ, even though it ended up costing him his life. He willingly dropped back into obscurity after the Lord came on the scene, and then he was willing to pay the ultimate price of his own life for the sake of the truth.

After John's death, the Lord eulogized him as the greatest man ever born of a woman (Matt. 11:11). His was a life of willing service to Christ. Our world has many ideas of greatness, but in God's kingdom the greatest are those who willingly and sacrificially serve, as John did.

So John's whole life was consecrated to Christ. This is what led him to de-emphasize the marks of earthly success. His modest diet and rough clothing were only reflections of a life that turned away from worldly success. He was unwavering in living for Christ. John the forerunner teaches us what being a follower of the Lord Jesus is all about. It is about consecration to the things of Christ, leaving in our wake a compelling and countercultural statement of the necessity of salvation and the ultimate futility of devotion to earthly attainments.

Let us be like John, a bold and burning light for Christ in the world (John 5:35). This is how to bring joy to a troubled and sad world. John pointed people to the joy of salvation. So today we are challenged to be lights to the world, bringing the joyful news of salvation to as many needy souls as we can.

—*Jeff VanGoethem.*

Heart of the Lesson

God always prepares the way for us. Sometimes He sends people ahead of us to pave a road for our easy travel. At other times He leads us by His Spirit so that we can make a way for others. John the Baptist was guided by the Holy Spirit; he prepared the way for Jesus.

1. Right place and right time (Luke 1:8-12). Our times and seasons are in God's hands. By God's divine plan He placed Zacharias in the temple, seemingly alone, to give him an encounter that would change his life forever. Zacharias went into the temple to burn incense while people outside the temple were praying. Incense is often symbolic of prayers. As incense burns, the fragrance rises upward, just as our prayers rise to heaven.

Zacharias and Elisabeth had been unable to conceive a child. In a culture that based one's worth on the ability to produce an heir, imagine the number of times they must have prayed for a child. As Zacharias was performing his priestly duty and lighting the incense, an angel appeared.

God knew Zacharias would be in the temple at that time. God knew Zacharias was praying when He sent a messenger to him. We would expect prayer to be a two-way conversation. We want God to answer our prayers. He may not answer immediately. He may not answer in the way that we expect. Nevertheless, when God answers our prayers, it is always for a greater purpose than solely fulfilling our desires.

2. Great joy and gladness (Luke 1:13-14). As Zacharias began to catch his breath, he heard the angel speaking to him. "Zacharias: . . . thy prayer is heard; and thy wife Elisabeth shall bear thee a son, and thou shalt call his name John." The angel continued to tell Zacharias that he would have great joy and gladness and that many would rejoice at John's birth.

When you have a child, the birth affects others as well. His or her addition changes the world of your relatives, your friends, and most significantly, your world. In most cases, when friends and family learn of the pregnancy, they are overjoyed and excited in anticipation of the birth of this bundle of joy.

3. Anything but ordinary (Luke 1:15-20). Even before his conception, John the Baptist was to be anything but ordinary. The Angel Gabriel announced his birth to Zacharias, told him to name the boy John, and stated that he would be great in the sight of the Lord. The angel also declared that he would "go before [the Lord] in the spirit and power of Elias, to turn the hearts of the fathers to the children, and the disobedient to the wisdom of the just; to make ready a people prepared for the Lord."

Because Zacharias did not believe the words of the angel, he was unable to speak until the day John was circumcised. This was a sign in and of itself that the words Gabriel spoke were true. Can you imagine the stories Zacharias and Elisabeth told John as he was growing up about how his birth and his destiny had been foretold by God?

After four hundred years of God's silence, John the Baptist was given the privilege of awakening the hearts of God's people and preparing the way for Jesus. We too need to make a way for God in our lives.

—*Kristin Reeg.*

World Missions

In the human experience there is always a first. Someone or something is at the head of every line. Inventors always have a prototype. Businesses have founders, industries have pioneers, nations have forefathers, and all people have Adam as their common ancestor.

Zacharias and Elisabeth were chosen to give birth to the most important herald in history. Their son John would proclaim the coming of the Messiah, the Lamb of God. As Zacharias listened to the angel, he had difficulty believing that he, an old man, had been selected to bring such a prominent prophet into the world. Because of his unbelief, Zacharias was made unable to speak until his son was eight days old (Luke 1:59-64).

Being first is often a difficult position. Missionary trailblazers often face dangers, diseases, the unknown, and often violence. As they scout foreign lands to find unreached tribes and nations, they are exposed to these and other risks. Because of their efforts, millions have heard, responded to, and further spread the message of our Lord Jesus Christ.

Will and Paula accepted the challenge of becoming missionary pioneers in a country that was known to be hostile to Christians. Amid reports of persecution, this couple insisted that God had laid this nation on their hearts, and He was sending them there to fulfill their missionary assignment. Many in their home church attempted to talk this courageous couple out of their intentions, but Will and Paula were steadfast in their resolve. Much like John the Baptist, Will and Paula were confident in their missionary calling and determined to complete their work, despite the danger.

Will and Paula landed in their target nation only weeks after its government had declared a non-Christian faith as their national religion. Local authorities were allowed to harass, threaten, and even arrest those who held to unsanctioned beliefs.

The first objective was to locate Christian pastors in a particular urban area. God provided miracles as Will met three pastors within the first week. Most church groups had been driven underground, having only secret meetings in house churches. Their aim became to teach, build up, and supply these pastors. They held conferences for leaders in the city to help them support and network with one another. They also kept a running list of the physical and financial needs of the churches in the area. God blessed the efforts of Will and Paula throughout their six-week stay.

When Will and Paula returned to their home church, they reported several accounts of the dangers they faced. The home they had lived in was damaged by vandalism, and windows were broken by rocks. Will was once stopped by two policemen and detained for what turned out to be mistaken identity. They accused him of a serious crime, and one of the officers pointed a gun at him and threatened to shoot him.

God showed many times that His hand of protection was upon Will and Paula. His miraculous providence for them can remind us of the miracle He performed when He caused an old man and a barren woman to give birth to the forerunner of Jesus Christ. God has not changed, so we can believe that He will perform miraculous works for us today.

—Beverly Medley Jones.

The Jewish Aspect

Zacharias the priest served at a very exciting time in the history of Israel and of the world. We noted in an earlier study that he and his wife had been filled with the Holy Spirit (Luke 1:41, 67). Their son John, the Messiah's forerunner, was filled with the Holy Spirit from his mother's womb (vs. 15).

The filling of the Spirit in Zacharias and Elisabeth is suggestive of a small coterie of believers centered on the temple, nearly all of whom shared the uncommon filling of the Holy Spirit. They seemed to share a ministry of keeping the covenant promises of the King before the righteous.

Simeon, a righteous layman filled with the Spirit, was charged with bearing witness to the Christ Child, Jesus, born under the law as Saviour and Lord (Luke 2:27-30). Anna, a prophetess, served a similar function. She "departed not from the temple, but served God with fastings and prayers night and day" (vs. 37). She had a testimony of the saving work of the Messiah (vs. 38).

It is appropriate to note that the high priesthood was in the hands of the Sadducees. Sadducees, Dr. Schurer tells us, were aristocrats and followers of the priest Zadok, who anointed Solomon king. The Sadducees accepted the authority of the Torah, the first five books of Moses, and held that the sayings of the fathers were without authority (Schurer, *A History of the Jewish People in the Time of Jesus Christ,* Hendrickson).

The Sadducees' doctrine generally alienated them from the traditionalist Pharisees. However, the two sects could cooperate when necessary. Some scholars suggest that the parties together incited Herod to slay John the Baptist (cf. Matt. 14:1-12).

In places the Old Testament speaks of "priests," without mention of the order of priests, the sons of Aaron, or the Levites in lesser service positions. Zacharias belonged to the sons of Aaron, "of the course of Abia" (Luke 1:5; cf. I Chron. 24:10). Elisabeth "was of the daughters of Aaron" (Luke 1:5), which shows that both were of Aaron's lineage.

The godly couple lived in the high country of Judah, mere miles from Jerusalem. Because there were so many priests at the time of Jesus' birth, Zacharias probably had only one day in a lifetime career to actually serve in the temple worship. Residing outside Jerusalem spared Zacharias a good deal of the pseudo-spiritual chicanery of the Pharisees and Sadducees.

The Sadducees of Jesus' day were opposed to belief in miracles or angels. This antisupernaturalism fits into the popular heresy of no life after death, and, of course, no Messiah. Sadduceeism is attractive to Reform (liberal) rabbis of our day.

The high priest of Jesus' day was both the spiritual and the civil ruler of the people, that is, except when they were under foreign rulers, like the Roman authorities. Life was good for the high priest, for he was required to preside only on the great Day of Atonement. The rest of the year, he could sacrifice or leave it to others as he chose (Schurer).

The high priest's robes were beautifully made and of rich material. They were to speak of the holiness of the high office. On the solitary day he entered the Holy of Holies, the high priest wore a simple, well-made robe.

The temple was a repository of great riches. Stacks and stacks of gold and silver utensils were held in reserve. Priests' robes were also plentiful. Great sums of money were in the treasury, and other nations knew of this and were anxious to plunder the riches.

—Lyle P. Murphy.

Guiding the Superintendent

Each January, the president of the United States presents his annual State of the Union address. Prior to his presentation, the sergeant-at-arms of the United States House of Representatives introduces the president. The sergeant-at-arms announces the president by saying, "Mister (or Madam) Speaker, the President of the United States."

This week's lesson shows the Lord's preparation for the Messiah's coming. We will be reminded that a forerunner was put in place to lead the way for the Saviour's ministry.

DEVOTIONAL OUTLINE

1. The promise of a son (Luke 1:8-14). Zacharias was a priest. As had been determined by lot, Zacharias was assigned to burn incense in the sanctuary. Exodus 30:7-8 gave the significance of this burning of incense. As Zacharias did this, people were praying outside the temple.

While Zacharias was completing his priestly responsibilities, he had an angelic encounter. When this happened he understandably was overcome with fear. The appearance of an angel was no doubt an overwhelming experience.

Understanding Zacharias's situation, the angel attempted to calm him. The angel told him that there was no reason to fear. The angel informed him that God had heard the prayers he and Elisabeth had spoken. God was giving them a son. He assigned the child a name—he would be called John. The angel promised Zacharias that John's birth would bring joy and excitement.

2. The promised forerunner (Luke 1:15-17). The angel provided Zacharias with more detailed information concerning John. In the Lord's eyes, John would be great. He would not drink wine or alcoholic beverages. He would be filled with the Holy Spirit even before he was born.

John's ministry pricked the hearts of the Jewish people. As the result of John's ministry, many would turn to God. John would be similar to Elijah in his tenacity, power, and anointing. He would have a commanding impact preparing Israel for Christ's ministry. People's lives would change from rebellion to willingly hearing words of godly wisdom.

3. Zacharias expressed doubt (Luke 1:18-20). After hearing the angel's message, Zacharias expressed doubt. He could not fathom how someone the age of Elisabeth and himself could have a son.

The angel identified himself as Gabriel. He indicated that God sent him to tell Zacharias the good news. However, because Zacharias doubted the message, he would be stricken, unable to speak until after John was born.

AGE-GROUP EMPHASES

Children: Show children the care God took to prepare for Jesus' coming. Explain to them how God used John to announce Jesus to the world.

Youths: Illustrate to the teens the importance of being people who are willing to be used by God to have an impact for Him. John was used to announce Christ. God wants to use your young people to lead people to Christ, as John did.

Adults: Despite the improbabilities of some of God's promises, adults need to remember to always trust God. They can learn from Zacharias that God's promises are always fulfilled.

—*Tyrone Keith Carroll, Sr.*

Scripture Lesson Text

LUKE 2:8 And there were in the same country shepherds abiding in the field, keeping watch over their flock by night.

9 And, lo, the angel of the Lord came upon them, and the glory of the Lord shone round about them: and they were sore afraid.

10 And the angel said unto them, Fear not: for, behold, I bring you good tidings of great joy, which shall be to all people.

11 For unto you is born this day in the city of Da'vid a Saviour, which is Christ the Lord.

12 And this *shall be* a sign unto you; Ye shall find the babe wrapped in swaddling clothes, lying in a manger.

13 And suddenly there was with the angel a multitude of the heavenly host praising God, and saying,

14 Glory to God in the highest, and on earth peace, good will toward men.

15 And it came to pass, as the angels were gone away from them into heaven, the shepherds said one to another, Let us now go even unto Beth'le-hem, and see this thing which is come to pass, which the Lord hath made known unto us.

16 And they came with haste, and found Ma'ry, and Jo'seph, and the babe lying in a manger.

17 And when they had seen *it*, they made known abroad the saying which was told them concerning this child.

18 And all they that heard *it* wondered at those things which were told them by the shepherds.

19 But Ma'ry kept all these things, and pondered *them* in her heart.

20 And the shepherds returned, glorifying and praising God for all the things that they had heard and seen, as it was told unto them.

NOTES

The Saviour's Birth

(Christmas)

Lesson: Luke 2:8-20

Read: Luke 2:1-21

TIME: 6 or 5 B.C.   PLACE: near Bethlehem

GOLDEN TEXT—"Unto you is born this day in the city of David a Saviour, which is Christ the Lord" (Luke 2:11).

Introduction

On December 17, 1903, the Wright brothers became the first to fly a powered airplane, with a flight lasting fifty-nine seconds.

Today Orville and Wilbur Wright are still honored for their achievement. However, more than two years earlier, Gustave Whitehead claimed to have accomplished the same feat in Connecticut.

The evidence for Whitehead's claim, however, is a grainy, inconclusive photo and an article by an unnamed reporter. The Wright brothers' flight, on the other hand, was well documented. If Whitehead was, in fact, first, his failure was lack of adequate documentation.

God cannot be accused of such a failure. He left for all the world indelible evidence of the most important events in history—the birth, death, and resurrection of Jesus Christ. The first witnesses to His birth were not the most esteemed people of the day, but that only adds to the authenticity of Luke's inspired account.

LESSON OUTLINE

I. THE ANGEL'S REVELATION OF THE SAVIOUR'S BIRTH— Luke 2:8-14

II. THE SHEPHERDS' WITNESS TO THE SAVIOUR'S BIRTH— Luke 2:15-20

Exposition: Verse by Verse

THE ANGEL'S REVELATION OF THE SAVIOUR'S BIRTH

LUKE 2:8 And there were in the same country shepherds abiding in the field, keeping watch over their flock by night.

9 And, lo, the angel of the Lord came upon them, and the glory of the Lord shone round about them: and they were sore afraid.

10 And the angel said unto them, Fear not: for, behold, I bring you good tidings of great joy, which shall be to all people.

11 For unto you is born this day in the city of David a Saviour, which is Christ the Lord.

12 And this shall be a sign unto you; Ye shall find the babe wrapped in swaddling clothes, lying in a manger.

13 And suddenly there was with the angel a multitude of the heavenly host praising God, and saying,

14 Glory to God in the highest, and on earth peace, good will toward men.

The angel's appearance (Luke 2:8-9). Verses 1-7 describe how God providentially moved the Roman emperor Augustus to call for a census for the purpose of taxation. This census brought Mary, now near the end of her pregnancy, and Joseph to Bethlehem, the prophesied place of the Messiah's birth (cf. Mic. 5:2; Matt. 2:4-6).

With many traveling to their ancestral homes to register for the census, Joseph and Mary could find lodging only in a stable for animals. There Jesus was born, and His mother laid Him in a manger, or feeding trough.

Here the narrative shifts to the fields in the vicinity of Bethlehem, where shepherds were "keeping watch over their flock by night" (Luke 2:8). Shepherds played an important role in Israel's pastoral economy, which depended on sheep and goats for food and wool, as well as for sacrifices in the temple. Yet shepherds were not highly regarded, in spite of King David's heritage as one. They were considered unclean and "unreliable and were not allowed to give testimony in the lawcourts" (Morris, *Luke,* InterVarsity).

As shocking as it might have been to people of that day—and even the shepherds themselves—God chose them to be the first human witnesses to the Saviour's birth. The choice of the shepherds reminds us that God is not bound by human conventions. The King of the universe would not be welcomed by nobles but by lowly, despised shepherds. These shepherds, however, proved to be dependable, faithful witnesses to the Messiah's coming, unlike the elite of the nation who, for the most part, rejected and opposed Jesus.

The sudden appearance of the angel before these shepherds recalls the unannounced and unexpected angelic appearances before Zacharias (Luke 1:11-13) and Mary (vss. 28-30). As in the previous cases, the angel's appearance elicited fear (2:9). Fear was a natural response to the sudden appearance of this being during the night, especially since "the glory of the Lord shone round about them."

As an angel of the Lord, this spirit being reflected God's glory. Glory here speaks of God's visible presence, which is often associated with brilliant light (cf. Exod. 40:34-38; Luke 9:28-32; Acts 22:6-11). Indeed, the angel had come from God's very presence. The impressive—and frightening—sight before the shepherds certainly was not something these men could easily dismiss. And this was probably the reason for it. They could not use their lowly status in society to avoid the special mission for which God had chosen them.

The angel's announcement (Luke 2:10-11). The angel's first words were "fear not." There was no reason for the shepherds to fear, for the angel came not to bring judgment but to deliver good news. The word "angel" means "messenger," and this angel was bringing a message that would result in great joy for all people.

The shepherds would naturally think the promise of joy for all people meant joy for all Jews, who were eagerly awaiting the arrival of the Messiah. Yet the angel's words can be seen as at least hinting at the universal blessing associated with Christ's coming into the world (cf. Gen. 12:3). This was quite appropriate since Luke was writing primarily to Gentiles (cf. Luke 1:3).

If joy would be the overall characteristic of the angel's message, its content is set forth concisely in Luke 2:11. That very day a child had been born in the "city of David." The city of David often refers to Jerusalem, but here it refers to King David's hometown, nearby Bethlehem (cf. I Sam. 16:1-13).

The One born in Bethlehem that day was "Saviour," "Christ," and "Lord" (Luke 2:11). The "Saviour," or Deliverer, was the One whom Israel longed for to deliver them from oppression. This Saviour, however, would deliver His people from their sins (Matt. 1:21).

The Greek title "Christ," like its Hebrew equivalent "Messiah," means "anointed one." The Jewish people were familiar with the anointing of kings and priests to set them apart for service. They eagerly anticipated the Messiah, or Anointed One, prophesied in the Old Testament, for He was the one set apart to be Israel's Deliverer and King.

"Lord" describes a master, or ruler. The Greek word here is also routinely used in the New Testament to translate the Old Testament term "Yahweh," the name of the all-powerful, self-existent Creator.

Whether the shepherds grasped the full significance of this last title is not clear, but it was certainly clear in their minds that the One whose birth the angel announced was Israel's long-awaited King. The angel left no doubt about that. He was Israel's Deliverer, Messiah, and Lord, and He had been born that day in Bethlehem, as the Prophet Micah had foretold seven centuries earlier (Mic. 5:2).

The angel's confirmation (Luke 2:12). The angel's message was not just an unconfirmed declaration of an event that had taken place. What the heavenly being stated could be confirmed by locating the newborn Child in Bethlehem. The particular "sign" that would identify the Child was this: "Ye shall find the babe wrapped in swaddling clothes, lying in a manger."

Swaddling clothes, or long strips of cloth, were commonly used to wrap newborn babies and would not be surprising. However, the fact that this Child would also be lying in an animal's feeding trough would serve as a sign to the shepherds that this was the newly arrived Messiah of Israel. The extremely humble surroundings, along with the arrival of lowly shepherds, is a reminder that the Almighty God of the universe is not concerned about human measures of greatness. He did not come to impress people but to save people, whether they were honored or despised in this world.

While the angel did not command the shepherds to seek out the newborn Messiah, the announcement of His arrival and the sign they were given compelled them to do so. Such good news had to be seen and declared to others.

The angels' praise (Luke 2:13-14). With his divine message delivered, the angel was now joined by "a multitude of the heavenly host praising God." This refers to a large army of angels (cf. I Kings 22:19). Praise was the only appropriate response to the good news the angel had announced. In fact, the news of the Saviour's birth warranted the praise of all heaven.

Luke 2:14 records the angelic words of praise that have become familiar and beloved to Christians down through the ages. "Glory to God" is an expression that ascribes honor or majesty to God. "In the highest" does not mean "to the highest degree" but rather "in the highest heavens" (cf. 19:38). The angels offered glory, or praise, to the One who dwells in the highest place.

Only when the God in heaven receives the glory He deserves can there be the peace on earth of which the angels spoke. The Saviour's arrival brings the hope of peace, yet we should not think of this peace as cessation of warfare. Rather, it refers to spiritual peace, or salvation.

The translation "good will toward men" (Luke 2:14) can be a bit misleading. The words do not emphasize the goodwill, or pleasure, given to men but rather the peace given to men with whom God is pleased. The phrase can be translated, "to men upon whom God's favor rests." The angels were speaking of the peace "the Messiah brings to those on whom God bestows his grace" (Barker and Kohlenberger, eds., *The Expositor's Bible Commentary, Abridged,* Zondervan).

The only true, lasting peace comes from knowing the Saviour, Jesus Christ. And we can know this deep, abiding peace regardless of the challenges and conflicts we experience in this life (cf. John 14:27; 16:33; Acts 10:36).

THE SHEPHERDS' WITNESS TO THE SAVIOUR'S BIRTH

15 And it came to pass, as the angels were gone away from them into heaven, the shepherds said one to another, Let us now go even unto Bethlehem, and see this thing which is come to pass, which the Lord hath made known unto us.

16 And they came with haste, and found Mary, and Joseph, and the babe lying in a manger.

17 And when they had seen it, they made known abroad the saying which was told them concerning this child.

18 And all they that heard it wondered at those things which were told them by the shepherds.

19 But Mary kept all these things, and pondered them in her heart.

20 And the shepherds returned, glorifying and praising God for all the things that they had heard and seen, as it was told unto them.

The shepherds' quest (Luke 2:15-16). The shepherds did not need any further evidence. They were convinced that the birth of which the angel had spoken had indeed come to pass. This assurance came from their recognition that the message, while delivered by an angel, ultimately had come from the Lord Himself. In fact, they did not even mention the angel but said, "The Lord hath made [this] known unto us."

With the departure of the angels, the shepherds immediately determined to go into Bethlehem and see what the angel had told them about. This, not their shepherding responsibilities, was now their priority.

The shepherds quickly made their way into the village of Bethlehem in search of the newborn Messiah. Considering both the sign the angel had supplied and the haste with which they searched, it probably did not take them long to find Joseph and Mary and the Baby, who was still lying in the manger.

The shepherds' testimony (Luke 2:17-18). We have no record of the shepherds' immediate reaction to finding Jesus or of any conversation between them and Joseph and Mary. However, having witnessed the scene in the stable in accordance with the angel's message, the shepherds began to spread the word about the newly born Child everywhere they went.

They did not simply tell what they had seen; they explained what they had been told about the Child, namely, that He was the Messiah and Saviour of Israel. These humble shepherds boldly proclaimed the arrival of the Messiah. This was not an easy task in that society, where shepherds were held in such low esteem. Yet those shepherds faithfully testified to what they knew to be true.

God honored the shepherds' testimony. People who heard them were amazed at what they were being told. The Greek word translated "wondered" in Luke 2:18 means "marveled" and often carries the idea of admiration. The shepherds' words left a lasting witness to the birth of the Saviour, thus laying the groundwork for His future presentation to the nation.

The shepherds' encouragement (Luke 2:19). Mary's response was to keep "all these things" and ponder them "in her heart." "All these things" may well include more than just the appearance of the shepherds in response to the angelic message. But the context suggests that the shepherds' testimony is primarily in view. While the shepherds spoke out publicly about Jesus, Mary "treasured all this, and retained it in the inmost recesses of her being" (Morris).

That Mary pondered these things indicates she did not fully understand everything at this point. The witness of the shepherds, however, confirmed what she knew to be true—that her son was Saviour, Christ, and Lord. The very fact that she and her espoused husband were not alone in this knowledge must have encouraged her through the years as Jesus grew up and neared the beginning of His public ministry.

The shepherds' praise (Luke 2:20). Verse 17 says the shepherds "made known abroad" what the angels had told them. It is not clear exactly how far and wide the shepherds took the good news of Jesus' birth, but verse 20 tells us they "returned, glorifying and praising God." They returned to their shepherding duties, whether that night or some time later, and they did so with continuing praise on their lips for what they had heard and seen.

Jesus Christ is no myth, and His birth is no fairy tale. He entered human history in a real place—Bethlehem. There were human witnesses to His birth as well as heavenly heralds of His coming. He is our Saviour, Israel's Messiah, and Lord of all. And we are privileged to declare to the world that He has come and that He has "come to seek and to save that which was lost" (Luke 19:10).

Like the shepherds of old, we are not called to impress people but to point them to our impressive Saviour. He is worthy of all heavenly and earthly praise, and the praise we offer Him through our words and our works is a testimony to the world of the peace He gives.

—*Jarl K. Waggoner.*

QUESTIONS

1. What reputation did shepherds in Jesus' day possess?

2. How did they initially respond to the angel's appearance? Why?

3. What did the angel say would result from the news he delivered?

4. What titles did the angel use to describe the newborn Jesus?

5. What is the meaning of the term "Christ"?

6. What sign did the angel give the shepherds? How would this aid them?

7. What is meant by the expression "glory to God in the highest" (Luke 2:14)?

8. To whom did the angels say that God's peace is given?

9. What did the shepherds do as soon as the angels departed?

10. How did people respond to the shepherds' testimony? How did Mary respond?

—*Jarl K. Waggoner.*

Preparing to Teach the Lesson

For Christmas, the challenge as a teacher will be to bring something of spiritual value to your students. They already know the Christmas story, and they may have a lot of distracting things going on. Their attention may be diverted from the true meaning of Christmas to friends, family, activities, and the gifts of the season. Pray that God, through His Holy Spirit, will work in the hearts of your students so that they will reach a new appreciation of what He has done in sending the Lord Jesus to earth to be born as a human and become our Saviour.

There may also be unsaved people in your class this week. They may have come because it is Christmas. This lesson may bring them to faith in the Lord Jesus. It is a great opportunity! Seize the moment!

TODAY'S AIM

Facts: to see that God can do miracles to bring us salvation.

Principle: God can do anything that is needed to bring about both His great eternal plans and our favorable eternal destinies.

Application: to live every day in the light of God's intervention in human history and in our personal destinies.

INTRODUCING THE LESSON

One might have expected the announcement that the long-promised Messiah had been born would have been made to a king, high priest, or prophet. The event certainly had great spiritual, political, and religious significance. To make the announcement to shepherds would not have been expected. But our God is the God of the unexpected. He is always creating new things and new approaches to people. He can surprise us today with a new sense of His presence and a new relevance of His Word to us.

DEVELOPING THE LESSON

1. The miraculous announcement to the shepherds (Luke 2:8-14). There were undoubtedly many shepherds throughout the land of Israel who were also out "in the field, . . . watch[ing] over their flock by night." The ewes would have been carrying lambs, and it would not have been wise to attempt to bring the flock back to the sheepfold every night. There would have been wolves and occasionally lions or bears out in the fields at night, and it was necessary to guard the flock. They did not know a heavenly announcement was about to be made, but they were available.

In the ordinary activities of life, it is always wise to be available in case God is about to do something. We are told to watch and be ready for the second coming of the Lord Jesus. We should pray about it daily and be spiritually ready for Him.

Shepherds were very common people; in fact, if one were to pick an occupation that was considered to be the lowliest in that day, he likely would pick shepherding. They may have been the last picked to witness an event and testify about it to others. However, in God's perfect plan, they were given the announcement that the Messiah had been born, the location of His birth, and a sign by which they would recognize Him. He would be wrapped snugly in strips of cloth and lying in a manger—a food trough for animals. They were not told what to do with this information, although a hint is found in the words "ye shall find the babe" (Luke 2:12). They were to go see the newborn baby.

2. The shepherds' reaction to the message (Luke 2:15-20). As soon as the angels returned to heaven, the shepherds hurried to Bethlehem to find Joseph and Mary and the Baby Jesus. Once they had found Him, they told many others what was told to them about this Child. The authority of the message did not depend on their occupation, experience, or credibility as shepherds. The only thing that mattered was that God had done something that the world needed to know about.

There are certain things God does once for all time and for the entire world, such as bringing about the birth, death, and resurrection of the Lord Jesus Christ. There are some things He does for people individually, like saving them, changing them, and making them part of His family. These acts of grace on God's part need to be known by others. These actions need to be humbly reported by those who have been so blessed. The shepherds heard the announcement, and their immediate response was, "Let us now go . . . and see" (Luke 2:15).

ILLUSTRATING THE LESSON

May our reaction be like that of the shepherds in sharing the message of the gospel with others.

CONCLUDING THE LESSON

We are common people. We would hardly expect to be the ones to whom God would send angels with an important announcement of a world-altering event. We might pale at the thought of the responsibility of being entrusted with some great spiritual truth. How would we react? What would we do? And yet we have been given a great deal of information about God and His salvation—not only about the birth of the Messiah but also about His death and resurrection. We have been told what these things mean and the eternal results of our faith in God. We have been given the written Word of God about God's plan of salvation and prophecies of His plans for the future. Is what we do with this information important, or do we ignore it and go back to our daily routine? We choose our reactions and profit or lose by them.

First, it is of absolute and ultimate importance to react in faith to God's Word about the Lord Jesus in this life. It is not possible to live the fulfilled life we can and should live without having Him as our Saviour. The presence and power of the Lord Jesus through the Holy Spirit is the only thing that will change us. Second, our eternal destiny depends on our faith in Him. When we come to know the Lord Jesus as our Saviour, the fact that He died for us does not depend on our authority, character, or experiences—no matter how interesting these things may be. It depends on the character and actions of God and His faithfulness in saving people. We must hurry to tell others that He was born and died for them too.

ANTICIPATING THE NEXT LESSON

Our next lesson introduces us to a unit on how all creation praises God the Creator.

—*Brian D. Doud.*

PRACTICAL POINTS

1. God will use us as we remain faithful in our calling (Luke 2:8-9; cf. 19:13).
2. God's good news is for everyone (2:10-11).
3. God does not play hide-and-seek. He will lead us to our destination (Luke 2:12; cf. Prov. 3:6).
4. God's awesome power and authority command praise (Luke 2:13-14; cf. Rev. 5:13).
5. We should want to investigate the things of God with great interest (Luke 2:15-16).
6. We should be willing witnesses for God (vss. 17-19).
7. Seeing God's will fulfilled brings rejoicing (vs. 20).

—Lendell Sims.

RESEARCH AND DISCUSSION

1. What is the significance of the angel coming to shepherds (cf. Matt. 11:25)?
2. The shepherds had no inkling that they would witness the coming of the Messiah. How will we know that Christ's return is drawing near?
3. The three titles—"Saviour," "Christ," and "Lord"—appear together only in Luke 2:11. What does each mean concerning Jesus?
4. Do we have the same reverence for God today as people did in biblical times? Explain.
5. Describe ways in which the Lord communicates with us.
6. How might people have reacted when the shepherds told them what they had seen and heard?

—Lendell Sims.

ILLUSTRATED HIGH POINTS

Let us now go . . . and see this thing

Recently, neuroscientists discovered a correlation between our brain's response to mere stories and actual experiences. When we read about scents, the part of our brain that processes odors lights up as if we had actually taken a whiff. If the hero kicks a ball, our brain neurologically kicks a ball. It was not enough for the shepherds to hear the angel's report; they wanted to actually insert themselves into this remarkable event.

The Prophet Ezekiel observed that, although the Israelites were listening to the words of God Ezekiel spoke, they had become (to them) merely like the words of "a very lovely song" (Ezek. 33:32). Are we existing vicariously through the accounts of preachers, only to awaken one day and find we have been deceiving ourselves (cf. Matt. 7:24; Rom. 2:13; Jas. 1:22)? We have heard what God can do through those who serve Him; let us experience it firsthand.

And pondered them in her heart

Mary was a ponderer. Even after twelve years, she was still musing in her heart regarding the nature of her son (cf. Luke 2:51).

Mere pondering is a thoughtful exercise of the mind, but pondering in one's heart is an emotional embracing of the matter—it is devotional. It is our privilege and responsibility to make daily deposits into our "ponder banks," or we might attempt to make a withdrawal, only to discover our treasury has gone bankrupt.

We may not need those provisions now, but a day will come when we will desperately need to tap into our own hearts. "The law of his God is in his heart; none of his steps shall slide" (Ps. 37:31).

—Therese Greenberg.

Golden Text Illuminated

"Unto you is born this day in the city of David a Saviour, which is Christ the Lord" (Luke 2:11).

These words were spoken by an angel to a group of lowly shepherds in the fields outside of Bethlehem. Joseph and Mary had already made their famous journey from Nazareth to Bethlehem, and the Lord Jesus had been born. The shepherds saw the glory of God in the night sky and received this angelic message explaining the extraordinary events that had occurred.

What can turn a group of common shepherds into a mighty band of evangelists (cf. Luke 2:17)? The same thing that can transform you and me: a personal encounter with the Lord Jesus Christ, the Son of God. The shepherds heard from an angel of God that the Saviour was born, and then they met Him. The consequence was a life-changing witness to the Lord Jesus' coming into the world.

The shepherds doubtless understood the message of Luke 2:11. They were in the city of David; it is likely that they knew the history of King David and God's dealings with His chosen people. The angel used the language of the prophets and the Old Testament, invoking the memories of the messianic promises. The newborn Child was the Christ, the long-expected Messiah. It was a glorious moment.

The language used invoked the coming gospel age. The Saviour was born—a Saviour who would be preached in the centuries to come in every corner of the earth, changing countless lives and delivering all who believe from the darkness of sin into the light of redemption. Jesus came to earth to be proclaimed, as the early reaction of the shepherds teaches us.

We also see the Saviour referred to in this text as the Lord. How could we forget that word? Lord, Master, Deity, King—all these names and titles belong to Him. He is Lord of creation. He is Lord of the church. He is Lord of every man, woman, and child. He is God's own incarnation. No wonder an encounter with Him is so life-changing!

Even when the shepherds met Jesus in His infancy, the experience was overwhelming. Their lives undoubtedly were changed forever; meanwhile, His mother "kept all these things, and pondered them in her heart" (Luke 2:19). The shepherds became the first evangelists, and Mary became the Lord's first devoted follower.

Have we pondered lately the greatness of the Lord's coming into the world? Have we sought to encounter Him afresh? The Christmas season affords us the opportunity to meditate on the coming of the long-expected Messiah, who brings light into this dark world. Do we need light in our lives? Do we need purpose and direction? Do we need hope? Do we need peace and joy? Look to the Lord Jesus as the humble shepherds did. Meet with Him. Thank Him for His coming, for His gospel, for His salvation, for His love, and for His soon return, when we shall meet Him face-to-face.

Our culture bombards us with many truth claims, many of them quite frivolous and even harmful. Well, the events of Christmas point to the most important of all truths. This is a life-changing reality. It brings salvation to all who believe. It brings purpose to all who desire to serve the Lord. The merciful God came into a harsh and difficult world. This changes everything.

—*Jeff VanGoethem.*

Heart of the Lesson

Merry Christmas! I love when Christmas falls on a Sunday. It helps us put life in perspective. As we sing "O Come, All Ye Faithful" and "Joy to the World," we remember why we celebrate the birth of Christ. Even as a baby, Jesus Christ was King. From His first few breaths of air, He was worthy to be adored. Jesus is 100 percent human and 100 percent divine. The stable was too small to hold the accompanying angelic choir, who overtook the night sky with their praise instead.

1. A night to remember (Luke 2:8-10). The shepherds were watching for predators, not angels, on the night Christ was born. They were unaware that Joseph and Mary had spent days trying to get to the city of David for the census. They probably had no idea that all the rooms were booked in the entire city. The shepherds were just trying to look after their sheep, unaware that their long-awaited Messiah would be born.

Imagine it—no streetlights, no lamps, no flashlights, and no cell phones. The only light the shepherds had was the light provided by the moon and stars. Suddenly, an angel appeared with a great light, and they heard a voice saying, "Fear not: for, behold, I bring you good tidings of great joy, which shall be to all people" (Luke 2:10). This was a night these shepherds would never forget.

2. Jesus Christ born (Luke 2:11-14). The angel told the shepherds, "For unto you is born this day in the city of David a Saviour, which is Christ the Lord." The angel continued, telling the shepherds where they could find the Baby Jesus. Suddenly, a multitude of angels joined the messenger and began to proclaim, "Glory to God in the highest, and on earth peace, good will toward men."

3. Coming to pass (Luke 2:15-20). When a messenger from God comes and speaks truth, it will come to pass. The shepherds believed that they had indeed been visited by an angel. Based on the information that was given to them, they immediately headed toward Bethlehem and found the Baby Jesus wrapped in a blanket and lying in a feeding trough. We can always trust God's words to come to pass.

God always breaks through the silence of night with the light of His presence. He does not hide from us; rather, He helps us find Him. Sometimes He sends an angel, as He did with the shepherds. Sometimes He sends a human messenger like you and me to share the story of His love, His grace, and His mercy. We who have found the Way, the Truth, and the Life carry the message of His goodness within us. The shepherds "made known abroad the saying which was told them concerning this child [Jesus]" (Luke 2:17). They went about "glorifying and praising God for all the things that they had heard and seen, as it was told unto them" (vs. 20).

We also must testify to the things we have seen, heard, and experienced. Remember, the birth of Jesus Christ on the earth signified the need of our spirits to be reborn. The Divine One humbled Himself to become a man; man humbles himself to submit to the Divine One and receive from Him love, guidance, and faith. As we celebrate Christ's birth this season, remember that you have been reborn into Christ's family through the death and resurrection of the One who came from heaven!

—*Kristin Reeg.*

World Missions

Merry Christmas! This special day, inaugurated as the celebration of the birth of Christ, generates goodwill and kind acts throughout the Christian-influenced world. Christmas is a day we gather as families and perform our traditions. I would suspect that not many of our Christmas routines include going to a small stable and laying our babies in a straw-filled feeding trough that animals use. Our traditions are far more glamorous. Many are born from legends, fables, and other extra-biblical sources.

Jesus was born in a stable, an unsanitary environment for the birth of any king. It is believed by most scholars that His birth was not actually on December 25. Nonetheless, true Christians celebrate Christmas sincerely and gratefully. Our children eagerly anticipate that day as a special day indeed. Christmas brings joy to those who celebrate its true meaning.

Missionaries are privileged to see the faces of adults and children around the world who experience highly anticipated days in their lives. The day may not be Christmas. It could be when a shipment of food packages enters a village, or when the first spurts of water gush from the new community well. The groundbreaking for a church, orphanage, or school can elicit the same or greater exuberance as a child on Christmas morning. Missionaries, having seen the joy that arises in people who receive the necessities of life, recognize that every good and perfect gift comes from God. Although all children desire toys, missionaries see equal enthusiasm when children in certain countries receive medicine, clothes, food, or water.

A few years ago, a church in my city rallied the community to donate money to purchase medicine for children in a country thousands of miles away. As reminders, the church gave out plastic baby bottles for everyone to fill with bills or coins. The shipment of filled bottles would be used to help children with HIV, tuberculosis, and other deadly diseases. The donations would also provide medications for common diseases, such as measles and influenza, and for children already weakened by malnutrition and unsanitary conditions. The joy of the participants who were giving to such a great cause could be increased only if they could have seen the looks on the parents' faces as they received the help they desperately needed for their children.

Christmas comes in a variety of forms. The birth of Christ came with good tidings of great joy. The King, our Saviour, is still bringing joy through the loving acts of His people in His name. Missionaries have many opportunities to take the glorious proclamation of God's love to those who need it. No matter what time of year, missionaries seek to bring improvements to the lives of those they encounter.

The baby bottle drive proved to be very successful. The missionaries raised thousands of dollars for the mission field. God is pleased when people give, go, and send. As the body of Christ imitates His life in unity of purpose, His love always shows through for His glory. We all should be encouraged to work together in support of missionary efforts. As we do, we can in one accord demonstrate Luke 2:14: "Glory to God in the highest, and on earth peace, good will toward men."

—Beverly Medley Jones.

The Jewish Aspect

The idea of our Saviour and King, Jesus Christ, lying in a manger, an animal's feeding trough, is a sobering thought. However, this was not His first association with earth. Indeed, with the Father and the Holy Spirit, He was the Creator of all things (Gen. 1:1-27; Col. 1:13-17).

The Scriptures give evidence of Christ's Old Testament visits to people on earth. These appearances are called theophanies. Theophanies corroborated the doctrine of the Trinity (Isa. 6:1-3, 8) and anticipated the miracle we celebrate today (John 1:14). They also confirmed the wonderful truth of God's eternally dwelling with His redeemed children (Harrison, ed., *Baker's Dictionary of Theology,* Baker).

In some appearances Jesus is seen as the Angel of the Lord, without the stunning, glorified appearance John later saw of the Jesus he had known so well before His ascension. John wrote, "And when I saw him, I fell at his feet as dead" (Rev. 1:17). As we shall see, some Old Testament saints saw unique appearances of Jesus long before His birth.

In the Old Testament appearances of Jesus as the Angel of the Lord, He is distinguished from angels by the fact that He accepted worship (Josh. 5:14) and is described as the Redeemer (Isa. 63:8-9). Theophanies were no idle visits but rather portended great events or some aspect of God's plans (Harrison).

Samson's mother was childless when the Angel of the Lord appeared and told her she would bear a son. Three times she and her husband were warned against strong drink, for it was God's plan that Samson should be a Nazarite (Judg. 13:4, 7, 14), one who was set apart to serving the Lord.

In his visits, the Angel declined to eat Manoah's food (Judg. 13:16), and He would not reveal His name (vs. 18). Manoah made an offering, and "when the flame went up toward heaven from off the altar, . . . the angel of the Lord ascended in the flame of the altar" (vs. 20).

Ezekiel had visions of the Lord that strongly rival the Revelation appearance. The first of these scenes was marked by a sapphire throne, with fire-like amber surrounding the man upon it (Ezek. 1:26-27). Not surprisingly, Ezekiel fell on his face (vs. 28).

A man of the same appearance—a body of fire-like amber—met with Ezekiel when he witnessed the Israelites' idolatrous defection within the temple compound (Ezek. 8:2).

Those early visions squared with what the Prophet Ezekiel saw in what will be the millennial temple. "And he said unto me, Son of man, the place of my throne, and the place of the soles of my feet, where I will dwell in the midst of the children of Israel for ever, and my holy name, shall the house of Israel no more defile" (Ezek. 43:7).

Today our Jewish friends are observing the feast of Hanukkah, or Dedication. Last evening they lit the middle candle of their nine-branch candelabra, which Jews call "the servant." But it is known as "the Messiah" for believing Messianic Jews, for He is the Light of the World (John 8:12). From the servant/Messiah's light, one candle is lit each of the eight evenings of Hanukkah.

In this observance, the Jews are reliving the miracle of two centuries before Jesus, when the temple was wrested from the Greeks. In rededicating the temple, they rekindled the seven-branch candelabra, but it had insufficient oil. Jewish sources report the lamp miraculously burned for eight days, allowing time for a fresh supply to be prepared.

—Lyle P. Murphy.

Guiding the Superintendent

There is an old cliché that states, "Good things come to those who wait." For centuries, the Jews eagerly awaited God's promised sending of the Messiah.

This week's lesson tells us of the jubilation experienced by the shepherds who saw the Saviour Jesus.

DEVOTIONAL OUTLINE

1. Common men had an uncommon experience (Luke 2:8-14). Near the birthplace of Jesus were shepherds watching their flocks. An angel with a radiant appearance that reflected God's glory appeared to them. Because this was so unusual, naturally the shepherds were traumatized with fear. The angel proceeded to calm them.

The angel assured the shepherds that his visitation was to bring them good news. The news he conveyed promised to bring the prospect of hope to all people. They would see the Saviour Jesus, who was born in Bethlehem.

To further solidify his message, the angel gave specifics about the Saviour. The child would be wrapped in swaddling clothes, strips of snugly wound cloth. The angel also revealed that the Saviour would be found in a manger. A manger is a feeding trough for animals. The shepherds' encounter with the angel became more spectacular. The angel, along with countless others who appeared in the sky, praised God. They uttered words of praise and declarations of peace toward mankind.

2. The shepherds visited the Saviour (Luke 2:15-17). After their angelic experience, the shepherds discussed going to the site of the Saviour's birth. It was apparent that they were ecstatic about the news. They moved expeditiously to Bethlehem. They found Jesus in the manger, with Joseph and Mary nearby. After this encounter, they could not keep the news to themselves. They joyfully spread the tidings of the Saviour's birth.

3. The shepherds returned home with joy (Luke 2:18-20). Upon hearing the shepherds' message, people were astonished. Mary had a different approach. She treasured the events and quietly pondered the significance of Jesus' birth. For Mary, Jesus' birth must have been an overwhelming experience.

The shepherds returned home. They expressed joy and praise to God. They understood the unique privilege they had in seeing the Saviour. They were grateful for the opportunity, which caused them to abound in joy.

AGE-GROUP EMPHASES

Children: Children are excited about Christmas. Due to modern-day commercialization, it is easy to overlook the real meaning of Christmas. Help the children understand the significance of Jesus' birth. In addition, communicate to them the hope that they have because Jesus was born.

Youths: Teens can learn about the positive impact one person can make in the world. Jesus' birth opens the way to transformed lives that can make a difference in the world. Encourage your students to submit to God's plan for their lives.

Adults: God used common men like the shepherds to spread the news of the Saviour's birth. Help the adults understand that regardless of their social status, they can be used by God to make a significant impact.

—Tyrone Keith Carroll, Sr.

Scripture Lesson Text

PS. 33:1 Rejoice in the LORD, O ye righteous: *for* praise is comely for the upright.

2 Praise the LORD with harp: sing unto him with the psaltery *and* **an instrument of ten strings.**

3 Sing unto him a new song; play skilfully with a loud noise.

4 For the word of the LORD *is* **right; and all his works** *are done* **in truth.**

5 He loveth righteousness and judgment: the earth is full of the goodness of the LORD.

6 By the word of the LORD were the heavens made; and all the host of them by the breath of his mouth.

7 He gathereth the waters of the sea together as an heap: he layeth up the depth in storehouses.

8 Let all the earth fear the LORD: let all the inhabitants of the world stand in awe of him.

9 For he spake, and it was *done*; he commanded, and it stood fast.

NOTES

Praising God the Creator

Lesson: Psalm 33:1-9

Read: Psalm 33:1-9

TIME: unknown   PLACE: Palestine

GOLDEN TEXT—"By the word of the Lord were the heavens made; and all the host of them by the breath of his mouth" (Psalm 33:6).

Introduction

It is common today to hear people marveling at the creation that surrounds us. Nature and science documentaries, the naturalists at the national and state parks, environmentalists, and New Age adherents all are effusive in praise for the wonderful world in which we live. And our growing knowledge of the universe and the microscopic world continually adds to that wonder. As Christians, we can join with all these people in appreciation for the remarkable things we see in creation.

Ironically, though, the world by and large rejects God as the Creator even as they praise the creation; and, sadly, even some Christians downplay God's work in creation. If we really believe what the Bible teaches, however, we cannot sep-

arate the creation from the Creator. Creation speaks eloquently of the One who created it all. It reveals His power, wisdom, goodness, faithfulness, and glory.

The wonders around us are not here simply for us to enjoy but to point us to the Creator. Our understanding of and appreciation for nature should drive us to praise the Creator continuously. This is something of which the Psalms frequently remind us.

LESSON OUTLINE

I. AN INVITATION TO PRAISE—
Ps. 33:1-3

II. REASONS FOR PRAISE—
Ps. 33:4-9

Exposition: Verse by Verse

AN INVITATION TO PRAISE

PS. 33:1 Rejoice in the LORD, O ye righteous: for praise is comely for the upright.

2 Praise the LORD with harp: sing unto him with the psaltery and an in-

strument of ten strings.

3 Sing unto him a new song; play skilfully with a loud noise.

While Psalms 32 and 34 were both written by David, the author of Psalm 33 is unknown. Yet it almost seems to pick up where Psalm 32 ended—with rejoicing in the Lord. Psalm 33 certainly seems to be "designed for use in Israel's congregational worship" (Craigie, *Psalms 1—50,* Nelson), and it serves as an appropriate model for our own worship today.

Rejoice in the Lord (Ps. 33:1). Verses 1-3 form a call to worship. Verse 1 addresses this call to the "righteous." A righteous person is one who conforms to God's holy standards. While no one but God is perfectly righteous, those who have put their trust in Him are counted as righteous before the Lord (cf. Gen. 15:6). Thus, a righteous person is one who is saved, a believer. "Upright," which appears at the end of Psalm 33:1, is a synonym for "righteous."

Only believers can truly worship God, for only they know Him. Yet even followers of the Lord must be reminded of the duty and privilege of praising Him.

To rejoice in the Lord is to sing aloud for joy in His honor. The parallel idea of praise carries the same emphasis. In fact, the Hebrew word here, *tehillah,* means "song of praise" and is the title of the book of Psalms in the Hebrew Bible.

To rejoice in the Lord is said to be a fitting thing to do. It is appropriate and, indeed, beautiful. It is befitting of the followers of God to rejoice in Him at all times. When we develop such a practice and attitude, we present a beautiful picture to the world of our great God.

The very fact that Scripture repeatedly calls the righteous to rejoice in the Lord (cf. Phil. 4:4) suggests that we may at times be prone to forgo this duty. When hardships come, it may be especially difficult to praise God. Failure to do so, however, robs God of what He deserves and robs us of the joy that such rejoicing brings.

Praise the Lord (Ps. 33:2). The word translated "praise" in verse 2 differs from the word for praise in verse 1. The word in verse 2 indicates praise in the form of thanksgiving. The psalmist called on his readers to offer thanks to God through music. Music is a wonderful means of praising God and thanking Him for His blessings, for music touches not only the intellect but also the emotions.

The musical instruments mentioned in Psalm 33:2 are stringed instruments. The "harp" refers to a lyre. The "psaltery" is more what we would call a harp. The "instrument of ten strings" could be yet a third instrument but probably is a further description of the psaltery, or harp.

This command might seem somewhat irrelevant to us since many people today have never heard of these items. They were commonly used instruments in Israel's worship, however. And, of course, the psalmist's point was not to limit praise to the use of two or three instruments but rather to emphasize the worship of the Lord musically, regardless of the instruments employed.

Strictly speaking, music is not worship; worship is an inner attitude. However, worship is to be expressed outwardly and publicly. Music is an important, God-given means of expressing our praise and thanksgiving to God. In so doing, we give testimony to God's character and works and we encourage fellow believers.

Sing to the Lord (Ps. 33:3). The third part of the invitation to praise is to "sing unto him a new song." The "new song" does not demand the creation of new lyrics and/or melody. A constant supply of newly written songs is certainly appropriate, though, since even the beloved songs so familiar to us can never fully and exhaustively express the praise God deserves.

As one biblical scholar noted, "As occasion demands, it may become necessary to compose new songs to fit the new occasions for praise which the Lord affords His people though, to tell the truth, any old hymn becomes new and fresh when it is sung with true devotion" (Leupold, *Exposition of the Psalms,* Baker).

Our songs of praise are to be offered with a devotion to excellence. Our abilities will vary, of course, but we should give our best to the Lord, for He deserves nothing less. The psalmist also said our songs should be given with loud shouts of joy. Here, "the emphasis is more on the 'jubilant' character of the praise offered than upon the more external character that it is 'loud' " (Leupold).

The invitation to praise God in Psalm 33:1-3 reminds us that whatever forms our praise and worship take, the object must always be the Lord Himself. He is the one we rejoice in, praise, and sing to. We must examine our attitudes to be sure we gather together to praise God, not impress other people.

REASONS FOR PRAISE

4 For the word of the Lord is right; and all his works are done in truth.

5 He loveth righteousness and judgment: the earth is full of the goodness of the Lord.

6 By the word of the Lord were the heavens made; and all the host of them by the breath of his mouth.

7 He gathereth the waters of the sea together as an heap: he layeth up the depth in storehouses.

8 Let all the earth fear the Lord: let all the inhabitants of the world stand in awe of him.

9 For he spake, and it was done; he commanded, and it stood fast.

"Praise the Lord" too often has become almost a meaningless phrase uttered because it is what believers are supposed to say. But those three simple words, if spoken alone, should raise this question: Praise Him for what? After calling for God's people to praise Him, the psalmist began to set forth the *reasons* to praise Him. In short, the psalmist said we are to praise God for who He is and what He has done.

God's attributes (Ps. 33:4-5). First, "the word of the Lord is right." God's "word" refers to whatever He has declared as recorded in Scripture. Whatever God says is "right." This is the same Hebrew word translated "upright" in verse 1. It literally means "straight," or "correct." God's words are dependable. We need never fear that He might be wrong or incapable of keeping His promises. He is entirely faithful.

The second half of Psalm 33:4 also emphasizes this same characteristic of God. In fact, the word for "truth" can be translated "faithfulness." The thought here is that God's faithfulness is seen not only in His words but also in His works. God speaks and acts faithfully. He is faithful to His word and to His people, especially in preserving them and answering their prayers. "His faithfulness expresses itself through His 'word' . . . all these are always 'right,' that is to say just what they should be and, therefore, normative and dependable" (Leupold).

This is who God is—the faithful God. Faithfulness is a part of His very nature, and His faithfulness calls for our praise.

Psalm 33:5 speaks of the attributes of righteousness, judgment (or justice), and goodness. The Lord not only loves righteousness and justice, but these are also attributes of His character. He loves these qualities because they reflect His glorious character. "Righteousness" is related to the word translated "righteous" in verse 1.

It describes God's conformity to His own perfect and holy nature. "Judgment," which is better understood as justice, means that "God gives to man what is due him. He rewards righteousness . . . and He punishes sin" (McCune, *A Systematic Theology of Biblical Christianity*, Detroit Baptist Theological Seminary).

Furthermore, the Lord is good, and His goodness fills the earth. The word is often translated "lovingkindness," and it conveys the ideas of love and faithfulness.

In spite of the evil and corruption in the world, God's goodness, or lovingkindness, fills the earth. It is found throughout the world in His dealings with humanity and in the works of His people.

If we seem to lack for reasons to praise and honor our God, we need only remember who God is. The righteous, faithful, just, and loving God we find in Scripture has not changed. He is still present, and His attributes can be seen even in this sin-darkened world. What a blessing that is, and what a reason that is to praise Him both privately and publicly!

God's work of creation (Ps. 33:6-9). God's attributes, the distinguishing characteristics of His nature, make Him worthy of our continual praise (vss. 4-5). Likewise, His mighty works demand our praise. Those works include not just His miracles but also His providential works in history and the preservation of His Word and His people.

The first and foremost work the author of Psalm 33 brings to our attention is God's work of creation. This mighty work by itself is reason enough to praise the Lord. And unlike many of the miracles described in the Bible, we still see evidence today of this divine work.

Some have argued that the Bible teaches that God is the Creator but does not tell us *how* He created.

However, the psalmist, like the book of Genesis, tells us exactly how God created: "by the word of the Lord" (Ps. 33:6; cf. Gen. 1:3, 14-15). He spoke, and the heavens came into existence.

The second part of Psalm 33:6 restates this thought, saying, "all the host" of the heavens was created by "the breath of his mouth." The "host" refers to all the heavenly bodies contained in the expanse of space. God's "breath" stands parallel to His "word" in this verse. It is that which proceeds from God. He commanded, and it was done.

If God truly is the eternal, all-powerful God and His Word is true, there is no reason to demand alternate explanations for the existence of the universe. God created everything, and He should be eternally praised for this mighty work (cf. Rev. 4:11).

Psalm 33:7 speaks of God gathering "the waters of the sea together as an heap." The wording here is the same as that found in Exodus 15:8, part of the song of praise for God's deliverance of His people through the Red Sea. At that time the Lord had divided the sea so that it stood like walls on either side of the Israelites as they passed through the waters (14:22). Perhaps that event was in the mind of the psalmist; in any case, that miracle vividly speaks of God's controlling power over His creation.

The poetic description of God laying up the deeps of the sea in storehouses pictures the Lord containing the seas "as easily as a farmer keeps the grain in the storehouse" (Barker and Kohlenberger, eds., *The Expositor's Bible Commentary, Abridged,* Zondervan). Again, the emphasis is on God's power over His creation. He created all things and as such exercises absolute control over all things.

God did not create our world and

then lose control of it. He is the sovereign Ruler over His creation. We live within His creation and are bound by the laws that govern it, but neither we nor those laws are in control. Only the Creator is, and that knowledge should redound to His praise.

God's power is manifested to all mankind through His creation (Rom. 1:20). This testimony to God's existence and power is such that "all the earth" should "fear the Lord" and "stand in awe of him" (Ps. 33:8). We know, of course, that unbelievers reject the revelation of God both in His creation and in His Word. Yet the revelation is adequate to reveal that there is a God who has created all things, and those who reject this are without excuse (Rom. 1:18-21).

If the psalmist can issue a call to the whole world to fear God, surely Christians, above all others, should cultivate an attitude of fear, or reverence, toward God. In fact, if we do not stand in awe of God as the One who stands infinitely above us in His character and power, we probably have too high a view of ourselves. "Man's littleness and weakness must always lead him to due reverence for the One who is so much greater than himself" (Leupold).

Psalm 33:9 returns to the truth pronounced in verse 6: "He spake, and it was done." God merely gave the command, and what He commanded was instantly accomplished. Here this truth is again presented as a reason to fear the Lord and honor Him with our praises. Of no other being in the universe can it be said that he merely speaks and his will is done. There is nothing remotely comparable to creation by *fiat,* or divine decree. There is no human explanation for creation *ex nihilo* (from nothing). "Nothing that man can attempt will come remotely near to this type of divine activity. The second half of this verse could be translated: 'He commanded, and there it stood.' Who could not fear such a Lord?" (Leupold).

That is the psalmist's point. God stands alone as the Creator, and no person or thing can compare with Him. As finite beings, we cannot fully understand the infinite, omnipotent Creator, and we are not called to do so. However, we are called to acknowledge who He is and the great works that have come from His hands. We are to praise the Lord. We are to rejoice in Him and sing to Him. Our lives are to be centered in Him, and they are to reflect His holy character. Let us heed the Scriptures and stand in awe of our Creator and God.

—*Jarl K. Waggoner.*

QUESTIONS

1. For what purpose was Psalm 33 designed?
2. What does it mean to "rejoice in the Lord" (vs. 1)?
3. What means can we employ to give thanks to God?
4. What should characterize the singing of our songs of praise, according to verse 3?
5. In what ways is God's faithfulness seen?
6. What attribute of God fills the whole earth? In what sense is this the case?
7. By what means did God create the universe?
8. What event in Israel's history does verse 7 recall?
9. What revelation has God given to all humanity?
10. What final reason did the author of Psalm 33 give for praising God?

—*Jarl K. Waggoner.*

Preparing to Teach the Lesson

Understand that your class has been repeatedly exposed to the de facto national religion of humanism. They have been told that humanity, and especially the individual, is the ultimate good, not God. The main tenet of humanism is atheistic evolution. Students have been told through many avenues that humans evolved from animals and were not created by God. Therefore, they are not responsible to God for their thoughts or actions and will never be called to account to Him for them. If people can eliminate God from their thinking, there are no ethical or moral restraints except those commonly accepted by their peers. That leaves very few restraints.

The revival of the old Greek religious ideas of naturalistic evolution, repopularized by Charles Darwin in the mid-nineteenth century, helped fuel at least three belief systems, or "isms," during the twentieth century: Nazism, which helped evolution along by eliminating all "inferior" races; communism, which says that the state is the highest good and that all people hold everything in common; and humanism, which teaches that people evolved from animals and have no god or moral authority over them.

If you do not believe that God created us through the special act of creation as revealed in Genesis, then you cannot possibly teach from our lesson text for this week. If you do believe it, you can teach this lesson with authority and conviction. If we cannot believe that God is our Creator, as He states repeatedly throughout Scripture, then we cannot believe that He can save us, either.

TODAY'S AIM

Facts: to see that Scripture urges us to praise the Creator.

Principle: to show that all that has been created by God needs to praise Him.

Application: to teach that we should center our lives around praising our Creator and appreciating what He has created.

INTRODUCING THE LESSON

We understand that a vast majority of people may not truly believe that God is our Creator. They cannot join in praising Him as Creator. They have neither the heart for it nor the ability to do so. However, for those who do acknowledge Him in faith as their Creator, it is right and good.

God is not affected by our praise. He will not be strengthened by our praise or weakened if we do not praise Him. Praise will not buy favor with Him. He will continue to be God even if no one believes in or trusts in Him.

We must understand that God does not want us to praise Him because of some selfish need He has for praise to boost His ego! God has no needs. We are the ones with needs. Humans need praise sometimes just to feel good about themselves.

DEVELOPING THE LESSON

1. Praising God is the right thing for godly people to do (Ps. 33:1-3). You and I may not think we are righteous, but remember that we were declared righteous when we believed in the Lord Jesus (Rom. 3:26). We do not need to wait until God takes us to heaven to be called righteous. We are freed from the power and the presence of sin and should always be ready to praise Him. We praise Him because of who He is, not because of who we are or may seem to be. We are told it is "comely," or fitting, for us to praise Him. A praising soul is a healthy soul. Our spirits need to praise God to be healthy just as our bodies need nutrition to be healthy.

It is appropriate for us to praise God for His greatness when we see a beautiful sunset. We see beauty and enjoy it. We become joyful when we see beauty and depressed when we see ugliness. So it is fitting to praise God. His is the ultimate beauty.

2. Praising God for His truthfulness and mercy (Ps. 33:4-5). Whatever God says is right and true. In a world where it seems as though a majority of people cannot be trusted to tell the truth, it is wonderfully refreshing that we can trust God to tell us the truth. He has no reason to lie to us; whatever He says is the truth. He never changes. He is supremely careful in exactly what He says.

While there are many injustices and wrongs perpetrated by sinful people, we can still see the righteousness and mercy of the Lord in His creation. God is good to the just and the unjust. The promised seasons bring their own particular good to all. The earth was originally made to be a perfect home for humanity.

We are urged to praise the Lord in song and to use musical instruments in praise. People have invented many forms of music, some of which may not be appropriate to use in praising God. Even when praising God for what He has done for us, we must be careful that we are really praising Him, not simply glorying in our own situation as though He has not done much.

3. Praising God for His power and thoughtfulness in creation (Ps. 33:6-9). Only the God of orderly thought could have made the orderly heavens. The stars do not do random things; they can be trusted to be in the appropriate spot every night. Sailors on the measureless oceans have trusted them for navigation for centuries. God spoke them into existence on the fourth day of Creation. The magnificence of God's creation gives us a hint of how much greater His magnificence must be.

Our lesson text for this week mentions that God established the boundaries of the oceans and created storehouses for them. The power and wisdom required to accomplish all that God did in Creation are way beyond our comprehension. We are in awe of the mind of God and His thoughts as He created. His intellect is so vast and His power so great that it is difficult to comprehend what God has done and continues to do.

ILLUSTRATING THE LESSON

We praise God for the wonders of His creation and His care for us.

CONCLUDING THE LESSON

Praising God as our Creator is essential for our spiritual health, just as nutrition is essential for our physical health. We were made that way. If we honor God as our Creator, He may honor us with a gift of creativity. We can praise Him in exercising creativity.

ANTICIPATING THE NEXT LESSON

In our next lesson, we will study how all creation joins in praise to the Lord.

—Brian D. Doud.

PRACTICAL POINTS

1. Praising God not only brings blessing; it attracts the sinner to God as well (Ps. 33:1; cf. 67:5-7).
2. Singers and musicians are ministers of God and should use everything at their disposal to bring Him praise (33:2-3).
3. Uprightness and truth are defining qualities of all that God does (Ps. 33:4; cf. Num. 23:19; Rom. 3:4).
4. Righteousness and justice are virtues that God loves (Ps. 33:5; cf. II Tim. 4:8).
5. God creates according to His divine will (Ps. 33:6).
6. The earth and all its resources belong to the Lord (vs. 7).
7. God's awesome power should cause all to reverence Him (vss. 8-9).

—Lendell Sims.

RESEARCH AND DISCUSSION

1. Why is there a command to those who have been redeemed to rejoice in the Lord?
2. How do we reconcile Psalm 33:5 with the fact that there is much evil in the world?
3. Why is it important that Scripture emphasizes that the universe was created by a word from God?
4. What or who is included in the heavenly host (cf. Gen. 2:1; Luke 2:13)?
5. What changes would we see in the world if the truth of Psalm 33:8 were realized in our time?
6. What evidence do we have of God's awesomeness?

—Lendell Sims.

ILLUSTRATED HIGH POINTS

Praise is comely for the upright

In a world where celebrities (whether they are from sports, entertainment, or cooking) are idolized, praise of God is considered unfashionable and uncultured.

A painting had been hanging on a man's lowly wall for ten years, but now his wife was gone. He had no use for it or several of her other things. He packed them up and sent them off to the auction house to collect whatever he could. That seemingly worthless painting went up for auction and brought in over a million dollars. There it had hung, year after year, enjoyed somewhat by his wife but considered worthless by him. It was in plain sight, but it was utterly undervalued.

And what of the One who died for the world on history's cross, the One for whom the world has little more than contempt? Yet there are those who consider Him of highest worth. To them, praising Him is beautiful.

Sing unto him a new song; . . . skilfully

Our ministries should reflect the fruit of diligence. Let us also, however, remember to retain our passion.

A journalist actually felt relieved the day he was laid off. It seems that although he had attained success in his field, he had long since lost interest. He had lost, as he put it, his "nose for news." Interestingly, one week later, a cold caused him to also lose his physical sense of smell. Concerned about this, he went about picking up objects just to smell them. Slowly, his discernment for both news and aromas returned.

Our worship and ministry may be skillful, but are they new, fresh daily, and passionate (cf. Rev. 2:3-5)? It is time to daily test our sense of worship.

—Therese Greenberg.

Golden Text Illuminated

"By the word of the Lord were the heavens made; and all the host of them by the breath of his mouth" (Psalm 33:6).

Psalm 33 is a psalm of praise. It calls for musical instruments to be played and for worshippers to sing. The object of the praise is the word of God, particularly the power of His spoken word. God is extolled for His power to speak and create out of nothing.

We can see that Psalm 33:6 has two clauses that are mirror images of each other; scholars call it "synonymous parallelism." Each clause is asserting the same thing: all the heavens—the vast universe above us—came into being through the power of God's spoken word. As we contemplate this glorious truth, we are led into the realm of praise to our great Creator.

There is an interesting circle of truth to be gleaned from this text. First of all, God spoke and created the heavens above. These heavens and all that God brought into existence by His power then give back to the great Creator the praise that is due Him. So God spoke His word, and His creation responds back to Him! And we, His people, join in on this circle of praise. Thus, all creation renders praise to God. Truly, everything that is made is made for the glory of God.

We live today in what many call the "me generation." Not too many people think this is a good thing. The "me generation" is considered selfish, short-sighted, self-indulgent, and ungodly. People in our society tend to think primarily of themselves and their interests and have a dim view of serving others and embracing community. It is not good for society, and it is not good for the church. What is the cure for this disease? Certainly a big part of it would be praise—a greater God-ward focus.

This text leads us back to consider how God is the center of all creation.

If we can begin our theology with God at the center—understanding the greatness of God's power and that His word began it all—then perhaps we will rebuild our lives around Him instead of ourselves. This text urges us to see that all things flow from God and all things must flow back to God. He must fill our minds, our hearts, and our lives. Without the "breath of his mouth," we have nothing and are nothing. Theology begins with the presence and power of God, and it flows down to us, His humble creatures, who are duty-bound to give Him praise.

Praise is not just singing a praise song at church. It is the acknowledgment that God is the center of life, that we owe our being and life to His creative power. He must be acknowledged first of all. And then when we find our way back to Him, or rather, when God rescues us through the cross of Christ, we become a people who worship and serve Him forever. The Shorter Catechism of the Westminster Confession had it right when in response to its question, "What is the chief end of man?" it answered, "to glorify God and to enjoy him forever." Our lives must be swallowed up in the knowledge of God, which leads to a life of service and praise.

Maybe what our generation needs is more of God—more teaching, more preaching, and more heartfelt study of Him. By God's grace this can become the means of spiritual growth, and praise then becomes the natural outflow of our lives.

—*Jeff VanGoethem.*

Heart of the Lesson

Have you ever read a psalm quickly, glanced over it, and determined that it was not really relevant to you because it was all about praising God? This may not be something you want to admit, but we have all done it. Sometimes in life we are looking for a word of comfort, and the last thing we want to be told to do is to praise God. However, when the Psalms say "Praise the Lord," it is not a suggestion. It is a command. Despite how our circumstances, trials, or tribulations may speak to our hearts, God is worthy of all our praise.

1. A new song (Ps. 33:1-3). I often take long car rides, and there is nothing better than when a favorite song plays on the radio. All of a sudden my mood lightens, the volume goes up, and I attempt to maintain the tune at the top of my lungs. It did not matter how I was feeling the moment before the song came on because once it started playing, my outlook shifted.

Music is a powerful force. This is why the psalmist commanded us to praise the Lord with instruments. Music can capture a mood in a way that makes words unnecessary. I love lyrics, and I do not enjoy much music that is devoid of them. But what do we do when there are no words? We should sing a new song to the Lord! Make up your own words. Make up your own tune. Sometimes we just need to express to our Creator how we are feeling in a song. It might not be a song you would want anyone else to hear. No matter. It is not for public consumption; it is for the Lord. So sing it out with all the gusto you can muster! He will delight in your offering.

2. The truth of God's word (Ps. 33:4-5). God is faithful. God is incapable of deceit. The words of the Lord are true; there is no error in them. "All his works are done in truth." In other words, everything that the Lord does supports the words that He has spoken.

Think about your favorite fruit, your favorite flower, an adorable puppy or kitten. Think about your best friend or soul mate. Now ponder this: God created them all.

The goodness of the Lord fills the earth. He loves righteousness and justice. God hates unfairness and will eventually right every wrong.

3. Created by the spoken word (Ps. 33:6-9). The psalmist took a moment to remember that the very land that he was standing on was created solely by the word of the Lord. God opened His mouth, formed words, and gave them voice. This is the process by which all things were created. We all have moments in which we need to be reminded of God's work in creation. Here is why: God does not change. He is the same yesterday, today, and forever. If something was created when God spoke, then when God speaks to us now, we know He has power to create again.

If we need something to shift in our lives, if we need assistance, if we need healing, or whatever it is that we are in need of—we just need God to speak it into existence. Why? "For he spake, and it was done; he commanded, and it stood fast" (Ps. 33:9). The same power that raised Christ from the dead lives within us. When we give voice to His Word (the Bible), that same creative power begins to work in our lives. God's word is true. It never returns void.

—Kristin Reeg.

World Missions

"So, how did you get here?"

"Well, my dad met my mom and—"

"No, José. I mean, why do you think you're on this earth?"

José dropped his gaze and began to kick the sandy soil beneath his feet. "I really don't know. I have no idea."

This is a sliver of a conversation between Steven, an American missionary, and José, a young Dominican husband and father. José believed in the existence of God but had not trusted in Jesus as his Saviour. He had heard the gospel many times as he was growing up, yet he struggled with the thought of committing his life to Christ. He understood that working to provide for his family was a noble endeavor. His family had instilled the values of honesty, integrity, and responsibility in him. But as the conversation continued, Steven became sadly aware that José was still without a Saviour. As José described his work, his family, and his lifestyle, Steven silently breathed prayers that God would guide the conversation toward the gospel. In His faithfulness, God led the discourse in the right direction.

Steven continued with the story of the Creation. He reminded José that God is the Creator of all things and all people. Then he reviewed some stories of Bible heroes whom José had learned about as a child. José agreed that Noah, Abraham, and David were specially made to do specific jobs. He was convinced, though, that his life was not like theirs and that he was not special to God. Steven's heart sank as he listened to José's misunderstanding of the love of God. At that moment Steven resolved to inform as many people as he could about how special they are to God.

Steven turned to Jeremiah 29:11 and asked José to read it out loud from his own Bible. "For I know the thoughts that I think toward you, saith the Lord, thoughts of peace, and not of evil, to give you an expected end."

"Me? God is thinking about me?" José asked. José suddenly received the revelation of God's personal interest in him. His face lit up, and he began to listen more intently to Steven's message. José had always known that God created everyone, but he was now enlightened to the fact that God specifically created him with a special purpose.

José asked Jesus to be his Lord and Saviour during that conversation. Once he recognized that the Creator of the universe had a personal interest in and love for him, José wanted to trust Him as King of his life. In the years following his conversion, José has learned much more from the Word of God. He has become a stable Christian and teacher on his island home. As Steven left his post in the Dominican Republic, he never forgot how the Creator led the conversation that brought salvation to José.

The golden text for this lesson depicts the message Steven wanted to express to José. God led the conversation into the deeper need within José to know that God cared for him intimately. Just as José came to know God's love for him, all who encounter the gospel must see that the Creator is the God of love.

When missionaries go into the mission fields, they communicate God's love to others. As we pray for missionaries worldwide, we should ask God to reveal Himself as the Creator of all and the One who cares for each person individually.

—*Beverly Medley Jones.*

The Jewish Aspect

In his book *The Genesis Record,* Henry Morris observes, "If a person really believes Genesis 1:1, he will not find it difficult to believe anything else recorded in the Bible. That is, if God really created all things, then he controls all things and can do all things" (Baker). This testimony is true and is relevant to our theme for today, "Praising God the Creator."

The Jewish people speak of creation in three particulars. First, they believe the land of Israel was created for them and given to them in perpetuity. During the dramatic term of Golda Meir, the American-raised prime minister of Israel, an American tourist suggested Mrs. Meir must be thrilled to sit where Moses sat. Weighing her words carefully, Mrs. Meir said, "I don't know about that. He wandered around here for forty years and settled on the only land without oil."

Second, the Torah, the five books of Moses, is seen as written in appreciation of creation.

Finally, the Jewish people believe themselves to be an accomplishment of divine creation. There is no arrogance in this contention.

Israel today is a land roughly 60 miles wide and 200 miles north to south. The center of it all is Jerusalem. For the Jew, the route to the city of David is always "up." Everywhere else is down. For example, a traveler "went down from Jerusalem to Jericho, and fell among thieves" (Luke 10:30).

At some time in their lives, nearly all Jews consider *aliyah,* "going up," in the larger sense of settling in Israel. The history of modern Israel is the story of nation building. The pioneers (*halutzim*) of the early twentieth century came to escape eastern European oppression. Mainly they were secular Jews who had little appreciation for God in their labors, although God had His hand upon them at all times.

Travel in Israel takes the visitor to varying terrain and unique sites and brings the Bible to life. Driving out to the Mediterranean coast, the warm-water beaches bid one to stay a while.

The most verdant fields in all of the Middle East unfold before Israel's visitors. The grape arbors of the Mount Carmel district are picture perfect. This is the breadbasket of the Middle East.

Galilee, so important to New Testament study, clusters around the Sea of Galilee, also called Tiberias and Kinnereth. Walking where Jesus walked with His disciples is the thrill of a lifetime.

The Jordan River flows out of the south end of the sea and threads its way to the Dead Sea, the lowest spot in the world. The high salt content means no fish swim there and no birds drink of it. On the north side of the Dead Sea are the caves where the Dead Sea scrolls, mostly Bible texts, were found.

On the west side of the Dead Sea loom the heights David knew so well in fleeing from King Saul.

The drive out to the Mediterranean once more takes one near the ancient cities of Arad, Beersheba, and Hebron. This is the Negev, the southern wilderness Abraham knew so well.

The Philistines, long a thorn in the side of Israel, lived along the Mediterranean and just inland of it. One day it will be possible to properly visit the area and thus complete a circuit of the Holy Land.

Christians in great numbers visit Israel each year. In spite of safety concerns, the Israelis keep risk to a minimum.

—*Lyle P. Murphy.*

Guiding the Superintendent

As Christians, we are blessed to have an awesome God. His acts of kindness, mercy, and love are too numerous to name. It is impossible to fully thank God for all of His wonderful acts. However, we still should cheerfully offer praise and worship to Him.

Today's lesson points us to reasons that we should praise the Lord. This lesson will help us develop a deeper appreciation for Him.

DEVOTIONAL OUTLINE

1. Give praise to God (Ps. 33:1-3). The unknown psalmist encouraged God's people to rejoice in the Lord. The Hebrew word translated "rejoice" can mean to cry out, to give a ringing cry and shout for joy. The psalmist expressed the beauty of God's people allowing praise to flow out.

The people of God are further encouraged to praise God through musical instruments. Sometimes musical instruments are looked down upon as a means to offer praise to the Lord. As indicated by the psalmist, however, God takes pleasure in them.

Psalms 33:3 informs us that God's people should sing songs of praise to Him. They are directed to sing songs with a new awareness of God. In addition, they are to sing with loud voices. This means that God's people should render their praise with joy.

2. Celebrate the righteousness of God (Ps. 33:4-5). The psalmist rejoiced in God's righteousness. He had an understanding of God's character. He viewed God as honest and lacking nothing. He elaborated on the trustworthy nature of God. He further emphasized that God's character is exemplified through His acts of kindness toward all creation.

3. Celebrate God's creation (Ps. 33:6-9). By God's declaration, the world came into existence. Seas, oceans, and rivers were formed. God separated the land from the sea. As the result of God's massive creation, the world should be in awe of Him.

AGE-GROUP EMPHASES

Children: At an early age, children need to learn the importance of showing appreciation. Enlighten them that their lives, blessings, and possessions are the result of a loving God. Encourage them to express praise and thanksgiving to God. This will help chart the course of their lives as they experience God's goodness.

Youths: Many teens are inundated with technology. This has prevented them from appreciating the natural wonders created by God. Through this passage, educate them about how detailed God's creative activity in the world is. Elaborate on the beauty of the seas, mountains, and heavens. Emphasize to them that technological advances are dependent on the natural resources created by God.

Adults: Adults are faced with many challenges. Because of this reality, they can occasionally be oblivious of the Lord's blessings. Sometimes they need reminders of the loving care of God. Share with them that they have a loving Father who is concerned about them. Tell them as well that they are privileged to be God's children.

—*Tyrone Keith Carroll, Sr.*

Scripture Lesson Text

PS. 96:1 O sing unto the Lord a new song: sing unto the Lord, all the earth.

2 Sing unto the Lord, bless his name; shew forth his salvation from day to day.

3 Declare his glory among the heathen, his wonders among all people.

4 For the Lord *is* great, and greatly to be praised: he *is* to be feared above all gods.

5 For all the gods of the nations *are* idols: but the Lord made the heavens.

6 Honor and majesty *are* before him: strength and beauty *are* in his sanctuary.

10 Say among the heathen *that* the Lord reigneth: the world also shall be established that it shall not be moved: he shall judge the people righteously.

11 Let the heavens rejoice, and let the earth be glad; let the sea roar, and the fulness thereof.

12 Let the field be joyful, and all that *is* therein: then shall all the trees of the wood rejoice

13 Before the Lord: for he cometh, for he cometh to judge the earth: he shall judge the world with righteousness, and the people with his truth.

NOTES

All Creation Joins in Praise

Lesson: Psalm 96:1-6, 10-13

Read: Psalm 96:1-13

TIME: unknown   PLACE: Palestine

GOLDEN TEXT—"O sing unto the Lord a new song: sing unto the Lord, all the earth" (Psalm 96:1).

Introduction

"God is great. God is good. Let us thank Him for this food. By His hands we all are fed; give us, Lord, our daily bread. Amen." Many of us learned this mealtime prayer as children. And although we probably recited it without thinking much about its meaning, the words, though simple, actually convey very sound theology. God truly is great, and He certainly is good.

In a similar way, the Psalms convey in very simple and poetic language profound truths about our God. They return again and again to God's greatness, glory, strength, goodness, and mercy; and they recall His mighty works on behalf of His people.

The Holy Spirit, who inspired the whole Bible, knew how much we need to be reminded of who God is, what He has done, and what He promises to do. It is the knowledge of these things—and the constant reminders of them in our songs and worship and meditation—that equips us to live joyfully and triumphantly in this often-cruel world and to declare to that world the wonders and glory of our great God and King.

LESSON OUTLINE

I. **TELL OF HIS GLORY**—Ps. 96:1-3

II. **ACKNOWLEDGE HIS GREATNESS**—Ps. 96:4-6

III. **ANTICIPATE HIS COMING**—Ps. 96:10-13

Exposition: Verse by Verse

TELL OF HIS GLORY

PS. 96:1 O sing unto the Lord a new song: sing unto the Lord, all the earth.

2 Sing unto the Lord, bless his name; shew forth his salvation from day to day.

3 Declare his glory among the heathen, his wonders among all people.

Psalm 96 "appears with slight variations in I Chron. 16:23-34" (Leupold, *Exposition of Psalms,* Baker). There it is sung on the occasion of David's moving the ark of the covenant into the tent constructed in Jerusalem. This is not proof that David wrote the psalm, whose author remains anonymous. However, the context in I Chronicles demonstrates how appropriate the words are for public worship even today.

Sing to the Lord (Ps. 96:1-2). The call to "sing unto the Lord" reflects a common emphasis in this section of Psalms (90—106), where praise, especially of the Lord's kingship, is very prominent (cf. 92:1; 93:1; 95:1; 97:1; 98:1; 99:1). This appeal initially is directed toward Israel, in contrast to the "heathen" (96:3). Verse 1 calls on the Israelites, the Old Testament people of God, to sing a "new song" in praise of God. This expression appears a number of times in Psalms (33:3; 40:3; 98:1; 144:9; 149:1).

Wiersbe noted that the expression "may mean new in time or new in expression. . . . The Spirit of God can make an old song new to us as we grow in our knowledge of God and His Word, or as we have new experiences, and He can also open our hearts to a song completely new to us" (*The Bible Exposition Commentary,* Cook). The point is that our worship should always be fresh and exciting, not simply thoughtless, boring, rote phrases.

The second half of Psalm 96:1 again calls for singing, but it expands the call to include "all the earth." The praises of Israel alone are not adequate to fully honor the Lord as He deserves. The earth here may include poetically the creation itself, but it certainly includes all humanity. The Lord is deserving of universal praise, and as His children, we are to lead the way.

The third call to sing to the Lord is followed in Psalm 96:2 by two other commands that explain the content of the singing. To "bless his name" means simply "to praise God." One of the chief reasons for praising the Lord is His salvation. The Hebrew word translated "shew forth" means "to preach (or bring) good news." "Salvation" can refer to various types of deliverance that come from the hand of God. His mighty works of deliverance call for praise, and the ultimate good news of deliverance is salvation from sin accomplished through the work of Jesus Christ. The good news of salvation should be on our lips daily, giving testimony to the world of the grace and mercy of God, which we have experienced.

Declare the Lord's glory (Ps. 96:3). Along with our songs of praise and testimony, we are to declare the Lord's glory among all peoples. In simplest terms, God's glory refers to the honor He possesses and deserves. His glory, or honor, is to be made known to the "heathen." Non-Jews is the normal meaning of the word for "heathen," but here the word basically means all those who have never heard of our God.

Typical of much Hebrew poetry, the second half of Psalm 96:3 essentially repeats the thought of the first half, using different terms. "Wonders" stands parallel to "glory" and refers to the mighty acts of God that reveal His glory. "All people" expands on "heathen." As we praise God for who He is and declare His mighty works in history and in our lives, His glory is revealed to others so that they can see what the Lord "is ready to do for all men" (Leupold).

There is clearly a missionary note here, but it is important to see that the call to declare God's glory to the world is not divorced from our personal worship and praise of Him but rather is an outgrowth of that worship and praise. As one writer has stated, "Where passion for God is weak, zeal for missions will be weak. Churches that are not centered on the exaltation of the majesty and beauty of God will scarcely kindle a fervent desire to 'declare *his* glory among the nations'" (Piper, *Let the Nations Be Glad!* Baker).

ACKNOWLEDGE HIS GREATNESS

4 For the LORD is great, and greatly to be praised: he is to be feared above all gods.

5 For all the gods of the nations are idols: but the LORD made the heavens.

6 Honor and majesty are before him: strength and beauty are in his sanctuary.

The Lord is above all (Ps. 96:4). With verse 4 the psalm begins to focus on the greatness of the God who has brought salvation and whose glory is to be declared worldwide. The very presence of the name Yahweh ("Lord"), which denotes His self-existence, speaks of His greatness. He is distinct from and far above His creation.

Because of His greatness, the Lord is to be praised greatly. Only lavish praise is appropriate for One who is so far above all else. In the highest terms and to the greatest extent, we are to offer praise to the Lord.

The praise of God is to be central to our lives, and the Word of God has a vital role in establishing such an attitude of praise in our lives. As we study Scripture, we learn more and more who God is and what He has done, and our praise and thanksgiving grows. And as we dwell on His glory, we understand more and more who we are; and as a result, our praise for Him grows even more.

The Lord's greatness demands fear surpassing all gods. Fear includes reverence, of course, and awe, and those ideas are present here. The word also is used frequently almost as a synonym for worship, and that idea is probably present as well. When we are genuinely in awe of the Lord—His character and His works—we do not just brush it off as an amazing experience; we fall before Him in worship.

The reference to "all gods" in Psalm 96:4 does not in any way affirm the actual existence of other gods, as the next verse will show. The psalm is simply exalting the greatness of God above anything human beings can conceive.

Our God is above all things—created and imagined. As such, He is to be feared and praised above anything this world exalts as a substitute. While God graciously gives us people, possessions, work, and experiences in which we often can take great joy, we must never let such things distract us from properly honoring the only One who is truly great.

The Lord is Creator of all (Ps. 96:5-6). The psalmist declared that "all the gods of the nations are idols." "Nations" is literally "peoples." The various so-called gods worshipped by people throughout the earth are nothing more than worthless idols.

The Hebrew word for "idols" means "something worthless (particularly as an object of worship)" (Harris, Archer, and Waltke, eds., *Theological Wordbook of the Old Testament,* Moody). The gods themselves do not exist (Isa. 45:5), and the objects that represent those false gods are utterly worthless.

The contrast between man-made idols and the one true God could not be greater. The idols are impotent and worthless. The Lord, on the other hand, created the heavens. His creative work is proof of His greatness and demonstrates the foolishness of elevating any person or thing above the Lord.

Psalm 96:6 further demonstrates

the greatness of the Lord. Honor, majesty, strength, and beauty are portrayed almost as persons standing before the Lord. This poetic device is used to communicate the idea that these characteristics of God are present wherever He is present. Especially in Israel's "sanctuary"—namely, the tabernacle and later the temple—God's glorious presence was manifested visibly (cf. Exod. 40:34-35; I Kings 8:10-11).

We know, of course, that God is omnipresent, or everywhere present at all times. As such, we can see these attributes of God revealed in His creation, in His providential works, and in our own lives.

The words for "honor" and "majesty" in Psalm 96:6 are very similar in sound and meaning in the Hebrew language. Both speak of the Lord's glory or splendor and together indicate "how everything in the presence of so great a King is of so high an order" (Leupold). "Strength" and "beauty" in the parallel phrase again emphasize the greatness of God. God's strength is revealed in His ability to create from nothing all that exists, and His beauty is seen in that which He has created. Though the world is marred by sin, great beauty still exists and testifies to the beauty of our Creator.

As important as it is to thank God for His blessings to us personally, true worship must also acknowledge God's greatness. He is awesome, and His creation reflects His strength and beauty. He is infinitely greater than anything human beings can attain, create, or imagine. The Lord is great, and He is worthy of great praise. If our lives are not filled with praise for our God, we are not fulfilling the primary purpose for our very existence: to glorify Him (cf. Isa. 43:6-7; I Cor. 10:31; I Pet. 4:11).

ANTICIPATE HIS COMING

10 Say among the heathen that the Lord reigneth: the world also shall be established that it shall not be moved: he shall judge the people righteously.

11 Let the heavens rejoice, and let the earth be glad; let the sea roar, and the fulness thereof.

12 Let the field be joyful, and all that is therein: then shall all the trees of the wood rejoice

13 Before the Lord: for he cometh, for he cometh to judge the earth: he shall judge the world with righteousness, and the people with his truth.

The Lord's rule (Ps. 96:10). The call here to proclaim to the unbelieving nations, or "heathen," that "the Lord reigneth" clearly points to Israel's Messiah, the Lord Jesus Christ. The Lord is King. He is, always has been, and always will be the Sovereign of the universe. However, the psalmist saw some future time when the Lord will come as Judge of all people (cf. vs. 13). So when the psalm speaks of the Lord's reign, it points "to a new and overwhelming assertion of sovereignty rather than a timeless theological truth" (Kidner, *Psalms 73—150,* Inter-Varsity).

This reign of the Lord will ensue when Christ returns to earth (Rev. 19:11—20:6). While few, if any, of the Old Testament saints saw or understood the distinction between Christ's first and second comings, the New Testament tells us that the Lord's earthly rule as King is fulfilled with His second—and still future—coming.

When Christ returns, the world "shall be established" with the result that "it shall not be moved" (Ps. 96:10). This suggests that there will be stability and security. The word for "established" can even be rendered "fixed." When Christ returns to reign on earth for a thousand years, the world's ills will be fixed. This is because the Lord Himself will be present, and "he shall judge the people righteously." "Judge" here refers not to condemnation but to governance. The Lord's rule will be marked by righteousness or perfect equity. There will be no injustice under His rule.

Nature's rejoicing (Ps. 96:11-12). Verses 11-12 describe the joy throughout the world when the Lord's kingdom is fully realized on the earth. Even the heavens and the earth, the trees, the sea, the fields, and all that they contain are called on to rejoice and be glad. The words are poetic and figurative, of course, in that these objects do not verbally praise the Lord. However, there is a sense in which nature itself, corrupted as it is by the curse of sin, longs for redemption (Rom. 8:22) and can rejoice with us in the coming reign of Christ.

The Lord's judgment (Ps. 96:13). This psalm ends with a repetition of the promise of the Lord's coming to judge, or govern, the earth. He will "judge the world with righteousness, and the people with his truth." "Righteousness" is the same Hebrew word that is also translated "justice" in the Old Testament. The Lord will dispense perfect justice.

The Bible tells us the Lord is just (cf. Deut. 32:4; Isa. 45:21; Acts 7:52), yet in this world we often see a lack of real justice. The psalmist declared that when the Lord comes, justice will be served. All will be judged justly and with steadfastness, or "truth," the final word in Psalm 96. It expresses the idea of faithfulness or complete dependability.

The promise that justice will be finally, fully, fairly, and perfectly dispensed on earth one day is a great comfort to God's people, who know Him as the just God and long for ultimate justice.

That promise also gives us yet another reason to praise our Lord and King. He is coming to do in this world what we can never accomplish.

The Lord is a God of glory and wonders. He is a God of honor, majesty, power, and beauty. He stands infinitely far above even His highest creation. And He is worthy of our highest and continual praise. He never changes, but our sinful world will change. It will change when the rulers of this world are replaced by the returning Ruler of the universe, and His people will reign with Him for a thousand years (Rev. 20:6). He will then establish a new heaven and new earth, "wherein dwelleth righteousness" (II Pet. 3:13).

—*Jarl K. Waggoner.*

QUESTIONS

1. In what other context do we see Psalm 96 employed?
2. What is involved in singing "a new song" (vs. 1)?
3. What salvation are we to show forth to the world (vs. 2)?
4. What is God's glory, and how do we declare His glory among the peoples of the world?
5. Why is the Lord to be greatly praised (vs. 4)?
6. In what sense are all the "gods" of the nations idols?
7. How is the greatness of God contrasted with the gods of the nations?
8. In what ways are God's strength and beauty revealed?
9. To what event does the Lord's reign in verse 10 refer?
10. What will characterize the rule of Christ on the earth?

—*Jarl K. Waggoner.*

Preparing to Teach the Lesson

You may remember that when the Lord Jesus made His triumphal entry into Jerusalem on a donkey, His disciples were praising Him. When He was asked to stop them, He said that if they did not praise Him, the very rocks would cry out in praise (Luke 19:40). When God declares that He will be praised, it will be done no matter who tries to stop it (Ps. 118:26). God created everything that exists. It was all meant primarily for His enjoyment and for mankind's enjoyment as well.

While the Fall and resulting curse has caused the created world to be flawed, it is still appropriate that all creation praise Him. We are never wrong to praise the Lord for what He has done for us, continues to do, and promises to do in future blessings. We honor Him for His beautiful character. Without it, we would never know about perfect character. No god conceived by humans has character deserving of praise.

TODAY'S AIM

Facts: to see how right and good it is for all creation to praise the Lord.

Principle: to see our privileged place in praising the Lord.

Application: to build an attitude and habit of praising the Lord daily.

INTRODUCING THE LESSON

There is a story of an older married couple. The husband was a man of few words. When his wife asked him whether he still loved her after so many years, he replied, "I said I loved you when I married you, and if there are any changes, I'll let you know." Clearly, he had not made a practice of telling his wife he loved her; he thought once was enough!

Any marriage counselor should, of course, advise couples to declare their love for each other frequently. So it is with praising God. His mercies are new every morning. His grace is richly poured out on us through the Lord Jesus, and we are daily surrounded with His blessing on our lives. All creation praises Him. As born-again Christians and part of His creation, we should always praise Him for who He is and what He has done. All creation praises Him in its own way.

DEVELOPING THE LESSON

1. Praise should be an outflow, not just an inward attitude (Ps. 96:1-3). We are urged here to sing a new song to the Lord. We are used to singing songs that we have used over and over. Not all of us are composers of songs; how, then, are we to reconcile this? Even if we sing a song that we have sung before, there needs to be a newness of our emotion and thoughts toward the Lord as we sing.

It is possible to sing along with others and not have any thought that we are singing to the Lord at all, much less a new expression of praise. He not only saved us; He also continues to save us daily, both in every spiritual way and in many practical physical ways. It will take constant spiritual renewal and diligence on our part to have a fresh love for the Lord, a fresh appreciation for His deeds, and a renewed heart of praise to Him. A godly attitude is crucial. Otherwise, we are not really praising Him at all.

2. Praise is appropriate because He alone is worthy of praise (Ps. 96:4-6). The gods created by humans down through the years have demanded praise and compliance with their demands, on penalty of death. They have demanded to be feared. But they are really weak and worthless nonentities when compared with the Lord. When we read that God is to be feared, we understand this to mean that we are to respect Him and hold Him in the highest esteem. God made the heavens and the earth and all that exists. One who can do that is the greatest. He totally transcends and eclipses all the false gods that people can invent.

We find in Psalm 96:6 that the concept we have of honor and majesty comes from our limited understanding of God's honor and majesty. Nothing else in all His magnificent creation is as majestic as God Himself. His strength and beauty are the origin of all we see as strong and beautiful in the created world. Without God as He is revealed in the Scriptures, we would have no concept of true beauty and honor.

There are major religions created by humans whose god must be corrupt indeed, for their approach to life results in ugly treatment of others rather than grace and mercy. We should praise God that He has revealed Himself to us enough that we can know such things as honor, strength, and beauty.

3. Praise should be universal and joyful (Ps. 96:10-13). We are to spread the word among all people of the earth that the Lord is worthy of praise. He alone can bring righteousness to our experience. There is so much inequity and persecution in the world. The good news about the Lord should bring great relief and encouragement to the oppressed and hopeless people of all nations. All creation is praising the Lord because He is coming to judge the world and right the wrongs people have inflicted on one another for centuries.

None of our political solutions answer everything. None of our educational solutions can offer everything we need. None of our financial fixes help enough. Only our magnificent God, with righteous judgment and just correction, can solve any of our significant problems. Lesser problems that we can correct must be answered in the light of His praiseworthy character and righteous actions.

ILLUSTRATING THE LESSON

All the earth praises the Lord.

ALL EXISTS BY HIS WORD!

SING UNTO THE LORD!

CONCLUDING THE LESSON

Our security and strength is in the Lord. As we worship Him, we are changed to be more like Him. It is true that no people have ever risen above their concept of God. We are drawn by the Holy Spirit to become like our God. His Word and the leading of His Spirit will always beckon us to praise and worship.

The word "worship" is a contraction of the older English "worth-ship." Our worship says that we believe our God has worth. If we fail to give Him glory and honor, we say He is not worth much. It would certainly be less than grateful to fail to thank and praise Him for what He has done in saving us from our sins and giving us His salvation. He has promised us His presence and power and has prepared a home for us in heaven. Praise the Lord!

ANTICIPATING THE NEXT LESSON

Our next lesson is about praising God as the great Provider and looking at what He provides.

—*Brian D. Doud.*

PRACTICAL POINTS

1. We should express genuine praise to God rather than methodical, empty worship (Ps. 96:1-2).
2. Evangelism is a Christian requirement (Ps. 96:3; cf. Mark 6:7-12; 16:15; Rom. 10:15).
3. The created are eternally subject to the Creator (Ps. 96:4-6).
4. God reigns over all whether men acknowledge Him or not (vs. 10).
5. There is peace in knowing that God's sovereign plan supersedes our circumstances (vss. 11-12).
6. Those who await Christ's return will be vindicated by God's judgment accomplished with righteousness and truth (Ps. 96:13; cf. Matt. 5:6; II Tim. 4:8).

—Lendell Sims.

RESEARCH AND DISCUSSION

1. Why do you think Scripture emphasizes singing so much? In what way is it possible for the whole earth to sing to the Lord?
2. How can we display God's salvation in our lives?
3. Why do you think Psalm 96:3 tells us to declare God's glory rather than His salvation?
4. Discuss the meaning of the term "modern-day idol." What are some examples of modern-day idols?
5. How can we as Christians help our nation realign itself with its core Christian tenets?
6. When will the world be judged? What part will the righteous play in this judgment (I Cor. 6:2)?

—Lendell Sims.

ILLUSTRATED HIGH POINTS

All the gods of the nations are idols

Since Ancient Greece, con artists have robbed curious bystanders with something called the shell game. It is played with empty containers, such as walnut shells, and a small item, such as a pea. Victims, or marks, are encouraged to gamble on their ability to identify the shell containing the elusive item.

This game is unwinnable. The hustler uses skillful sleight of hand to move the item to any position he wishes; the player always comes up empty. Furthermore, once the person begins to play, the scammer's friends surround him, obstructing his exit path.

What are we seeking—money, prestige, true worth? We try to find them everywhere. Friends, beware—this game is rigged. All our pursuits are but empty shells. There is, however, the One who made the heavens. He is not an empty shell but a living, feeling, powerful Being—God. He does not hide but promises that He will be found by all who truly seek Him.

The fulness thereof. . . . all that is therein

The dictionary defines a false front as a "facade extending beyond and especially above the true dimensions of a building to give it a more imposing appearance" (www.merriam-webster.com). It is an architectural device often used by set designers for films. Might we be "fronting" with God?

Observe the concept expressed in Psalm 96:11-12: "Let the sea [an entity] roar, and the fulness thereof [that which fills the entity]" and "let the field [an entity] be joyful, and all that is therein [that which fills the entity]." God is calling for both our outer man and our inner content to enter into worship.

—Therese Greenberg.

Golden Text Illuminated

"O sing unto the Lord a new song: sing unto the Lord, all the earth" (Psalm 96:1).

Throughout the Psalms we find that we are to sing of God's wondrous works, triumphs in history, glorious attributes, and wonderful characteristics. God Himself is to be the focus of our singing.

But this text goes so much further. Notice that it has a worldwide focus. It calls on the whole earth to join in praise to God through singing. The psalm goes on in verse 3 to mention the importance of declaring His glory among the "heathen," in fact, among "all people" (every kind of person in every place). So this is not just a text speaking about praise; it is also a text that speaks of mission. Since God is to be praised by the whole of His creation, we are given the foundation for our worship and also a solid foundation for worldwide missions and evangelism. God is to be praised by every creature in every place.

Have we grasped the greatness of the scope of the doctrine of praise? It is more than singing our favorite songs in church. It is a commitment to lift up our great God's name wherever it can be taken in this wide world.

The song that is to be sung is a "new" song. There is to be a fresh expression of praise permeating our testimony and witness in the wider world. This is not a command to come up with new songs for singing in our churches. It is a command to tell the story of God's creation and salvation in a fresh way, reflecting a refreshed heart, wherever we go. Remember, the focus is worldwide. The psalm is urgently telling us that God's glory and salvation must be made known everywhere. Let us find new ways to tell the gospel and new ways to praise Him, engaging all of our faculties and creativity to reach the world with the glory of God!

We know that this command that God be praised in all the earth is routinely violated by countless souls in innumerable locations around the globe. Day after day men and women in places around the world ignore the living God, believe falsehoods about Him, fight against Him, or trivialize His nature and glory. This command is testimony that God is to be worshipped by those who are currently not doing so. That is why we have missions, because God has commanded worship everywhere.

Worship and praise lead to missions, seeking to bring lost men and women in "all the earth" into right relationship with Him through Christ so that they too may fulfill their proper destiny, turning with true worshipping hearts to the One who made them.

When men are singing a new song unto the Lord in every place, our mission will be nearing fulfillment. Until that time we have work to do. Missions is not just about church planting or theological education or Bible translation; it is about planting the name of God where it is not known and leading others to become worshippers, filled with authentic praise. That is God's heart.

Through praise we fulfill our mission. We commit ourselves to spreading the knowledge of God all over the earth and calling each person to understand why he exists and how to return praise to the living God. What an exciting adventure!

—*Jeff VanGoethem.*

Heart of the Lesson

There is something so refreshing about starting a new year. Perhaps we want a new beginning when the snow covers the ground like a layer of glue and we feel as though spring will never come. Truthfully, we have the opportunity to start something new every day; however, the onset of a new year tends to give us that extra boost of motivation.

1. Sing to the Lord (Ps. 96:1-3). Sing! Make a melody! Awaken your heart to the things of God. Look at Psalm 96 as an invitation to join with all creation to tell God how great, wonderful, and marvelous He is!

Have you ever been at a sporting event when almost everyone in the stands was on their feet, screaming at the top of their lungs and encouraging their team? As you scan the crowd, every once in a while you will see one or two people still sitting in their seats. Let us presume that those who refused to stand were able-bodied and just chose not to join the celebration. They may have missed the best part of the experience of going to a game by choosing not to participate.

It can happen to us in regard to our worship of God. We can miss what could be some of the high points of our lives because we choose not to join in the celebration of Jesus Christ. We choose to enter the sanctuary just as the worship time ends. We choose to sing the songs with our mouths but not our hearts. The psalmist is not just inviting us to sing; he is inviting us to participate in an ongoing worship service to our King.

2. The Lord is great (Ps. 96:4-6). "The Lord is great, and greatly to be praised: he is to be feared above all gods." Our God is very great! He is much more powerful than we can imagine. The psalm really captures this in verse five: "All the gods of the nations are idols: but the Lord made the heavens." In other words, it does not matter what other people tell us their gods did for them; our God created the heavens and the earth. All other gods are created beings, but our God *is* the Creator! Other gods are made of gold, silver, bronze, or wood. Our God is clothed with majesty and dignity, strength and beauty, and justice and truth.

3. The Lord is coming (Ps. 96:10-13). Let the nations of the world know that our God is King; our God reigns. Let joy and gladness erupt everywhere because the Lord is coming to the earth!

"He cometh, . . . he cometh to judge the earth: he shall judge the world with righteousness, and the people with his truth" (Ps. 96:13). When we talk about judgment, we have a tendency to fear. It is similar to the feeling that many of us get when we are driving and realize that a police officer has been following us a little too long. Here is the good news, and this is truly something to cause joy and peace. If we have been following the laws of the land, there is no reason for the police officer to pull us over and write us a traffic ticket.

In the same manner, when the Lord comes to judge the earth, we have nothing to fear. We are on the right side of the court! The Judge is going to rule in our favor! Why? Because Jesus already paid the price for our acquittal.

—*Kristin Reeg.*

World Missions

Music is a powerful missionary force. David was assigned to play for King Saul, and the evil spirit fled (I Sam. 16:23). An earthquake shook the prison when Paul and Silas were singing praises to God (Acts 16:25-26). According to Zephaniah 3:17, God sings over us. And we are admonished to speak to one another in psalms, hymns, and spiritual songs.

God loves music. He wants all the earth to sing to Him. Songwriters, musicians, and singers, though not typically acknowledged as missionaries, are explicitly included in God's plan for drawing people to Himself.

Roger Jones is a songwriter, recording artist, and bandleader of the Spiritual Hi-Lites. Although he knew music was his calling, at first he had not considered himself a missionary in this area. He travels the country singing the gospel. He sees lives change before his eyes as people commit their lives to Jesus at his concerts. Roger insists that the band only sing songs that are biblically sound. Every song he writes has a scriptural origin. His heart is set on reaching the lost and hurting with the good news of Christ. He truly takes the gospel message everywhere he goes. Because he had not been formally commissioned in the mission field, however, Roger did not describe himself as a missionary. But one encounter changed his mind.

One evening the Spiritual Hi-Lites held a concert in a small country church. They passed out a list of their song titles to each person who entered. Roger had insisted that Scripture references be included with each corresponding song. He wanted the listeners to have an outline for later study.

When the concert ended, many from the audience came to the stage to speak to the band members. Eighty-four-year-old Ellen slowly made her way to the front, finding a place to sit on the first pew. She waited until Roger was free and motioned for him to come to her. Roger took a seat beside Ellen to hear her weak voice. She started by telling Roger how much she enjoyed the concert. Then she thanked him for including the corresponding Scriptures. She told Roger she would take the list home and read the verses that night. Roger was encouraged by Ellen's words and decided that including the Scripture with the song list had been an idea God had given him.

The next day, Roger received a telephone call from a member of Ellen's church. Ellen had been found that morning in her bed. She had gone to be with the Lord during the night. Roger did not find out whether Ellen had been able to read the list of Scriptures, but he was satisfied to know that his band had blessed her before she died. After this experience, Roger and his band began to consider their traveling concerts as musical mission opportunities.

God expects all the earth to sing to Him. As we sing to the Lord, He will bless us and those around us. Ellen was blessed when the Spiritual Hi-Lites sang to the Lord. God's people all are blessed through singing. When we sing, we praise God.

There are innumerable mission opportunities God has targeted around the world. This week, we illustrate one of those missions—music. Roger and his band discovered how vital music is in missionary work. All creation should join in praise through music and singing to the Lord.

—*Beverly Medley Jones.*

The Jewish Aspect

Charles Haddon Spurgeon, the great preacher of London, called Psalm 96 "a missionary hymn" and a "millennial anthem." Spurgeon enlarged on those ideas by calling its purpose "to give forth a song for the Gentiles . . . to celebrate the conversion of the nations" (*The Treasury of David,* Hendrickson).

In the last verses of Psalm 95, God grieved over the rebellion of the Jews, typified by the ten spies of Kadesh-Barnea (Num. 13:30-33). Now Psalm 96 points to a future day when all the nations will worship God.

It is easy to emphasize the defection of the ten spies, but what of the faithfulness of the other two—Joshua and Caleb? A look at Jewish history reflects the interesting story of the two groups that left Jerusalem as the Roman army approached the great city in A.D. 70. One group, "those who accepted Jesus of Nazareth as the Messiah, indifferent to the national cause, sought safety in flight from Jerusalem; the small community settled in Pella beyond the Jordan" (Margolis and Marx, *A History of the Jewish People,* Jewish Publication Society). Jesus had warned His followers to flee when the siege appeared imminent (Luke 21:20-21).

A second group of Jews walked through the siege lines, made a deal with the Romans, and established a bloodless Judaism in Yavneh, Israel. This was the founding of the Judaism of today (Margolis and Marx). The eighteen synagogues in my own city carry on the Yavneh doctrine of no personal Messiah and no new birth needed for mankind.

W. Graham Scroggie, commenting on Psalm 96, wrote, "The Israelites are made the Lord's evangelists" (*Psalms,* Revell). Wilhelm Baum was rescued from the menace of the Nazis in Germany in the 1930s. An American Jewish family brought him out of the terror that would in a few years destroy six million Jews. Settled in America, Wilhelm became "Bill" and an American citizen. When World War II began, he enlisted and was trained as an aerial photographer.

The gospel of grace touched Bill, and he trusted the Messiah Jesus. He immediately sought Bible training and began to reach the nations. Youth for Christ, a dynamic soul-winning organization, trained the young believer. Bill became the "Gospel Magician!"

From that beginning Bill felt the call of God to take the gospel to the nations. He felt a special calling to the islands of Japan. He and his wife, Augusta, went to Japan and spent a lifetime reaching a very challenging people. Many Christians thought he should have gone to Israel and the Jews, but he did not feel led in that direction. At the close of their missionary service, the Baums returned to the heartland, but continued to proclaim the gospel in over twenty-six countries. No servant of Christ was ever appreciated more than Bill Baum, now with the Lord.

One of the most important groups in Jewish evangelism today is the Lausanne Consultation on Jewish Evangelism. LCJE is a gathering place of worldwide missionaries to the Jewish people. Currently, the LCJE has exposed the false teaching that the gospel was only for the Gentiles rather than the Jews. This claim is based on the contention that God has rejected the Jews. Dr. Ashley Crane, an Australian missionary, found this charge without basis (*LCJE Bulletin 117,* August 2014).

—Lyle P. Murphy.

Guiding the Superintendent

In sporting events, there is usually a home (host) team and an away (visiting) team. The home team usually has a larger number of fans attending than the visiting team. This creates a benefit that is commonly referred to as the home-field advantage. This is because there are more people cheering, praising, and encouraging the home team.

This week's lesson points us to the importance of directing worship and praise to the Lord. The psalmist will give encouragement to celebrate God through multiple methods.

DEVOTIONAL OUTLINE

1. The call to praise (Ps. 96:1-3). There is debate over who authored this psalm. Some scholars believe it was David, while others suggest that there is not enough evidence to identify an author. Regardless of the author's identity, he encouraged all to praise God.

The first method of praise emphasized by the psalmist is singing. The people were directed to sing a new song to the Lord. This meant that songs to God should interpret afresh His salvation. God's people are encouraged to declare His wonderful works to the world.

2. Reasons to praise (Ps. 96:4-6). The psalmist moved from encouraging people to praise God to offering reasons to praise Him. The first reason presented is the greatness of God. God is greater than and is to be feared above all other gods.

Because of His majesty, power, and character, God is worthy of all praise. Other gods are mere creations formed through man's ideas. They do not have the capacity to sustain, bless, or protect their followers. In contrast to idol gods, the Lord alone created the universe. Glory and majesty describe Him, and His temple radiates power and beauty.

3. Let the universe praise (Ps. 96:10-13). God's people are encouraged to declare the Lord's supremacy. He is forever established as King. He is the Judge of all humankind, who will execute fairness and justice to all humanity. The psalmist called on the universe—heavens, earth, and sea, and all creatures in them—to express adoration to the Lord. Not excluding any form of creation, he also commanded the fields and trees to rejoice.

The psalmist spoke of the future coming of the Lord. When He arrives, God the Righteous One will judge the world.

AGE-GROUP EMPHASES

Children: Children need to understand the beauty of offering praise to God. Explain to them that the animal kingdom, seas, and heavens declare the glory of God. Encourage the children to begin expressing praise to God through prayer, singing, and testimonies.

Youths: Convey to teens the importance of expressing gratitude to God. Encourage them to daily practice it. Help them understand that worship and praise should be rendered to God for His goodness.

Adults: God calls His people to share their faith. Christians sometimes overlook this responsibility. However, this lesson demonstrates to adults the importance of being a witness to a lost world. Encourage them to express God's goodness in their testimonies to others.

—*Tyrone Keith Carroll, Sr.*

Scripture Lesson Text

PS. 65:1 Praise waiteth for thee, O God, in Si'on: and unto thee shall the vow be performed.

2 O thou that hearest prayer, unto thee shall all flesh come.

9 Thou visitest the earth, and waterest it: thou greatly enrichest it with the river of God, *which* is full of water: thou preparest them corn, when thou hast so provided for it.

10 Thou waterest the ridges thereof abundantly: thou settlest the furrows thereof: thou makest it soft with showers: thou blessest the springing thereof.

11 Thou crownest the year with thy goodness; and thy paths drop fatness.

12 They drop *upon* the pastures of the wilderness: and the little hills rejoice on every side.

13 The pastures are clothed with flocks; the valleys also are covered over with corn; they shout for joy, they also sing.

NOTES

Praise God the Provider

Lesson: Psalm 65:1-2, 9-13

Read: Psalms 65:1-13; 67:6-7

TIME: about 1000 B.C.   PLACE: Jerusalem

GOLDEN TEXT—"Thou visitest the earth, and waterest it: thou greatly enrichest it with the river of God, which is full of water" (Psalm 65:9).

Introduction

There is an old adage that says, "You never miss the water till the well runs dry." On the surface, those words express the obvious. How could we miss the water as long as we have it? The proverbial meaning, however, is that we often do not appreciate what we have until it is gone.

How true that is! When no water comes from the tap, we begin to realize how dependent we are on water. When a health crisis arises, we really understand the great blessing of good health.

It is true that we thank God when we recover from illness or when unexpected blessings come our way, but we frequently overlook those daily blessings that are always present. The water, the sun, and the food we have are almost always present, and we

tend to take them for granted. Yet these blessings are as much from the hand of God as those "big" answers to our prayers.

It is instructive that the New Testament lists ingratitude alongside such sins as covetousness and blasphemy (II Tim. 3:2). As followers of Christ, we need to cultivate an attitude of thanksgiving. Like other portions of Scripture, Psalm 65 reminds us to be thankful for those blessings we so often take for granted.

LESSON OUTLINE

I. GOD GRACIOUSLY HEARS—
   Ps. 65:1-2

II. GOD GRACIOUSLY PROVIDES—
   Ps. 65:9-13

Exposition: Verse by Verse

GOD GRACIOUSLY HEARS

PS. 65:1 Praise waiteth for thee, O God, in Sion: and unto thee shall the vow be performed.

2 O thou that hearest prayer, unto thee shall all flesh come.

Psalm 65 was written by David. Given its emphasis on the blessings related to the harvest, many have surmised that it was written "to be sung annually when the first grain of the year's barley harvest was brought to the Lord and waved by the priest as a dedication offering (see Lev. 23:9-14)" (Walvoord and Zuck, eds., *The Bible Knowledge Commentary*, Cook).

Psalm 65 begins with a rather interesting statement: "Praise waiteth for thee, O God, in Sion." The picture seems to be that of worshippers gathered in "Sion," or Zion, waiting to offer praise to the Lord.

While the name Zion is sometimes applied to the whole city of Jerusalem, it originally referred to the hill on which the temple was eventually built. The temple was not built until after David's death, but the ark of the covenant resided there on Zion until the temple was completed in Solomon's reign. David thus pictured the people gathered at the sanctuary of the Lord on Zion to praise God.

The Hebrew word translated "waiteth" in Psalm 65:1 literally reads "silence." The opening phrase therefore could be translated in any of several ways: "Praise is silence for You," "Silence is praise," or "There will be silence before You, and praise." We usually think of praise as taking the form of songs and verbal testimony to God's greatness, but "silence is also a part of worship, and we must learn to wait quietly before the Lord" (Wiersbe, *The Bible Exposition Commentary*, Cook). Quiet contemplation of God's blessings in gratitude for them is an appropriate form of praise.

While today there is no central sanctuary where God's people are to worship, we are to gather together to praise Him from the heart, whether in silence or in song. Worship can also include the performance of vows. Vows played an important part in Israel's worship, though there is not much emphasis on them in the New Testament. Vows were voluntary, but one who made them was obligated to fulfill them before God. To take a vow and act on it was a means of expressing gratitude to God.

Psalm 65:2 stresses the character of God as One who hears our prayers. The Hebrew expression literally reads, "O You, Hearer of prayer." When the Bible says that God hears our prayers, it is not talking about audibly hearing the sound of them; it means that He hears and responds. He is a compassionate God who hears the prayers of His people and is eager to answer.

This does not mean we always get what we want when we pray, of course, for we do not always know what is best for us, others, or God's glory. But it is reassuring to know that God is the Hearer of prayers. This great truth is all the more reason we should offer continual praise to Him.

The declaration that all people will come to Him emphasizes that it is only the God who answers prayer who can meet the needs of mankind. All *should* come to Him in their need, and indeed when the Lord Jesus reigns on earth, all *will* come to Him. We know, however, that in the present world, not all do come to Him. In fact, the verses that follow speak of sin keeping people from the Lord and of the sinners' need for God to purge them of their sin and cause them to approach the Lord.

God is worthy of the praise and worship of all His creation. In this fallen world, however, He does not receive the praise He deserves. Sadly, He often does not even receive the praise that He should from His own children. If we are to fulfill our very purpose in life, we must be people who express gratitude and praise to our Creator. Whether in the quiet of our own hearts or in the worship of the congregation of believers, let us be sure we are praising the Hearer of our prayers.

GOD GRACIOUSLY PROVIDES

9 Thou visitest the earth, and waterest it: thou greatly enrichest it with the river of God, which is full of water: thou preparest them corn, when thou hast so provided for it.

10 Thou waterest the ridges thereof abundantly: thou settlest the furrows thereof: thou makest it soft with showers: thou blessest the springing thereof.

11 Thou crownest the year with thy goodness; and thy paths drop fatness.

12 They drop upon the pastures of the wilderness: and the little hills rejoice on every side.

13 The pastures are clothed with flocks; the valleys also are covered over with corn; they shout for joy, they also sing.

Psalm 65 begins with a focus on Israel, the sanctuary in Zion, and the chosen people (vss. 1-4). It then expands to include all nations, "them that are afar off upon the sea" (vs. 5) and those who "dwell in the uttermost parts" (vs. 8). The psalm concludes with a universal perspective, as God's provision for the earth and all who dwell therein is pictured poetically and beautifully in verses 9-13.

For the earth (Ps. 65:9-10). David's psalm addresses God directly in verse 9, attributing the blessings that fall upon the earth to the sovereign and providential actions of the Lord. First, God is described as the One who visits the earth. In the Bible, the word "visit" carries the idea of exercising "oversight over a subordinate, either in the form of inspecting or of taking action to cause a considerable change in the circumstance of the subordinate, either for the better or for the worse" (Harris, Archer, and Waltke, eds., *Theological Wordbook of the Old Testament*, Moody).

Thus, the word can be used in reference to God's pouring out judgment (cf. Lev. 18:25; Jer. 5:9). Here, however, the word refers to God's acting to bring blessing to the earth, or land (Ps. 65:9; cf. Gen. 50:24; Ruth 1:6).

In Psalm 65:9 the particular blessing of God in view is His bringing water upon the earth. In fact, the earth is enriched with "the river of God, which is full of water." The rain is not just an act of nature; it is the providential work of God established in the natural order to benefit all humanity. The "river of God" is a poetic expression for rain, which in fact comes from God and makes the earth rich and fertile. Again this is a blessing for all, the just and the unjust (Matt. 5:45).

"Thou preparest them corn" (Ps. 65:9) means that God thoroughly establishes it. "Corn" is a general term for grain. God is ultimately the one responsible for producing the grain because He is the one who brings the rain. "Them" refers to people. God blesses the earth so that He can bless people. In the typical fashion of Hebrew poetry, the final line in verse 9 essentially repeats the thought that God establishes the grain for mankind through the rain He brings upon the earth.

Psalm 65:10 continues the thought of verse 9, adding precise details of *how* God prepares the earth for the growing of crops. The plowed fields with their furrows and ridges are pictured as being watered by the rain, which causes the loosened soil to be softened and to settle down. The water that comes is attributed to the Lord, as is the growth that springs from the moist soil.

As Leupold noted, "The poet . . . attempts to ascribe each successive step in the process to direct divine action. In the Bible nature does not work autonomously" (*Exposition of Psalms,* Baker).

The blessing of abundant water for the land presupposes that the Israelite nation was in right relationship to the Lord and His covenant. We must understand that the Old Testament nation of Israel was in a covenant relationship with the Lord, and as long as they obeyed Him as a nation, He would provide them with abundant rainfall (Deut. 28:1-2, 12; cf. vss. 15, 23-24). Since Psalm 65:3-4 speaks of the forgiveness of the Lord and His satisfaction with His people Israel, it followed that the blessing of adequate rainfall would come. And for this, David's people could—and should— praise the Lord.

Today the world experiences droughts and famine, abundant rainfall, and devastating floods. Because the nations of the world today are not related to God by covenant, however, we cannot specifically and directly connect such blessings or curses to national obedience or disobedience to God. There are two things to keep in mind, however. First, whatever blessings we enjoy come from the gracious hand of God, and for them He deserves our gratitude and praise. Second, the spiritual principle remains for both individuals and nations: obedience to God brings His blessing; disobedience to God brings only trouble.

For the year (Ps. 65:11-12). In very poetic language, David further described the provision of God for His people as the Lord crowning the whole year with His goodness. The fact that the entire year receives His blessing suggests God's continuing faithfulness to His covenant promises to obedient Israel.

To crown literally means to surround. God's goodness is seen as enveloping the year, revealing His moral perfection and His gracious nature toward mankind.

"Fatness" is a common idiom in the Bible to express prosperity and God's blessing (cf. Ps. 92:14; Prov. 11:25; 13:4; 28:25). Psalm 65:11 pictures God passing through the land, and everywhere along His "paths" the land flourishes. Verse 12 shows the extent of God's provision. The prosperity that follows on God's path reaches "the pastures of the wilderness."

The wilderness is usually depicted as a barren area with sparse vegetation because of the lack of rainfall. God's blessing extends even to these uncultivated lands, however, bringing fertility so that it can be said that they drip with the fatness, or prosperity, the Lord has brought.

The author used the poetic device of personification in the remainder of Psalm 65, beginning with the last half of verse 12, where the "little hills" are described as if they were people. Translated more literally, this portion of the verse would read, "The hills gird themselves with rejoicing." God's blessing on the land is such that the hills themselves are pictured as completely engaged in rejoicing. Just as our clothes enwrap us and are obvious to all who look at us, God's creation bears obvious testimony to His blessing for all to see.

For His people (Ps. 65:13). Verse 13 continues the description of the Lord's provision for His creation. The emphasis here, however, is more directly related to the benefits enjoyed by His people. "The pastures are clothed with flocks" continues the idea from the previous verse, where the hills are "clothed" with rejoicing. A different Hebrew word is used here, but the idea is very similar. The flocks of sheep and goats are so abundant and so thick that they look like clothing on the pastures.

As a one-time shepherd himself, David certainly could appreciate such a sight, but in the economy of ancient Israel, sheep and goats were especially important as sources of milk, meat, and wool for clothing, not to mention their important role in Israel's sacrificial system of worship. The sight of large, prosperous flocks in the pastures was a beautiful sight and evidence of God's gracious provision for His people.

Likewise, the valleys are described in Psalm 65:13 as being "covered over with corn," another obvious sign of fertility and prosperity. The word for "corn" here is not the same as is used in verse 9, but it essentially means the same thing, referring to grain of one sort or another. Barley and wheat were very valuable commodities, providing food for both people and livestock. Seeing the fertile, cultivated valleys producing an abundant harvest assured the Israelites that the Lord had provided the food that they needed.

Like the hills in Psalm 65:12, the pastures and the grainfields in verse 13 are pictured as shouting for joy and singing in praise of the God who had blessed them. Here David employed the very same Hebrew words that are used elsewhere to call God's people to "shout unto God" (47:1) and to sing to Him (cf. 33:3; 68:4, 32; 96:1-2).

Wiersbe observed, "The meadows would feed the flocks and herds, and the valleys would produce the grain. All of them would unite as one voiceless choir shouting for joy to the God of the universe, the Creator of every

good and perfect gift."

David the psalmist understood that such rich blessings could be anticipated by his obedient nation because of God's special promise to Israel. Yet we too enjoy the blessings of God every day in the sun and the rain, in family and friends, in our Saviour and our churches. God has graciously given us physical life and eternal life. Let us never be guilty of overlooking God's blessings or being ungrateful for all He gives us. If even the earth itself—the hills, the pastures, and the valleys—give silent but powerful praise to God, surely we can rejoice, shout for joy, and sing His praises aloud.

—*Jarl K. Waggoner.*

QUESTIONS

1. Who was the human author of Psalm 65?
2. In what sense can worship be silent?
3. What does the Bible mean when it says God hears our prayers?
4. What is the meaning behind the idea that all people will come to God (vs. 2)?
5. What does it mean that God visits the earth (vs. 9)?
6. What particular blessing of God is in view in verse 9?
7. To what does "corn" refer? How does God prepare the corn?
8. What promise did God give to Israel regarding rainfall?
9. What does the term "fatness" often signify in the Bible?
10. How did the author use the device of personification in verses 12-13?

—*Jarl K. Waggoner.*

Preparing to Teach the Lesson

Taking things for granted is probably the opposite of praising God for what He does. There are many things in life that seem to come to us rather automatically. We typically do not give them any thought until they become unavailable. Then we panic and frantically try to get them back again. Breathable air and drinkable water are prime examples of this. Daylight and enough warmth to function are high on our list of necessary "givens." God knows about all our needs. He is the great Provider and Sustainer of a multitude of factors that are essential and that make us comfortable.

The most important provision is the light of salvation in Christ. A huge portion of the world, both here and abroad, is in spiritual darkness. It is a great habit to daily thank and praise God for His wonderful provision for every need in our lives.

TODAY'S AIM

Facts: to see more clearly our need to praise God for His provision.

Principle: to see how properly aligning ourselves with God's pattern for our spiritual lives will bring great and lasting blessings.

Application: to daily thank and praise God for the blessing of His gracious provision for all.

INTRODUCING THE LESSON

Most of us have lived for so long in such abundance, and even in luxury, that we can become jaded. We either do not see that God is providing for us, or if do we see it, we no longer have any deep appreciation for it. Our lesson this week will show us that people everywhere are blessed by God's provision and need to praise Him for it.

DEVELOPING THE LESSON

1. Praise for God's general provision (Ps. 65:1-2). The phrase "Praise waiteth for thee, O God, in Sion" lets us know that praise belongs to God. We may compliment people on their accomplishments and even praise some people, but ultimate, heartfelt praise belongs to God alone. It belongs to Him for what He has done and continues to do.

Praising God is also necessary for human beings. We need to know that we have God watching over us and providing for us in order to be secure and fulfilled. Not only do we have a "God-shaped void" in our spirits without Him; we also are born spiritually dead because of our sinful human nature. We are not truly alive until we are born again by the Spirit of God in His grace. We then have spiritual life. Praising God for His provision of grace, salvation, and all the material things we need is not only natural for our spirits, it is also essential for our spiritual health. This includes the health of our minds and emotions.

God hears prayer. God answers prayer. That alone is cause for great praise. He is not obligated to do anything for us. In His total sovereignty, He could refuse to answer our prayers. However, He provides for us so lavishly that praise for His provision should be spontaneous, frequent, and fervent toward Him.

2. Praise for God's provision of food (Ps. 65:9-11). People talk about "Mother Nature" in connection with the weather or other facets of the natural world. This man-made deity is held responsible for the weather, both good and bad! But the truth is that God controls the rain and all facets of the weather. As the psalmist put it, He "visitest the earth." The "river of God" is the ecosystem that causes evaporation, clouds, and the resultant rain to fall to sustain the life and growth of plant life on earth. Not only is this "river" full of water; it also is self-replenishing. Then too, droughts and floods are part of His provision, even though they may be destructive at times.

Forest fires may have "natural" causes, such as lightning. They also may serve a special purpose; it is known that sequoia seeds will not germinate unless there has been a forest fire to replenish nutrients in the soil. For many years before the development of herbicides, farmers used to burn the dead grass and weeds on their farmlands to control the weeds. The weed seeds were thus killed and did not produce new weeds.

God provides for the corn and cereal grains to grow for both animals and humans. It is hard to imagine a world in which these did not play a big part. It is appropriate to praise God for this specific provision. Thanksgiving Day has a proper focus that we should perpetuate. We should be thanking and praising God daily for His provision of produce in the world. The way He has designed grains to reproduce many times over the amount needed for reproduction so that there is a great surplus for our consumption is a reality for which we may praise Him. Harvesttime with the abundance it usually reveals is a time of rejoicing and praise for the bountiful provision.

3. Praise for God's provision of the earth and the animals (Ps. 65:12-13). Our existence would be greatly impoverished without animals. That we are able to domesticate, train, and utilize animals is also a great blessing. The use of eggs and milk is common in our diets. We use animals as beasts of burden and keep them as pets. All these benefits would be absent had God not provided them for us. The psalmist portrays the hills, pastures, and valleys as singing and shouting for joy over the Lord's provision of rain and food for the animals. It is as though the world God created cannot be silent but must praise Him for His gracious provision.

ILLUSTRATING THE LESSON

All the world praises God for His provision.

CONCLUDING THE LESSON

We need to praise God. Praising Him aligns our spirits toward Him and contributes greatly to our spiritual health. We owe Him our praise because He has been so thoughtful and concerned for our welfare. We praise Him for His power in bringing about all the factors that contribute to our physical lives and our spiritual well-being.

Praise belongs to God; we owe it to Him. God hates the sin of ingratitude as much as anything we might regard as a major sin (such as murder). It is easy to be less than grateful. It is also easy to praise Him when we read His Word and understand what He has done for us as our great Provider.

ANTICIPATING THE NEXT LESSON

In our next lesson, we will look at God's wisdom and see why He is to be praised for it.

—Brian D. Doud.

PRACTICAL POINTS

1. We worship God in spirit and truth. Our access to God is made possible through Jesus. We should have compassion on those who are separated from Him (Ps. 65:1-2; cf. Jer. 29:12).
2. We often take for granted God's provision for all mankind and for us personally (Ps. 65:9).
3. There is a season for all things. Winter will inevitably lead to spring. God does everything in His own time (Ps. 65:10-11; cf. Eccles. 3:1-8; II Pet. 3:8).
4. God elicits praise from the earth as it basks in His provision (Ps. 65:12-13; cf. Matt. 5:45).

—Lendell Sims.

RESEARCH AND DISCUSSION

1. In ancient Israel, why was praise to God so closely connected to the city of Jerusalem?
2. Other than ministry work, why is it thought that farming is the profession most closely associated with godliness?
3. The secular world does not acknowledge God's provision. How sensitive is the food chain to disruption?
4. Because God is so caring, what can we do to avoid becoming like spoiled children?
5. How do we have access to the abundance of the Lord?
6. Other than by our Sunday church attendance, how can the non-Christian world witness Christians bringing praise to God?

—Lendell Sims.

ILLUSTRATED HIGH POINTS

Waterest it: . . . with the river of God

Water (physical or spiritual) is a life-giving gift from God. In the New Jerusalem, a great river will flow from heaven's throne (cf. Rev. 22:1). This quickening current is a visual manifestation of a spiritual truth. It speaks of the life-giving quality of the Holy Spirit (cf. John 4:14; 7:38-39).

Do we pray in earnest for spiritual rain? Without an outpouring of the Holy Spirit, how dry will our souls become?

"And the Lord shall guide thee continually, and satisfy thy soul in drought, and make fat thy bones: and thou shalt be like a watered garden, and like a spring of water, whose waters fail not" (Isa. 58:11).

Waterest the ridges . . . makest it soft

There is an old English proverb that says, "The more furrows, the more corn." Furrows are deep, irrigating grooves often dug by use of ox and plow into unyielding, crusty soil. Without them, the harvest would starve for want of moisture and nutrition (cf. Prov. 12:11). Furrows catch rain—that is their beauty.

Many things cut deep furrows into our hearts and lives: enemies (cf. Ps. 129:3), trials (cf. Ps. 119:71), and even the Word of God itself (cf. Heb. 4:12). But furrows are only a means to an end. They prepare the ground to receive the rain when it comes. Then the harsh ridges are watered, and the furrows are settled by the soft showers—the earth is comforted from her trial.

God sees the cuts and blows we have suffered. We can let them make us hard and severe, or we can look to Him for comforting, heart-softening rain—"showers of blessing" (Ezek. 34:26) "in due season" (Lev. 26:4).

—Therese Greenberg.

Golden Text Illuminated

"Thou visitest the earth, and waterest it: thou greatly enrichest it with the river of God, which is full of water" (Psalm 65:9).

This is a text about water, a topic that the Bible mentions at length. God created water. Water is vital to life on earth, including the whole cycle of evaporation, rain, and collection upon the earth. Water will be present in the New Jerusalem, the final home of believers. Scripture mentions all of these things.

In this psalm God is given praise as the generous provider of water to sustain our lives. Water is seen in this text as a sign of God's abundant blessing—His benevolent desire to provide for His people upon the earth.

Of course we know that the Bible was written in an agricultural society. Think of how dependent the people were upon a regular supply of water. Everyone, of course, needs water, but it is easy for us to take it for granted. Israel, though, was a land where rainfall and fresh water could be sparse. The rains normally came in the fall. This water would cause growth. This text marks out God's provision of water as a sign of His blessing.

First, God is always interested in "visiting" His people, that is, in being present and active in their lives. We often speak of God's visitation in the sense of His care and intervention in the circumstances of our lives. Life is not random; God is sovereignly present with us, which makes both prayer and praise possible and fruitful. When God sent the provision of water, He was visiting His people with His care and love, just as He visits us in our lives now in many ways, both seen and unseen.

Next, God has a "river," or channel, of water. Perhaps this is a metaphorical reference to how the rains are directed from the heavens above to the earth. It speaks of direction and purpose. God's blessings purposely come to us. God knows what we need, and He is to be praised for His thoughtful provision.

Finally, we see that this text speaks of God's abundant provision. He waters the earth and enriches it. The earth becomes "full of water." When God supplies, it is generous and abundant. How many of us can testify that God has dealt bountifully with us? This is another reason why we praise Him. As we look around at creation and see the ample nature of His provision, we are led to give Him praise and thanksgiving.

So in the midst of this very positive psalm of blessing and praise, the believer is led to confidently contemplate God's wonderful care and provision. The Lord is sovereign over the elements of nature and sovereign over our lives. We are happy that the creation is in subordination to Him, and we happily place our lives in subordination to Him. We who are sustained by His provision have a duty to render praise to Him.

So this text gives us a picture of a Heavenly Father who is like a devoted gardener, moving about in the garden He has fashioned in order to carefully and generously care for it. He purposefully pours out His provision upon His people. We receive this provision gladly and turn thankfully to Him to render praise and thanksgiving.
—*Jeff VanGoethem.*

Heart of the Lesson

Our God always keeps His promises. He is faithful to all generations. His love endures forever. Whatever we have need of, He will make available. Sometimes He makes us till the soil; other times a ram will appear in the bush. Regardless of how we obtain what we need, God always provides.

1. The people praise and pray (Ps. 65:1-2). Zion is the city of God. It is where His people dwell. In this psalm, King David is saying the people stand in awe of God and are waiting with excitement to praise His name.

It is similar to being at a conference and waiting for the keynote speaker. Once the speaker has been introduced and begins to take the podium, then the people stand, clap, and give honor to the one who is about to speak. In Psalm 65, David was explaining that God's people are just waiting to see what He will do next. They anticipate praising Him for His marvelous works.

God's people will keep the vows that they have made to Him. We should take a moment to recognize that a vow is much stronger than a promise. At a wedding ceremony the bride and groom make vows to each other. They are entering into a covenantal agreement that binds them together and that should be broken only by death.

We have a covenant with the Lord. When we enter into an agreement with Him, He expects us to keep our commitments just as He is faithful to uphold His. Because He hears all prayers, one day all people will seek out the Eternal God.

2. God loves the details (Ps. 65:9-13). Have you ever planned a party? The larger the party or event, the more details there are to check to ensure that nothing goes awry. Is there enough seating? Is there enough food? Did we remember to purchase the plates, cups, plasticware, and napkins? Is there coffee? Cream and sugar for the coffee? These are just the beginning of the details. The type of event will determine which additional items should be provided. Nevertheless, all the particulars should be taken care of and supplied so that when the guests arrive, they can enjoy the party without worry or care.

This is how God cares for us. When David was king, there was no Internet. There were no manufacturing plants or offices—just a lot of land and a lot of animals. Therefore, the care of the land was imperative. Whether the people ate or starved, lived or died, depended on whether the land yielded a crop.

David was acknowledging God and giving Him praise for taking care of the land. "Thou visitest the earth, and waterest it: thou greatly enrichest it with the river of God, which is full of water: thou preparest them corn, when thou hast so provided for it" (Ps. 65:9). If the land is dry, God waters it. If the land is uneven, God levels it. If the land is too hard to germinate seeds, God softens it.

God blesses the year with His goodness. The carts that carry the crops are overflowing and leaving remnants behind on the paths. The hills are green with food for the cattle and sheep. The valleys are full of grain. God takes care of the details. He provides for His people in ways we cannot. Our God is the God who hears and responds to the needs of His people.

—Kristin Reeg.

World Missions

Two years ago, I attended the funeral of a very special lady. We assembled to celebrate the life of a faithful woman who demonstrated the love and generosity of God throughout her life. Sister Small was the president of the missionary outreach at her church. To see Sister Small coming meant to expect her to ask for a donation to help the many missionary efforts she oversaw. She sent offerings to missionaries in Ghana, Liberia, Sierra Leone, Burkina Faso, Zimbabwe, and other countries far from her home.

Domestically, Sister Small would collect toiletries, clothing, hats and mittens, and books to be donated to organizations helping families in need. An exquisite cook, she rarely turned down an opportunity to lend her talent when her church provided meals for the homeless shelters. In spite of all her missionary activities, she still found time to volunteer at a local women's shelter to teach a weekly mentoring program.

Above all, Sister Small was a giver. She regularly donated furniture and household items to my ministry, Reach & Rescue Ministries, Inc., to be donated to families in transition from homelessness into housing. Her generosity did not stop at giving to the poor. Each time she called me to pick up her donations, she would slip in a gift for me. As my team and I loaded the truck with her items, she would hand me a bag and whisper, "This is for you." I would find a pretty blouse, a scarf, a plant, or a selection of vegetables from her garden. Sister Small went beyond expectations by giving with a very generous spirit.

God is a giver. He rains on the earth to water it. He refreshes us and provides for our necessities. David recognized God's overwhelming provision as he wrote in Psalm 65:11, "Thou crownest the year with thy goodness; and thy paths drop fatness." Just as God is the Provider, so those who belong to Him share in His giving character quality. Sister Small, an ardent example of the giving spirit, illustrated God's love through her life and missionary work. John 3:16 tells us that God gave His most precious gift, His only Son, because He loved the world very much. Love makes a person give. Our lesson's focus on God the Provider shows us that God is love. The love of God in our hearts leads us to give. We should freely give time, money, resources, energy, talent, and all we have to others. In that giving we glorify God, who has given us all the things we need.

The water mentioned in our lesson comes from God for growth. As we give to others, we participate in their growth—physical, spiritual, and in many other ways. Sister Small experienced the joy of giving, participating in the divine provision God had for those who received from her. I thank God for selfless people who sacrifice their own time and energy to help others. Such people will always be remembered as vessels of honor for God. Those who freely give are truly missionaries, whether they are in their own hometowns or thousands of miles from home. Since we know we are made in the likeness of our Father, we should examine our progress in becoming more like Him in the area of our giving. "The liberal soul shall be made fat: and he that watereth shall be watered also himself"(Prov. 11:25).

—Beverly Medley Jones.

The Jewish Aspect

Your community might lie in the icy grip of winter today, but it might encourage you to think that spring, summer, and fall are waiting in the wings.

Our theme for today, "Praise God the Provider," suggests the growing season, when God's plan for the health and strength of man once more bursts forth in life-sustaining produce. On our way to church in the country last fall, we viewed rolling fields of golden corn, tasseled and ready to turn. Soybeans grew abundantly. Farmers cheerfully spoke of bumper crops.

Psalm 65:9-13 speaks of God visiting the earth to ensure its abundance of moisture. The showers the Lord sends soften the furrows of the field so that it produces abundant crops. This is because the "river of God" is full. W. Graham Scroggie called this psalm "the most perfect harvest song ever" (*Psalms,* Revell).

Perhaps most Jews have at some point asked themselves, "Could I survive as a worker on an Israeli collective farm?" This question arises out of admiration for the hardscrabble lives of those who work the fields under the threat of attack without warning.

For just over a century, pioneers (*halutzim*) have volunteered to take on backbreaking labor amid war and bloodshed to build a commercially successful agricultural system in Israel that is the envy of the world. Early in the last century, secular Jews of eastern Europe slipped into the Holy Land in what is called *aliyah,* a one-way journey to escape oppressive regimes.

At first the small communal farms were largely family enterprises. The formula was "From each according to his ability, to each according to his needs" ("The Kibbutz & Moslav: History and Overview," www.jewishvirtuallibrary.org).

The small communal farms produced good food, but by reason of size they could not educate their children or provide employment for new Jewish immigrants. The socially conscious pioneers were seeking freedom from oppression. Out of this, the kibbutz (kee-boots) was born.

Kibbutz Degania was planted in 1909 with great care on the south end of the Sea of Galilee. It must have seemed like heaven on earth for secular Jews. The Jordan River pours out of the Sea and wends its way southward to the Dead Sea. Degania is in three parts, on both sides of the Jordan River. Degania A is an agricultural model, while B and C are into light manufacturing. The driveway into Degania A has a burned-out Syrian tank just inside the front gate. It is a memorial to the valiant pioneers who withstood the Syrian invasion in 1948.

No one owns a kibbutz. Volunteers for service are well fed, clothed, and housed with free medical benefits. Their days are long and exhausting. They are given some military training, for they are expected to help defend the farm. If you leave a kibbutz, you leave everything. There is no retirement pay, just the clothes on your back.

Israelis are among the world's leaders in agricultural research. In fact, Israeli scientists have carefully studied dew, the naturally occurring moisture provided by God, which is so valuable to southern Israel's wilderness.

Israel has the institutions of higher learning to make agricultural economics a profitable undertaking. Indeed, Israel provides food for many parts of the world. The abundance of God is freely shed abroad upon the earth.

—*Lyle P. Murphy.*

Guiding the Superintendent

When needs are met and life is going well, people sometimes can forget the source of their blessings. They can become complacent. They may start to believe that they are fully responsible for their blessings.

This lesson reminds us of the Person truly responsible for all the good we enjoy. We will be reminded that God is our Provider. Through Him, our lives are sustained.

DEVOTIONAL OUTLINE

1. Praise belongs to God (Ps. 65:1-2). King David is the author of this psalm. He declared that praises belonged to God.

Allen P. Ross wrote that the psalm "is a song of harvest blessing in celebration of God's goodness to His people. In this song David declared that God, who hears prayers, atones for sin, a provision that results in God's bounty. David also announced that God uses His supernatural power to aid His people. Based on these displays of God's good pleasure, the songwriter anticipated God's blessing on the land, which would bring the people prosperity" (Walvoord and Zuck, eds., *The Bible Knowledge Commentary,* Cook).

The inhabitants of Zion were identified as the people who should declare praises. Zion is another name for Jerusalem, thus indicating that it was particularly the people of God who should render praise. They were direct recipients of God's love, protection, kindness, and provision.

David indicated that the Jewish people's gratitude resulted in their fulfilling their vows. More specifically, they would give their offerings to Him. The Jews' dependency on God was reflected in their prayers to Him. Since their inception as a people, they had often sought His help. They were aware that their care and protection came solely through Him.

2. Praise for God's care of the earth (Ps. 65:9-13). God is the ruler of the earth. He controls the land, heavens, and seas. To ensure that His people are adequately cared for, the Lord preserves the earth. This means that God provides rains to water the earth. The result is that the ground yields a harvest of crops at the appropriate time.

As we look at the lush and beautiful landscape of forests, hillsides, and wildernesses, we can see the handiwork of God. When we observe all this beauty, we can say, as God said repeatedly in the Creation account, that it is good.

Food, shelter, water, and land are basic commodities that are daily life essentials. As believers, we can rejoice because we have a Father who provides His children with the essential things that are needed for our sustenance.

AGE-GROUP EMPHASES

Children: Show children that the result of God's creative work provides them with the means for survival. Help them understand that the Lord loves them and has provided for their necessities. Help them understand that God will always ensure that they are properly cared for.

Youths: Teens need to be cognizant of the Lord's care for them. Help them to develop an appreciation of God's detailed work in providing for their needs.

Adults: Adults sometimes lose sight of the Lord's care for them. This care can be easily overlooked as they become spouses, parents, and caregivers for others. Remind them that God is their great benefactor.

—*Tyrone Keith Carroll, Sr.*

Scripture Lesson Text

PS. 104:1 Bless the LORD, O my soul. O LORD my God, thou art very great; thou art clothed with honour and majesty.

2 Who coverest *thyself* with light as *with* a garment: who stretchest out the heavens like a curtain:

3 Who layeth the beams of his chambers in the waters: who maketh the clouds his chariot: who walketh upon the wings of the wind:

4 Who maketh his angels spirits; his ministers a flaming fire:

24 O LORD, how manifold are thy works! in wisdom hast thou made them all: the earth is full of thy riches.

25 *So is* this great and wide sea, wherein *are* things creeping innu- merable, **both small and great beasts.**

26 There go the ships: *there is* that leviathan, *whom* thou hast made to play therein.

27 These wait all upon thee; that thou mayest give *them* their meat in due season.

28 *That* thou givest them they gather: thou openest thine hand, they are filled with good.

29 Thou hidest thy face, they are troubled: thou takest away their breath, they die, and return to their dust.

30 Thou sendest forth thy spirit, they are created: and thou renewest the face of the earth.

NOTES

Praise for the Creator's Wisdom

Lesson: Psalm 104:1-4, 24-30

Read: Psalm 104:1-35

TIME: unknown   PLACE: Palestine

GOLDEN TEXT—"O Lord, how manifold are thy works! in wisdom hast thou made them all: the earth is full of thy riches" (Psalm 104:24).

Introduction

The United States, like the Western world in general, was founded on the presupposition that the Bible is true and truly reveals God as the eternal, holy, righteous, and just Creator. Yet today, we find America following the religious lead of the European nations, as atheism becomes more dominant in our culture—or at least louder—and public expressions of Christianity are increasingly banned in the name of protecting some poor souls from being "offended."

The change did not happen overnight. Indeed, it seems the devil understands that outright denial of God's existence must be built on a long-term strategy that begins with subtle yet systematic attacks on the foundations of our faith. This is why he indoctrinates people with the evolutionary claim that all creation, including human beings, is purely the natural result of random chemical reactions. Thus, God does not exist or at least is considerably less than what the Bible reveals Him to be.

As Christians we cannot allow the winds of culture to erode our view of God and thus rob Him of the praise due Him. The Bible fully reveals who God is.

LESSON OUTLINE

I. THE GREATNESS OF GOD—Ps. 104:1-4

II. THE WISDOM OF GOD'S WORKS—Ps. 104:24-30

Exposition: Verse by Verse

THE GREATNESS OF GOD

PS. 104:1 Bless the LORD, O my soul. O LORD my God, thou art very great; thou art clothed with honour and majesty.

2 Who coverest thyself with light as with a garment: who stretchest out the heavens like a curtain:

3 Who layeth the beams of his

chambers in the waters: who maketh the clouds his chariot: who walketh upon the wings of the wind:

4 Who maketh his angels spirits; his ministers a flaming fire.

Many commentators have observed that Psalm 104 presents a poetic view of the Creation recorded in Genesis 1. In fact, "the structure of the psalm is modelled fairly closely on that of Genesis 1, taking the stages of creation as starting-points for praise" (Kidner, *Psalms 73—150,* InterVarsity). The author of Psalm 104 is not given, but it begins and ends exactly as does Psalm 103, a Davidic psalm; so it quite likely was composed by David.

Revealed in His character (Ps. 104:1-2a). Like so many of the psalms in this section of the book (cf. 95—96; 98; 100; 103; 105—106), Psalm 104 begins with a call to praise the Lord. To "bless" the Lord is to praise Him, with the distinctive emphasis being on "grateful praise" (Girdlestone, *Synonyms of the Old Testament,* Eerdmans). "Soul" simply refers to the person or self in this context. While the psalm was written to be sung corporately, the emphasis is on the individual's participation in praise. Like the psalmist, we need to remind ourselves frequently to praise God.

The Lord is to be praised because of how great He is. The following phrases picture this greatness. The Lord is clothed with honor and majesty, and He wraps Himself in a robe of light. The Lord is presented as the King, and the imagery is of Him clad in royal garments. The terms speak of His splendor but also of His beautiful and attractive character. The fact that He puts on these attributes suggests that His character is displayed in His outward actions.

Light was the first of God's creations after the initial creation of the heaven and the earth (Gen. 1:3). The picture presents God as separate from His creation but closely identified with it.

Revealed in His dwelling (Ps. 104:2b-3). God's greatness is then highlighted in four successive phrases. First, He is the one who stretches out the heavens "like a curtain." The word for "curtain" here refers to a tent. So while the phrase speaks of how the Lord created the visible heavens as easily as one constructs a tent, it also speaks of the heavens as His dwelling place.

Second, the Lord is the one who "layeth the beams of his chambers in the waters" (Ps. 104:3). "Chambers" is more literally "roof chambers," like those that were built on the roofs of houses to take advantage of evening breezes during the summer heat. The beams of the chambers, however, rest on the waters. In the Creation context, these are the waters above the firmament (cf. Gen. 1:6-7). "He was like a builder making a private room by laying the foundation beams above the waters of the sky" (Walvoord and Zuck, eds., *The Bible Knowledge Commentary,* Cook).

The third description of God is of how the clouds serve as His chariot, and the fourth depicts Him riding on the wind as if it had wings. These highly poetic pictures present the Lord as Master of heaven and Ruler over nature. They clearly contrast Him with the false god Baal of the ancient Near East, who was believed to control rain and fertility and was described as "'the rider of the clouds'" (Tenney, ed., *The Zondervan Pictorial Encyclopedia of the Bible,* Zondervan).

Revealed in His servants (Ps. 104:4). Finally, the Lord who is to be praised "maketh his angels spirits; his ministers a flaming fire." The wording is difficult to understand, and it is complicated by the fact that the word for "angels" simply means "messengers" and "spirits" can also mean "wind." Some take the verse to mean that God makes the wind His messengers and the fire His ministers.

Hebrews 1:7, however, quotes the verse with reference to angels. Based on the Hebrews quotation, it seems the meaning is that God makes His angels like the winds and His ministers—another reference to angels—like fire. The angels who serve the Lord are indeed powerful and impressive in appearance. It is true that they cannot compare to God the Son, but the fact that these exalted beings serve the Lord further emphasizes His greatness.

To remind ourselves to bless, or praise, the Lord is to also remind ourselves of His greatness. Let us recall often that He is the Creator, the One who stands above His creation in majesty and honor, the One who rules His creation as Master, and the One who is honored and served by the mighty angels.

THE WISDOM OF GOD'S WORKS

24 O Lᴏʀᴅ, how manifold are thy works! in wisdom hast thou made them all: the earth is full of thy riches.

25 So is this great and wide sea, wherein are things creeping innumerable, both small and great beasts.

26 There go the ships: there is that leviathan, whom thou hast made to play therein.

27 These wait all upon thee; that thou mayest give them their meat in due season.

28 That thou givest them they gather: thou openest thine hand, they are filled with good.

29 Thou hidest thy face, they are troubled: thou takest away their breath, they die, and return to their dust.

30 Thou sendest forth thy spirit, they are created: and thou renewest the face of the earth.

His work of creation (Ps. 104:24-26). Verses 5-23 detail various aspects of God's creation, reviewing the distinction made between the land and the seas and describing the rain God brings to the trees and the vegetation and the role of the sun and the moon in God's plan. Before going on to cite other specifics of God's creation, the psalmist stopped to marvel at the great number and extent of the Lord's works.

The vast number and variety of God's creative works reveal the Lord's wisdom. It was in wisdom that all of them were made, the psalm proclaims. Wisdom can refer simply to skill, but more is involved in creation than mere skill. God's understanding, discretion, and omniscience are all part of His wisdom, which is revealed especially in His work of creation (cf. Prov. 8:1-4, 27-31; Jer. 10:12).

So many are the mighty works of God that Psalm 104 declares, "The earth is full of thy riches" (vs. 24). "Riches" can refer to either possessions or creatures. Certainly both ideas are true. The earth is filled with the creatures God made, and everything in the world belongs to Him (cf. 24:1). This is a reminder of our solemn responsibility as stewards of all that God has entrusted to us. Things on earth are not ours to use as we please; they belong to God, and we are to use them to please Him.

Psalm 104:25 turns to more of God's creations that display His great wisdom—namely, the sea and all the creatures that inhabit it. The sea is "great and wide." "Wide" speaks more of its size; "great," which picks up on the "great" seen in verse 1, emphasizes its importance and impressiveness.

Which sea is in view here? While the Sea of Galilee was very important to the economy of the northern part of Israel, the Israelite author of the psalm almost certainly had the Mediterranean Sea in mind. This sea was the only large body of water accessible to most Israelites that could be described in the terms used here. One could look out over the wide Mediterranean and see nothing but water, and in it were creatures beyond number, both small and large.

The creeping creatures are those that seem to glide along and so could describe any number of animals. The incredible variety in God's creation is especially evident in the sea, where tiny creatures swim side by side with the largest animals on earth.

The author seemed struck by the fact that the sea that carried the great ships and their cargo from one port to another also served as the home to living creatures as large or larger than those ships. The man-made vessels are introduced in Psalm 104:26 only as a means of exalting the greatness of God. "Leviathan" refers broadly to a large aquatic animal (Harris, Archer, and Waltke, eds., *Theological Wordbook of the Old Testament,* Moody). A whale may well be in mind, though some have argued that leviathan was a sea-dwelling dinosaur.

His work of providence (Ps. 104:27-30). Theologians use the term "providence" to refer to God's "power in bringing the movement of the universe to its predetermined goal and design" (McCune, *A Systematic Theology of Biblical Christianity,* Detroit Baptist Theological Seminary). God's providence is evidenced in the way He provides for the sustenance of all creation, including the sea creatures mentioned in verses 25-26.

The creatures of the sea, the psalmist said, "wait all upon" the Lord for Him to "give them their meat in due season" (Ps. 104:27). The thought here is that the fish and other sea creatures are totally dependent on the Lord to provide for them, and He faithfully provides in "due season," or the appointed time. He regularly provides what is needed at the time it is needed.

The waiting of the creatures of the sea points to their dependence on God, but they do not wait in the sense of doing nothing to obtain their food. They gather the food He provides, and they do so without comprehending that it comes from Him. Yet the Lord is the one who gives it from His open hand, and they are satisfied.

The psalmist illustrated God's providence with regard to the vast amount of sea life, but He is providentially at work in all of His creation, including mankind. While fallen, sinful people like to think they are the masters of their own fate and can care for themselves, in reality all people are dependent on God's sustaining power and provision for their existence and continuing existence in this world.

As the Apostle Paul said, "In him we live, and move, and have our being" (Acts 17:28). This is true whether people acknowledge the Lord's provision or not. However, if we understand this truth—and as Christians we certainly should—we will acknowledge the Lord and His greatness, and we will praise Him with all our being.

Psalm 104:29-30 reinforces God's providence by pointing to His control over the life and death of the creatures of the sea. If He chooses to hide His face from them, the animals are "troubled," or disturbed. To hide one's face is an idiomatic expression that means to withhold favor (cf. Ps. 13:1). When God hides His face from His creatures, they are indeed in trouble.

Likewise, if the Lord chooses to take

"away their breath, they die" (Ps. 104:29). This stands parallel to the previous line but is much more specific. The Hebrew word translated "breath" can also be translated "spirit." However it is understood in this context, it refers to life being taken away. Any creature whose breath or spirit is taken away dies, and that one's body decomposes and returns to "dust" (cf. Gen. 3:19). All living things live because God has put life and breath in them. When He takes this away, they die. Thus, they are utterly dependent on Him.

Psalm 104:30 focuses not on death but on the life God gives to His creatures in the first place. When He sends forth His "spirit, they are created." "Spirit" is the same word translated as "breath" in verse 29. This makes it clear that God is the one who gives life to all living things. Without Him, they would not be created.

In Genesis 1:21 we read that God "created" all sea life; the same Hebrew word is used in Psalm 104:30. Yet here the idea does not seem to be that God is constantly creating new life but rather that He is providentially working to see that life continues. As some of the sea creatures die, new ones are born. Each generation is succeeded by another, for the Lord in His wisdom has established this cycle, and He provides what is needed for it to continue.

This is explained in the final words of our text. It is by God's plan that the earth is renewed in this way, for He continually gives new, fresh life with each new generation of His creatures.

While the psalmist spoke of God's wise providence in reference specifically to the living beings found in the seas, it applies equally to all of humanity. The Lord gives us what we need when we need it to sustain our lives. Yes, there are those who suffer and die from deprivation, yet we can be sure that God will provide all we need until His purpose for us is complete.

Most people look at all this as simply the natural order of things. But it is not natural. It is by God's faithful, loving, and continual work that we live, and we continue to live in this world as long as He sees fit to keep us here.

It is easy to acknowledge God's miraculous works and thank Him for them. Yet miracles, by definition, are rare events. God's providential works, on the other hand, are present and ongoing and just as much divine works. Together, they give ample evidence of the wisdom of our Creator and ample reason to prompt ourselves to praise the Lord.

—Jarl K. Waggoner.

QUESTIONS

1. How does Psalm 104 relate to Genesis 1?
2. What does it mean to "bless the Lord" (Ps. 104:1)?
3. What royal imagery is used to picture the greatness of God? King
4. How does the mention of angels in verse 4 exalt God's greatness?
5. According to verse 24, what attribute of God is revealed by His works?
6. To what does the term "riches" refer?
7. What is the one man-made thing the psalmist mentioned? Why did he do so?
8. What is providence? How is God's providence revealed?
9. How does the providence of God relate to our lives?
10. Is God continually creating new life (vs. 30)? Explain.

—Jarl K. Waggoner.

Preparing to Teach the Lesson

The main alternative to the concept of God creating everything is the theory of evolution. It suggests that everything we see is the product of blind chance, fortuitous luck, and random changes that add up to order out of chaos and complexity out of simplicity. It takes a great leap of faith to accept evolution as fact. It would be easier to accept evolution if we began with the idea that we must rule out God or any effect He might have on the physical world if He does exist.

It is sheer folly to suggest that God used evolution to produce the world as we know it because He plainly tells us He created the world, including humans, in a logical and orderly sequence. This theme runs throughout the Bible in such depth that you would have to cut out a huge percentage of the Scriptures to blot out the idea. The Bible mentions creation often. We learn from John 1, Colossians 1, Hebrews 1, and many other passages that Jesus is the Creator. Blind chance could not possibly have resulted in the wisdom we see all around us in the created world.

TODAY'S AIM

Facts: to see the wisdom of God in His work of creation.

Principle: to understand that we will be better off if we accept His wisdom instead of our own.

Application: to frame our approach to the realities of life and death according to God's wisdom.

INTRODUCING THE LESSON

An in-depth study of the created world reveals great wisdom on the part of its Creator. In this week's lesson, we cannot touch on very many examples of this, but we can get an overall view. Someone has said that expecting to see an organized world such as ours as a result of chance is like expecting to find an encyclopedia as a result of an explosion in a print shop. However, that is practically what we have been told in the big bang theory. There are so many flaws in that theory that it takes a huge leap of faith to acknowledge it at all.

Psalm 104 in its entirety gives more examples of the Creator's wisdom. We also know facts about the natural world that show God's wisdom in creation—like symbiotic relationships, where one creature is dependent on another for existence. They could not logically have evolved independently and then somehow become dependent.

DEVELOPING THE LESSON

1. God's wisdom as seen in His dwelling place (Ps. 104:1-3a). We do not have a complete description of heaven as God's dwelling place, but here we get a glimpse. We see God clothing Himself with "honour and majesty" and covering Himself with light. He "stretchest out the heavens like a curtain" and "layeth the beams of his chambers in the waters." There really are not adequate words to describe where and how God abides. We know He exists eternally, without beginning and end. He is also omnipresent, or everywhere all the time. Yet perhaps as a concession to our thinking, He gives us a "location" in heaven.

While many have written and spoken about heaven, the reality of heaven and its makeup is so far beyond us that our speculations are worse than useless; they are even dangerous. It is best to go with what God tells us in Scripture and not to add or subtract and thereby risk being found at fault. God is wise to give us suggestions and figures of speech that we can understand rather than a description we could not understand.

2. God's wisdom as seen in His ways (Ps. 104:3b-4). God has repeatedly intervened in human history. His primary goal is to redeem mankind from sin and destruction. He uses the natural world, the inclinations of individuals, and the deeds of nations to bring about His desires. His choices of these elements and factors are infinitely wise. We make blunders with wars, natural resources, and finances; but He coordinates the works of nature and nations to bring about the fulfillment of His plans and purposes. He is wise enough to do this without violating our free will or relieving us of the ultimate responsibility for our choices.

3. God's wisdom as seen in His creation (Ps. 104:24-30). We see the statement that the earth is full of God's riches. This is true in phenomena such as electricity, nuclear energy, light, gravity, and many other "givens" around us. God has placed oil and other desirable commodities in the ground for us to find and use. Scientists have recently discovered that there are vast reservoirs of water, as much as in all the oceans, trapped far underground that could possibly be tapped and used if necessary.

ILLUSTRATING THE LESSON

By God's wisdom the world is created and continues to function.

ALL BY HIS DESIGN

PRAISE HIM FOR HIS GREAT WISDOM

CONCLUDING THE LESSON

While we test and measure the IQ of people, there is no calculating the knowledge or the wisdom of God. The earth is under the curse, but we still see the wisdom of God in creating it all. He gave the earth just the right balance of land and water. The creation of water with its states of freezing, liquidity, and vapor at just the right conditions shows amazing wisdom. There are so many forms of symbiotic relationships that we marvel at the wisdom it took to conceive the patterns, much less put them into practice. God's wisdom in preparing the earth as our home is beautiful as well as useful.

The wisdom of God's plan of salvation for humans is beyond telling or understanding. The wisdom of God in giving us His Word, the Bible, is immense. We are told enough that we can trust God and live His way, but not so much that we cannot understand what He has said.

ANTICIPATING THE NEXT LESSON

With our next lesson, we wrap up this unit on praising the Lord as the great Creator of everything. This central theme of the Bible is basic and essential to our understanding of God.
—Brian D. Doud.

PRACTICAL POINTS

1. The majesty of God leads to reverence of Him. We must appropriately respond to God's greatness (Ps. 104:1-4).
2. The variety and magnitude of God's creation are on display in the world around us. God's wisdom and power call for our admiration (vss. 24-26).
3. It is God who provides for the survival of His creation (Ps. 104:27-28; Matt. 6:26).
4. It is God who sustains and upholds the created order and who continues to renew it. The earth is the Lord's. Evolution cannot explain its origin or operation (Ps. 104:29-30).

—*Lendell Sims.*

RESEARCH AND DISCUSSION

1. The psalmist used a human convention (clothing) in speaking of God. What is the significance of Jesus being disrobed before He was hung on the cross?
2. God allowed Adam to name His creation. What does this say about people's mental capabilities prior to the Fall? Do we have the same capabilities today?
3. Psalm 104:30 reads, "Thou renewest the face of the earth." How does God, in the geophysical sense, give the earth a facelift? When did this happen in the past?
4. What does it mean that God hides His face from His creation (vs. 29)? What are the consequences of this?

—*Lendell Sims.*

ILLUSTRATED HIGH POINTS

Stretchest out the heavens like a curtain

According to Einstein and many who have followed him, space bends, folds, and wraps itself around planets like flowing fabric. Scientists also refer to the concept of an expanding universe. Scripture also depicts a stretching universe, but one created by the will of God, not a big-bang event.

It seems I cannot fold sheets or make a bed without my playful cat believing it is an activity exclusively for his wonderment and pleasure. While I may want to create order and structure in our home, it also pleases me to spend this time bonding with my precious pet.

Creation can be studied through the eyes of science, causing our minds to be impressed with its complexity and precision, but it can also be experienced with simple, heartfelt wonder, causing us to bond with our Creator. Surely, this is His desired outcome (cf. Rev. 4:10-11). After all, the fabric of the universe will "wax old like a garment" (Isa. 51:6), but the Lord remains the same forever.

How manifold are thy works!

With 1,093 United States patents, Thomas Edison once held the unofficial title of "world's most prolific inventor." Then came Shunpei Yamazaki, who surpassed Edison's record in 2003, only to be surpassed himself by Kia Silverbrook in 2008 with his 4,673 United States patents. How manifold were their works! However, there is a qualitative difference between invention and creation. While invention manipulates existing matter for new uses, creation brings matter into existence from nothing. God alone is the Creator, and how manifold are His works!

—*Therese Greenberg.*

Golden Text Illuminated

"O Lord, how manifold are thy works! in wisdom hast thou made them all: the earth is full of thy riches" (Psalm 104:24).

I have often encouraged Christian young people to study science. If a person enters the study of science and nature with a heart for God, he or she will find much for which to praise God.

Some have made the study of science into a battleground for truth. And certainly we must seek to make a strong defense for our faith to the wider world. For the believer, however, the study of science is a life of discovering over and over the great wisdom of the divine Maker of all things. And so the first step must be to learn to give God praise.

This text is an eruption of praise. It comes in the midst of a great psalm of praise. The writer is overwhelmed with a sense of God's majestic wisdom and power as he takes in all the details of Creation. So the world around us is not first of all a battleground. It is a scene for worship.

God's wisdom has resulted in "manifold" works; that is, the results of God's creative wisdom are of many kinds and are shaped in many ways. This psalm mentions God's creation of light, the heavens, clouds, angels, animals, seas, and more.

What depth of intelligence and creativity lies in God's nature! How can we even search it all out? We cannot do so completely, so what do we do? We praise Him, and our hearts are enlarged to worship and adore His great wisdom and power. We take in what we can, but always with a view toward adoration and giving glory to God.

Our text next makes the straightforward declaration that God's immense and eternal wisdom is at the root of all the creative work of God. There is no debate. There is no consideration of scientific and worldly theories. The plain truth is that everything in the natural world reflects the wisdom of God.

Any true student of the creation must become a worshipper of God. All that we see and study points to a loving being of awesome intelligence. It overwhelms the soul and the mind to think about it. Thus we give God praise for His wisdom.

Finally in our text, all that God has made and created upon the earth is spoken of as "riches." They are the rich gifts of God. We should experience the world around us with this understanding. All of His creative works—whether an angel (Ps. 104:4), an animal of the wild (vs. 20), a man engaged in labor (vs. 23), or a creature of the sea (vs. 25)—are rich gifts to be received, studied, and appreciated by the worshipping heart. God has made all things for His purposes, and they fit together in His divine plan for life on earth. Let us enjoy His provision of all things, taking each one of them to heart and spending our lives living in awe of the wisdom of the Creator.

If the number and kinds of created works are so varied and innumerable, what can we say about the God who is the Author of them all? We often marvel at the inventions of man, especially in this age of technology, but let us always look to the ultimate, creative Author of all things, remembering His glorious wisdom and seeking to live in harmony with Him.

—*Jeff VanGoethem.*

Heart of the Lesson

Wisdom is supreme. We should desire it more than silver or gold. When God asked King Solomon what he wanted, the king asked for wisdom. Wisdom is the ability to use the knowledge we gain from experience. It is also the ability to have insight into a situation that gets straight to the heart of the issue or gives clear direction to maneuver through a circumstance. Our God is wise beyond our ability to comprehend. The good news is that if we need wisdom, He will give it to us freely.

1. Praise the Lord (Ps. 104:1-4). It can be easy to praise the Lord on a Sunday morning. After all, that is what we expect to do as Christians. However, on Monday morning when the coffeemaker breaks, the kids are crying, or the car will not start, we may find it a bit more difficult to praise God. At first glance, the Bible does not give us an indication of what the psalmist was going through when he penned this psalm. What we do know is that he directed his soul and his emotions to praise the Lord. He praised the Lord as the Creator of the material and immaterial world.

2. God's great works (Ps. 104:24). There is a gospel song titled "Count Your Blessings" (Oatman). The chorus says, "Count your blessings, name them one by one. Count your blessings, see what God hath done!" Have you ever tried to actually count your blessings? If we truly tried to, we would find that they are too numerous to count. The psalmist said, "O Lord, how manifold are thy works! in wisdom hast thou made them all: the earth is full of thy riches." God's works and deeds are too numerous to try to count. If we are unable to count them in our own lives, it would be impossible to count them for the whole earth!

3. God's care (Ps. 104:25-30). Have you ever wondered why products come with warranties? Well, if items do not work as they were supposed to after a certain amount of time, we can return or exchange them. Most of the time we cannot return products to the retailer after sixty days; we have to contact the manufacturer. The company that created the product has promised to take care of it.

Our God created every living creature on earth; therefore, He ensures that their needs are met. The sea and its creatures impressed the psalmist, as did the great seagoing vessels. God feeds the creatures of the sea. God takes care of their needs. If God were to hide Himself, the creatures would be troubled. "Thou hidest thy face, they are troubled: thou takest away their breath, they die, and return to their dust" (Ps. 104:29).

There are times in life when our problems are overwhelming, when the camel's back was broken ten straws ago, when we feel as if life is a rollercoaster ride that goes only one direction—down. The psalmist reminded himself how strong, mighty, awesome, and powerful our God is and, in the light of His vastness, how small his own problems were. Think about it. God clothes Himself in light. He opens the heavens as if they were curtains. The wind is His messenger; fire is His servant. Is there really anything too difficult for our God? When times get tough, ask God for wisdom. Then compare your issue to your God. Who is bigger?

—Kristin Reeg.

World Missions

God is magnificent! His power is indescribable. And, as our lesson discusses, His wisdom is beyond measure. No matter where our vantage point is, one look around us will reveal the wondrous works of our Creator. Even through his tears, Job reverently acknowledged the wisdom and authority of God. Noah lived in close quarters with nature's creatures, interacting with his environment as few have ever done. As he authored psalms, David described the richness of creation in vivid imagery. Those of us who carefully observe our environment today will notice the Creator's signature all around us.

Christians working in the field of science have long been bridging the gap between God's creation and man's understanding of it. The majesty of God's handiwork is intriguing to mankind, especially to those interested in investigating it. Even though they are generally characterized as people set out to disprove creation, scientists have within their numbers a group of lesser-known participants—Christians. Christians in the laboratory, in research, or studying in, on, or above the earth can be considered missionaries. "Missionary science" places the Christian in two worlds—the world of observation, experimentation, and human explanation and the world we understand through faith in the Word of our Creator.

William Hearn, author of *Being a Christian in Science* (InterVarsity), has drawn numerous conclusions from science that have proved creation. He encourages young Christians to enter the science fields, not only as a profession but also as a missionary calling. In a review, Rich Milne wrote, "If scientists are to be reached with the good news of Jesus Christ, the church must see that scientists too are a mission field, and like most mission fields, they are best reached by the 'natives', other scientists."

Botanists, astronomers, mathematicians, biologists, geologists, physicists, chemists, and all other science enthusiasts are driven to investigate. They delight in discovering the parts and particles of their chosen disciplines. The missionary scientist has the unique privilege to discover God's handiwork, which reveals His magnificent wisdom. But this delight is coupled with the challenge of convincing other scientists to accept the truth that God is indeed the Creator of all they study. The opposition from non-Christian scientists may find its origin in the requirement to obey the truth we know. Hearn put it this way: "Scientific conclusions generally take the form of statistical generalities making no demands on the knower. In contrast, the moral aspect of religious knowledge puts doing the truth on a par with knowing the truth."

Our lesson demonstrates our opportunity to proclaim the truth by praising our Creator for His wisdom. Scientists agree that our earth is full of riches, and missionary scientists declare that God is the Creator of all that exists. Many reading this section may feel a call into one of the sciences. Notable on its own, a science profession would be further enhanced by Christians who accept the vocation as missionary scientists. Science and God are not competing cultures. God reveals His greatness through scientific discoveries, and science proves to mankind the wisdom, order, and grandeur of our God's creation.

—*Beverly Medley Jones.*

The Jewish Aspect

The cantor at the synagogue may chant Psalm 104. He or she might also echo our theme, "Praise for the Creator's Wisdom." Yet it will be mere lip service, for Judaism is mute on biblical creationism.

In Nathan Ausubel's *The Book of Jewish Knowledge* (Crown Publishers), there is no entry for Creation, and the sole entry for God refers the reader to the topic of monotheism (belief in one God). The general subject of monotheism consists of Judaism's attempt to deny that God has a Son, who is the Creator (Col. 1:16) and the Saviour of men. Judaism's discussion of end-time events centers on the statement, "The righteous of all nations will have a place in the world to come." These righteous then are to be employed on the world man plundered. This is the concept of *Tikkun Olam,* repair of the world.

Why is Judaism monotheistic? Sadly, Ausubel attributed this to human wisdom. He credited the god-kings of the Egyptians and the Zoroastrians of Persia with the basic concept. Jews, he said, then embraced the idea. He wrote, "The majority of knowledgeable people is in agreement that the great contribution of the Jews to the religions of the world was their development of the One God idea."

Psalm 104, however, clearly states that it is God's great wisdom that men should applaud. Monotheism is not a clever invention of human wisdom.

The brilliant Hebraist Merrill Unger pointed out the inconsistencies in the history of Israel. For thirty-two centuries, the Jews have revered Moses. Heroically leading his people, Moses did his best, but discipling and mentoring succeeded only partially and rarely. For example, in Leviticus 17:1-7, the Lord ordered the Israelites in the wilderness to slay their sacrificial animals at the entrance to the tabernacle to prevent them from going into the desert to sacrifice to demons called the *seirim,* thought to have the appearance of he-goats (Unger, *Biblical Demonology,* Kregel).

How advanced is the wisdom of the most rigorous of Jewish religionists? The Orthodox Jew will not pronounce the ineffable name of deity, rendered YHWH or Yahweh in the Old Testament (the pronunciation is uncertain). Yet God would have His name spread throughout the world, for this is the Saviour God.

The Orthodox Jew heads to the shul (synagogue) before the last three stars of heaven vanish away. It is time for the dawn prayer time. The first thing he will do at the service is to don his prayer shawl and his phylacteries, two leather boxes with thongs. The two-inch-square boxes contain Scriptures, especially Deuteronomy 6:4-6, the injunction to teach and obey the Law.

One phylactery is placed on the forehead just above the hairline. The second box is placed on the underside of the left bicep. The thong then is wound down the arm, ending with the binding of the two middle fingers of the left hand. The Jew is now ready to pray.

Unger said the word "phylactery" is from the Greek, meaning "safeguard." The needed safeguard is against demonic oppression. Unger quoted the Jewish Targum on Canticles 8:3, which says phylacteries "were regarded as amulets with magical power to avert evils and drive away demons" (Unger).

Christian admiration for the Jews is well deserved, but one can only mourn a Judaism that has robbed the Jewish people of their rich heritage in the great name of God and of the sacrifice of the Messiah Jesus.

—*Lyle P. Murphy.*

Guiding the Superintendent

Paintings by Vincent van Gogh are considered artistic masterpieces. Composer Ludwig van Beethoven is considered one of classical music's most brilliant composers. Although these two men are known for their artistic and musical brilliance, they pale in comparison to the brilliance of the Lord.

This week's lesson demonstrates the Lord's wisdom. We will discover that only God had the wisdom and power to create the beautiful world and its contents.

DEVOTIONAL OUTLINE

1. The Creator of infinite greatness (Ps. 104:1-4). The psalmist started this psalm with praise to God. He emphasizes that his praise flows from the depths of his soul. He speaks of the Lord's greatness. God illuminated Himself with honor and majesty. The Lord displayed His power in His creative acts. He took the heavens and spread them across the universe.

The psalmist used metaphors: He "layeth the beams of his chambers in the waters: . . . [He] maketh the clouds his chariot: . . . [He] walketh upon the wings of the wind" (Ps. 104:3).

According to the *Old Testament Survey Series,* "God is depicted constructing his own dwelling above the waters that in the beginning surrounded the earth (Gen 1:2). The storm cloud and tempest are the symbols of his approach to earth. Even his spiritual agents are viewed as manifesting themselves in the physical phenomena of wind and lightning" (Smith, College Press).

2. God's infinite wisdom in creation (Ps. 104:24-30). The Lord's works are superior and glorious to behold. It was through His wisdom that all creation came into existence. Every breathtaking natural wonder exists through the Lord's creative touch.

Through God's wisdom, the seas were created with depth and width. Ships are able to float upon the seas. The seas are filled with innumerable creatures, both small and enormous. The psalmist mentioned the leviathan, an ancient sea creature known for its menacing activity. Also referred to as a sea monster, it is mentioned in three other places in the Bible. The leviathan was a powerful beast, but was under God's control.

The psalmist declared that the sea creatures are dependent on God to supply them with food. Through His provision, they eat with satisfaction. However, the sea creation would be hungry and lifeless if God were to withhold His provision. Like the sea creatures, we need God to sustain us. We should be grateful for His provision.

AGE-GROUP EMPHASES

Children: Children need to understand the significance of God's provision. Although they have parents who provide for them, they need to understand that the source of their blessings is God. The parents themselves are provided by God.

Youths: Teach teens the importance of depending on God. Share with them that as they progress in life, they will need God's help to overcome many challenges.

Adults: Adults need to remember the importance of offering praise to God for provision and blessings. Encourage them to consistently praise God for their blessings. Help them understand that even as adults they are His children and under His care.

—*Tyrone Keith Carroll, Sr.*

Scripture Lesson Text

PS. 148:1 Praise ye the LORD. Praise ye the LORD from the heavens: praise him in the heights.

2 Praise ye him, all his angels: praise ye him, all his hosts.

3 Praise ye him, sun and moon: praise him, all ye stars of light.

4 Praise him, ye heavens of heavens, and ye waters that *be* above the heavens.

5 Let them praise the name of the LORD: for he commanded, and they were created.

6 He hath also stablished them for ever and ever: he hath made a decree which shall not pass.

7 Praise the LORD from the earth, ye dragons, and all deeps:

8 Fire, and hail; snow, and vapour; stormy wind fulfilling his word:

9 Mountains, and all hills; fruitful trees, and all cedars:

10 Beasts, and all cattle; creeping things, and flying fowl:

11 Kings of the earth, and all people; princes, and all judges of the earth:

12 Both young men, and maidens; old men, and children:

13 Let them praise the name of the LORD: for his name alone is excellent; his glory *is* above the earth and heaven.

14 He also exalteth the horn of his people, the praise of all his saints; *even* of the children of Is'ra-el, a people near unto him. Praise ye the LORD.

NOTES

All Creation Praises the Lord

Lesson: Psalm 148:1-14

Read: Psalm 148:1-14

TIME: possibly 516 B.C.   **PLACE: possibly Jerusalem**

GOLDEN TEXT—"Let them praise the name of the Lord: for he commanded, and they were created" (Psalm 148:5).

Introduction

Concern for the world in which we live is a legitimate issue for Christians. After all, we are stewards of the world God created. Although the world itself has been affected by sin, to do harm to the earth through neglect or abuse is to further mar this testimony to the greatness of the Creator. On the other hand, we realize this world is not our ultimate destination. It will one day be replaced by a new earth (cf. II Pet. 3:13; Rev. 21:1).

However, we live in a day when unbelief is growing and Christianity is increasingly under attack. Perhaps it should not be surprising in such an environment that pagan nature worship is on the rise, even among very educated people of the West. Nature has become God to many people, to the point that some even advocate violence against companies that in their minds exploit natural resources.

The Bible, especially passages like Psalm 148, stands as a powerful rebuke to those who would elevate the earth and its resources to the place of deity. Heaven and earth are not God; rather, they testify to God the Creator. In fact, the Bible calls on—and expects—all that is in heaven and earth to give praise to the one true God.

LESSON OUTLINE

**I. THE PRAISE OF HEAVEN—
Ps. 148:1-6**

**II. THE PRAISE OF THE EARTH—
Ps. 148:7-14**

Exposition: Verse by Verse

THE PRAISE OF HEAVEN

PS. 148:1 Praise ye the LORD. Praise ye the LORD from the heavens: praise him in the heights.

2 Praise ye him, all his angels: praise ye him, all his hosts.

3 Praise ye him, sun and moon: praise him, all ye stars of light.

4 Praise him, ye heavens of heavens, and ye waters that be above the heavens.

5 Let them praise the name of the

LORD: **for he commanded, and they were created.**

6 He hath also stablished them for ever and ever: he hath made a decree which shall not pass.

It is not difficult to categorize Psalm 148. From beginning to end, it is a psalm of praise and worship. As Warren Wiersbe noted, "The word *praise* is used thirteen times in these fourteen verses. The psalm begins in the highest heavens and ends with the little nation of Israel. If any psalm reveals the glory and grandeur of the worship of the Lord, it is this one, for it is cosmic in its dimensions and yet very personal in its intentions" (*The Bible Exposition Commentary,* Cook).

The call for praise (Ps. 148:1). Like the two psalms that immediately precede it and the two that follow, Psalm 148 begins with "Praise ye the Lord," or, in Hebrew, *Hallelu Yah.* It is an imperative call to laud the superior qualities of the Lord (Harris, Archer, and Waltke, eds., *Theological Wordbook of the Old Testament,* Moody). This particular call is for praise to be given from "the heavens." "In the heights" is simply a poetic way of restating "heavens." It refers to everything beyond the physical realm of the earth.

The praise of heavenly beings (Ps. 148:2). Verse 2 calls on the angels to praise the Lord. While at times in the Bible angels appear on the earth in visible form, their normal dwelling place is considered to be the heavens. These created spirit beings are superior to human beings in power and rank; yet, like us, they are called on to praise the Almighty. "Hosts," which often refers to armies, functions here as another name for the angelic throng in heaven.

The praise of heavenly bodies (Ps. 148:3). The psalmist's call for praise is extended to the heavenly bodies in this verse: the sun, the moon, and the stars. God created these luminaries on the fourth day of Creation (Gen. 1:14-19). They were created to provide light and distinguish the seasons, but they were also given as signs that testify to the Creator (cf. Pss. 8:3-4; 19:1-2).

The praise of all that is in the heavens (Ps. 148:4). Praise is also commanded from the "heavens of heavens." This expression is sometimes translated "highest heavens." It might be used here to distinguish the dwelling place of God or the outer reaches of the heavens from the "heavens" at the end of the verse, which is equivalent to the earth's atmosphere. The waters "above the heavens" (cf. Gen. 1:7) probably refers to moisture in the earth's atmosphere, which falls to the earth in some form of precipitation. This also is exhorted to praise the Lord.

The reasons for praise (Ps. 148:5-6). Everything in heaven is to praise the Lord. We can understand how angels can be told to praise the Lord. But how can inanimate things such as the sun, the moon, the stars, and the rain praise Him? This is probably a use of the poetic device of personification: attributing human characteristics to nonhuman things. However, all creation does in a sense continually praise God, for the very design and function of nature points to the divine Designer to whom all praise is due.

He deserves praise because He issued His command, and everything came into existence. His power in creating all things and the wisdom displayed in His creation warrants universal praise. The Lord's glory is revealed through His establishment forever of the inhabitants of heaven. By an unalterable decree, He has "permanently ordered and regulated the world of nature" (Barker and Kohlenberger, eds.,

The Expositor's Bible Commentary, Abridged, Zondervan), which speaks eloquently of God's glory (Ps. 19:1). The orderly operations of nature also testify to the faithfulness of the God who established the laws that govern it (Jer. 31:35-36). It is only appropriate that everything God has created should give praise to Him.

THE PRAISE OF THE EARTH

7 Praise the LORD from the earth, ye dragons, and all deeps:

8 Fire, and hail; snow, and vapour; stormy wind fulfilling his word:

9 Mountains, and all hills; fruitful trees, and all cedars:

10 Beasts, and all cattle; creeping things, and flying fowl:

11 Kings of the earth, and all people; princes, and all judges of the earth:

12 Both young men, and maidens; old men, and children:

13 Let them praise the name of the LORD: for his name alone is excellent; his glory is above the earth and heaven.

14 He also exalteth the horn of his people, the praise of all his saints; even of the children of Israel, a people near unto him. Praise ye the LORD.

The call for praise (Ps. 148:7a). The second call to praise God introduces a section of the psalm that focuses on things of the earth. Praise is to come "from the earth," that is, from everything on the earth.

The praise of earth's seas (Ps. 148:7b). First to be addressed on the earth are "dragons." The Hebrew word is frequently rendered that way in the Old Testament, though sometimes it is translated "whales." It is not clear exactly what creature is in view here, but it is not a mythological beast. That would be completely incongruous with the real animals and forces listed in the psalm. This is a real creature, one that inhabits the "deeps," or the seas.

Perhaps it is best to understand the word simply to mean a large sea creature. The vast array of life in the seas, including even the largest, most impressive animals, are the creations of God and thus should offer praise to their Creator.

The praise of earth's forces (Ps. 148:8). Various forces on the earth are likewise to praise—and are designed to praise—the Lord. These include fire, which can be both extremely helpful and extremely destructive. Hail is used figuratively in Isaiah 28:2 of divine judgment upon His wayward people, Israel, but here it is a reminder of God's power and glory (Harris, Archer, and Waltke).

Snow, like hail, is precipitation. Vapor is either smoke from fire or the appearance of thick clouds. All these forces, along with strong, stormy winds, occur naturally. They remind us that we cannot control nature. Yet nature, under God's control, fulfills His word. He uses these forces of nature to accomplish His purposes, whether those purposes are to water the earth, clear land, or judge His people.

The praise of earth's features (Ps. 148:9). Various features of the earth also testify to God's creative power and are called on to praise Him. These include the lofty mountains and the lower hills. The Israelite author of the psalm might have thought of the nine-thousand-foot Mount Hermon in the north or the mountains of central Israel and the Shephelah, or hill country, between the mountains and Israel's coastal plain.

The many varieties of fruit trees provide food for humans and animals. Cedar trees, so prized in ancient Israel, represent trees that are useful for construction.

The various features of the land and the vegetation that covers the earth exist because the Lord created them for our enjoyment and benefit. Like all creation, they exist to bring glory to Him.

The praise of earth's animals (Ps. 148:10). This verse lists four groups of animals. The "beasts" are literally "living things." This is a very general category, of course, but when it is used in contrast to "cattle" as it is here, it refers to wild animals. "Cattle" are livestock or domesticated animals. "Creeping things" refers primarily to reptiles. Together with the "flying fowl," or birds, these terms are meant to encompass all animal life on the land (cf. Ezek. 38:20).

Animals are the creation of God (Gen. 1:24-26), and as such they too are called on to praise their Creator.

The praise of earth's people (Ps. 148:11-12). The call to "praise the Lord from the earth" (vs. 7) is directed to the seas and all that is in them, the various forces of nature, the mountains, hills, and trees, and all the land animals. This lengthy list finally culminates with man. The idea being stressed is that all creation is to worship the Lord, the Creator.

The comprehensive nature of the list is further emphasized by cataloging various groups of people who are to worship the Lord (Ps. 148:11). "Kings of the earth" represent the most powerful people among mankind. Coupled with kings is "all people." This term seems to group people together and thus could be translated "nations." "Princes" are leaders, whether royal officials or military or religious leaders. "Judges of the earth" may be those who rule in legal matters or, more generally, those who carry out governmental functions.

People who have authority over others possess that authority because God has given it to them (cf. Rom. 13:1-7). They are to be respected, but they are also to praise the God who empowered them.

Psalm 148:12 makes it clear that no one is excluded in this enumeration of people. "Young men" are coupled with "maidens," or young, unmarried virgins. They represent those in the prime of life. "Old men" and "children" are also included in this list. The word for children is applied in the Old Testament to people from infancy to young adulthood. The term is masculine, but the idea is not to limit the people of the earth by gender or age but to include everyone. All are equally God's creation, and all are equally to praise Him.

The reasons for praise (Ps. 148:13-14). Just as the first call to praise the Lord (vss. 1-4) was followed by reasons for the praise (vss. 5-6), so the second call (vss. 7-12) is followed by more reasons to praise the Lord. "Let them praise the name of the Lord" (vs. 13) repeats the idea that everything on the earth is to worship Him (cf. vs. 5). To praise the Lord's "name" is to praise Him in all His fullness. "Name" speaks of "the sum total of all the things that He has achieved, or which are known concerning Him—popularly stated: His reputation" (Leupold, *Exposition of Psalms,* Baker).

The Lord is worthy of praise because only His name, or reputation, is exalted. The idea being expressed here is that God's name is "inaccessibly high" (Harris, Archer, and Waltke). It is beyond the reach of any person or creature. This thought is reemphasized in the next idea. The Lord's glory towers over the earth and heavens. God's glory is His majesty or splendor; it is very similar in concept to His name.

While God's wonderfully varied, intricate, and amazing creation reveals His glory (cf. Ps. 19:1), the glory it reveals is far above anything we can see in the heavens or on the earth. Creation points to the Creator, but it can never fully and exhaustively reveal His character and His works, and it can never replace the Creator. Creation is subservient to the Creator, and its role is to glorify Him forever.

Psalm 148:14, the final verse of the praise hymn, gives another reason the Lord's creation should praise Him, and it centers on His work on behalf of the nation of Israel. The book of Psalms was Israel's "hymnbook." It provided songs for the Israelites' worship, especially their congregational worship. So while the psalm reminds all creation of the Lord's glory, it also reminded Israel of the personal blessings they had experienced from the Lord.

How had the Lord blessed Israel? He had raised up a horn for His people. A horn represented strength and power and often a powerful ruler (cf. Pss. 89:17, 24; 132:17). Much of Israel's history, of course, was a recounting of disobedience, defeat, and subjection. So it seems a particular and relatively recent event may be in view here. This has led many to conclude that Psalm 148 was written after the return of the Jews to their land from the long Babylonian Captivity.

Whatever the exact circumstances, Israel had much for which to thank the Lord. They were the special, chosen objects of His blessings, and those blessings brought praise to them, His saints, or holy ones, who were near to Him. The implication is that Israel was near to God because of their obedience to Him. And when they were obedient, they enjoyed power and prosperity as the Lord had promised them in His covenant (Deut. 28:1-14).

Leupold summarized the thought of these last verses: "The destiny of Israel is so important, and what God had recently done for His people in their Restoration is of such vital importance to all nations and creatures that, if they grasped what it involved, they would be glad to add their praises to Israel's praises."

Psalm 148 ends as it began: "Praise ye the Lord." It is a command that is equally appropriate for us today. If all the created universe should rise up in united praise to our God, surely we, the redeemed, whose lives have been so favored by the grace of God, should never cease to praise the name of the One whose glory is above the earth and heaven. Indeed, "How anyone could trivialize the privilege and responsibility of worship after pondering this psalm is difficult to understand" (Wiersbe).

—Jarl K. Waggoner.

QUESTIONS

1. To whom is the first call to praise the Lord addressed?

2. Why were the sun, the moon, and the stars created?

3. What is personification? How is it used in Psalm 148?

4. To what does the term "dragons" in verse 7 refer?

5. How do natural forces on the earth fulfill the word of the Lord (vs. 8)?

6. What created features of the earth are called to praise God?

7. What terms did the psalmist use to encompass all animal life on the land?

8. What earthly leaders did the psalmist list as owing praise to the Lord?

9. In what sense is only the Lord's name "excellent" (vs. 13)?

10. For what could Israel personally praise the Lord?

—Jarl K. Waggoner.

Preparing to Teach the Lesson

The last five psalms start and end with the phrase "Praise ye the Lord," so in case we have not yet grasped the message, here is a major encouragement, even a command, to praise the Lord! If we as teachers are persons who praise the Lord throughout every day, we will be much better prepared to encourage our class to also be praiseful persons. If we are not praiseful teachers, our words will be only theory and will not urge others to action.

The challenge of teaching is to visibly be examples of that which we are attempting to teach. This is not accomplished by just saying "Praise the Lord" all the time but in our heart attitude of thanks and praise to God. We praise the Lord for the way He orders our lives so that the events we experience are for our good and His glory. We can praise Him during the bad as well as the good things that happen.

TODAY'S AIM

Facts: to see the full meaning of scriptural encouragement to praise the Lord.

Principle: to see that all of God's creation is to bring Him praise.

Application: to teach that the most important activity in which we can engage is to praise the Lord.

INTRODUCING THE LESSON

We have already touched on many of the facets of praising the Lord in previous lessons. Psalm 148 gives us a perspective of just who and what is meant to bring praise to the Lord. The scope of this psalm is complete and universal. It elevates praise to the highest level possible. We do not have to be perfect people to praise the Lord, although He will not accept insincere or phony praise. He is not pleased with praise from those who do not trust or obey Him. What we need to do is come to Him with our sins confessed and forsaken and our spirits thus cleansed by the Holy Spirit. Praise from a pure heart will always please the Lord.

DEVELOPING THE LESSON

1. Praise the Lord from the heavens (Ps. 148:1-6). Praising the Lord from the highest heavens includes the outer reaches of the universe. We do not know the size or shape of the universe. Albert Einstein thought it was cylindrical. I believe it has no boundaries because it exists primarily in the mind of God, who is infinite. That is not to say that it is not real, such as a dream or a thought. Someone who can say "Let there be" something, and it happens, can will anything into existence or nonexistence.

Praise is elicited from the angels and "all [God's] hosts" (Ps. 148:2). God has revealed Himself as the Lord of Hosts throughout the Scriptures. We have no idea of how many angels there are or if the "hosts" are just angels or some other beings God has not defined for us. There could well be many more of them than there are people on the earth. There could be billions and billions of spirit beings praising Him right now.

The next things mentioned praising the Lord are the sun, moon, and stars. Next are the heavens and waters above the earth and every created thing. There is nothing in existence that He did not create! The reason given for all creation praising the Lord is that they came into being at His command. God established them and decreed their existence and purpose. From passages such as this we understand that every human soul is eternal. God alone knows where each soul will ultimately reside, but all will be brought to bring praise to Him.

2. Praise the Lord from the earth (Ps. 148:7-14). In commanding that praise should come from the earth, the psalmist first mentioned the huge and inexplicable creatures of the oceans. The oceans themselves are to praise the Lord also. What we call the elements—fire, hail, snow, fog, and windstorms—are also called to praise the Lord. They are almost given personality because they fulfill His Word. We remember that the Lord Jesus said, "Peace, be still" (Mark 4:39), and the wind and waves became calm. He is Master over all the elements.

The psalmist then moved on to describing the physical landscape, the fruit trees and other trees, as praising the Lord. Also mentioned as praising the Lord are the beasts, cattle, creeping things, and birds (domesticated and not domesticated). When all the millions of pieces of the "earthly puzzle" the Lord has made all work together harmoniously, it brings praise to the Lord.

All people—rulers, judges, and common folk—are meant to praise the Lord, no matter their age or social status. The reason given is that His name alone is excellent and His glory is transcendent. What God has done is perfect and beautiful, as well as practical, and for the benefit of all. The natural and normal state of human beings should be to appreciate who God is and what He has done and to praise Him for it all.

Last mentioned are God's people who are strong in Him and "a people near unto him" (Ps. 148:14). It is a wonderful thing to know the Lord and to be near Him. We can draw near to Him through His Word. We can be near Him through praise and prayer. We can draw near Him when we obey His Word and hold Him in the forefront of all our deliberations and plans. We can praise Him in our daily activities as well as in our church activities.

ILLUSTRATING THE LESSON

Everything created should praise the Lord at all times.

ALL CREATION PRAISES HIM

CONCLUDING THE LESSON

If we wonder whether or when praising God is appropriate, we should wonder no longer. All created things should praise the Lord all the time. The heavens and the earth praise Him. They did not take part in Adam's sin, and they still praise Him all the time. They obey His wishes completely and flawlessly. We can praise the Lord in good times and bad, in joy or in sorrow. We can praise Him in adversity or in plenty. We can praise Him during political or governmental success or disaster. We can praise Him if we really want to. It should be our natural, normal state of mind to praise Him. It will be fulfilling and uplifting to us and pleasing to God to do so.

ANTICIPATING THE NEXT LESSON

Our next lesson begins a unit titled "The Church Is Born," with teachings from the book of Galatians.

—*Brian D. Doud.*

PRACTICAL POINTS

1. Praise is a command, not an option (Ps. 148:1; cf. I Thess. 5:18).
2. All of creation is commanded to praise God. He is Creator of all (Ps. 148:2-5).
3. God oversees all creation—we should trust Him and praise Him (vss. 6-10).
4. No matter the age or the station in life, we must respond to the Lord's call for praise (vss. 11-13; 150:6).
5. God has shown His care of His people by giving them strength ("horn") through His provision of the Messiah (148:14). This calls forth praise.

—Lendell Sims.

RESEARCH AND DISCUSSION

1. The Bible mentions different levels of the heavens. What does this complexity tell us about the Creator?
2. "Dragons" (Ps. 148:7) may refer to seagoing dinosaurs such as the plesiosaur. What import might this have on evolutionists' view of dinosaurs?
3. Scripture commands rulers and judges to praise God. Is it proper to point this out to those in authority?
4. Since Jesus and the Father are one, what is verse 13 telling us about the name of Jesus?
5. Psalm 148:14 speaks of God exalting "the horn of his people," the Messiah. Why is a ram's horn an appropriate symbol of power and strength for Christ?

—Lendell Sims.

ILLUSTRATED HIGH POINTS

Praise ye the Lord

In 2014, the American Institute of Architects posthumously honored Julia Morgan with a gold medal for her more than seven hundred buildings, including the Hearst Castle in California. As a female architect who began working in the late 1800s, she was not readily accepted. However, she often expressed her desire that her buildings would speak for themselves—and they did. Morgan designed the first college bell tower for Mills College, which amazingly survived the 1906 San Francisco earthquake unscathed.

Like the pages of an architect's portfolio, Psalm 148 puts the works of God on display. Creation after creation is presented in near chronological order. The day will come when the works of man will crumble while His Word continues to stand (cf. Prov. 19:21). Then the world will give Him the praise He has long deserved (cf. Phil. 2:10-11).

Exalteth the horn of his people

The Battle of the Little Bighorn (or Custer's Last Stand) is noteworthy for its intensity and decisive outcome. This conflict is named for its location on the banks of the Little Bighorn River, which eventually flows into the wider Bighorn River. The Native Americans named this river for the fierce bighorn sheep that gather at its shores.

In Scripture, the horn is symbolic of strength in battle (cf. Deut. 33:17; I Sam. 2:1,10; I Kings 22:11). Although He came as a tiny baby, Jesus, the Horn of our salvation (cf. Luke 1:69), shall be exalted in the end. He has fought a definitive battle for our souls (cf. Ps. 18:2) and will fight a final fierce conflict (cf. I Sam. 2:10; Ps. 92:9-10). He will not be tiny when He returns; He will be exalted solely as the Horn (cf. Ps. 89:17).

—Therese Greenberg.

Golden Text Illuminated

**"Let them praise the name of the Lord: for he command-
ed, and they were created" (Psalm 148:5).**

Throughout this unit the golden texts have spoken of God's creation, and we have seen that the knowledge of the creation and its Creator logically leads us to worship. One cannot encounter and embrace the immensity of creation without turning in worship to the Creator. This text tells us the who, what, and why about praising the Lord for His creation.

Who should praise the Lord? Our text simply says "them." Who does this refer to? It is everything in creation. The list is impressive, given to us in verses 1-4 and 7-12. That which is above should praise Him: the heavens should sound forth His greatness. Angels should join in, as well as the host of heaven—including the sun, moon, and stars. The heaven of heavens and the waters above the heavens should praise Him.

Also joining in on the praise should be what is on the earth and in the earth. The dragons and the depths should praise Him. Fire, hail, snow, and wind should extol Him as well. Along with the mountains, the hills, and the trees, all the beasts—from cattle to creeping things and all fowl—should call out with joy. And finally, all people, including kings and rulers, the young and the old, should glorify the Lord. Obviously, this is meant to speak comprehensively. Nothing God has made should refrain from praising Him. He is worthy of such honor as the Creator of all things.

So we see *who* should be rendering praise—everything and everyone. Now let us ask, *What* should be praised? This question is answered with the phrase "the name of the Lord." His name stands for His character and His attrib-
utes. What are some of the attributes of God that come to mind when you ponder His creative power? If I were teaching a class, I would ask students to take some time and make a list. All of God's attributes should be extolled. God is to be praised for who He is, based on what He has done in creation.

Now let us ask the final question: *Why* should God be praised in His creation? The answer is twofold. First, we praise God because of His primacy. He commanded that all things come into existence. He is the first cause and the reason for all things. He is Lord of all creation. We all owe our existence to His glorious power and love. So it is only right to return thanks and praise to Him, extolling all of His glorious attributes. Praise and worship is the right response when there is a firm conviction that God is the center of life.

Second, we render praise to God because it is spiritually profitable and beneficial for us to do so. It aligns us with God. It causes worship and submission and love. God's love comes to us in creation, and our love returns to Him in praise. Psalm 148:14 also reflects on this truth. Scripture strengthens us to praise God and helps us to stay near to Him.

Sometimes the most thrilling things in life are the simplest. We take a walk outside and see the sky above, or a sunset, or a hill or mountain or tree, or an animal—something that God has created and designed. We are able to see His handiwork. That observation becomes a blessing and leads us to worship. All creation points to God and calls for us to praise Him.

—*Jeff VanGoethem.*

Heart of the Lesson

good

Praise the Lord! Sometimes it is spoken as a command. Sometimes it is spoken as a response to what God has done. But what does it mean to praise the Lord? When we praise the Lord, we give Him the glory and honor He deserves; we exalt His name.

1. Praise the Lord (Ps. 148:1-4). Who should praise the Lord? First and foremost, we should praise the Lord. The heavens should praise the Lord. The angels should praise the Lord. The armies of God should praise the Lord. The sun, the moon, the stars, and the waters should praise Him too. What the psalmist is illuminating here is that everything that God has created needs to give Him praise. What we praise and what we glorify we recognize as having some attribute or characteristic that is praiseworthy. Since God is perfect and His love knows no end, we have an abundance of reasons to give Him praise!

2. God created all (Ps.148:5-6). With a word, God spoke the heavens into existence. He placed the sun and the moon in their spaces. He scattered the stars throughout the sky. With a word, He created the earth and everything within it. It was by His command that even we came into existence; therefore, everything that He created by His word should praise His name. He is the Alpha and Omega, the beginning and the end. By His word something is created, and by His word something is destroyed. What God says will surely come to pass. Praise Him!

3. Who should praise (Ps. 148:7-14)? Sometimes when we come across a certain truth, we choose to believe that it is not meant for us. We unconsciously believe a lie instead. For example, the truth is that God loves the world. We are in the world; therefore, we are loved by God. However, I may believe that God loves you but have trouble believing that He loves me.

What does this have to do with Psalm 148? Well, the psalmist began listing the elements of creation to show that everything, in a sense, praises God. Sometimes when we use broad terms like "all" or "everything," it is easier to believe that the words are *not* really all-inclusive. We can subconsciously exclude ourselves when making such a wide-ranging statement. But the psalmist wants to emphatically make the point that everything in creation reveals the greatness of God, and so we too must praise Him.

The psalmist is stating in poetic terms that all creation praises God. The "praise" of rain is different from the "praise" of fire, but both offer their praise to the great I AM. Whether we are in positions of authority or subservience, we need to praise God. Whether we are in abundance or in want, we need to praise God. Whether we are young or old, we need to praise the Lord. Whatever stage of life we find ourselves in, as long as we still have breath in our bodies, we are to give Him the praise.

It is not always easy to praise the name of the Lord. When our hearts are broken, when our bodies ache, or when our lives are in turmoil, it is not easy to give God praise. But just because something is difficult does not mean that we should avoid it. Praise God that He mends our hearts. Praise God that He heals our bodies. Praise God that He calms our storms. Praise Him!

—*Kristin Reeg.*

World Missions

All of nature obeys the intentions of the Creator. Dogs bark, waters flow, winds blow, birds fly, stars shine, and tree branches reach toward heaven, all in response to the natural order of God's universe. Lions do not chirp, and robins do not roar, for God has chosen the manner of expression He prefers from each member of creation.

From the first week of Creation, each creature, whether animal, plant, or mineral, has been faithful and obedient to the command of God to praise Him. The one exception in the universe is man. Man, God's premier achievement and most precious possession, has used his free will to choose to detour from God's perfect paradise. The psalmist urged his readers to join with nature to express praise to God. "Let them praise the name of the Lord: for his name alone is excellent; his glory is above the earth and heaven" (Ps. 148:13).

Mona is a lover of nature. Born and raised in West Bengal, India, she spent the first eighteen years of her life among scenic landscapes, magnificent forests, rippling streams, and the majestic Himalayan Mountains. The wildlife sanctuary in her local Jalpaiguri was home to indigenous creatures such as the elephant and the leopard. Mona respected her environment and grew up to enjoy all of nature with her family. Mona was of the Hindu religion, as were a large percentage of the citizens in the region. Christian missionary teams came to Mona's community with crusades, children's programs, and church plantings, but Mona showed no interest in attending. Then she met Kyra.

Kyra was a member of a missionary team whose sponsors had built a school in a neighboring community. She was the same age as Mona, who was at that time twenty-seven years old, and married with two children. The women met outside a produce market as they were returning to their bicycles. The conversation began with a polite dialogue about the beautiful weather that day after the two days of rain they had experienced. It quickly advanced to a description of Kyra's programs for children. Mona mentioned her six- and four-year-old sons and how they might enjoy the art classes. "But we don't just worship your one God. We have gods and goddesses. Is that all right?"

Kyra was stunned that a Hindu would be so open to a Christian program for her children. God had opened this door so smoothly that Kyra was amazed at the ease of this conversation. The two women exchanged telephone numbers. A few days later Mona and her children visited the school. Mona's eyes went first to the decorative interior of the building. Enlarged photographs of animals, architectural structures, bodies of water, and, of course, the Himalayas enhanced the walls of the halls and classrooms. Mona quickly realized that the missionaries in that school had eyes for beauty and appreciation for the nature she loved. "I'll speak to my husband about enrolling the boys."

Mona did send her sons to Kyra's art program. Though her religion was not Christian, she and her husband agreed to allow their children to be exposed to the gospel message through the lessons they attended. This happened because of the design of God to use nature to bring Him praise.

—Beverly Medley Jones.

The Jewish Aspect

Charles Haddon Spurgeon, a skilled expositor, could easily discern the various stanzas in many of the psalms. However, of Psalm 148, he said, "It is one and indivisible" (*The Treasury of David,* Hendrickson). It is appropriate, then, that our lesson text covers all fourteen of the psalm's verses.

Our theme, "All Creation Praises the Lord," speaks of *fiat creationism,* the idea that the One in authority creates by the power of His spoken word. Psalm 148:5 says, "He commanded, and they were created."

The psalm concludes with a remark about "the praise of all his saints; even of the children of Israel" (Ps. 148:14). Spurgeon cited one James Smith, who related the quotation to the church, the body of Christ, ignoring the reference to Israel. This error proliferates today. Many believers think Israel's promises are now ours.

Most would agree that singing and music are important elements of worship. Nathan Ausubel noted, however, that music also was clearly related to prophecy, citing Elisha's request for a minstrel in II Kings 3:15: "And it came to pass, when the minstrel played, that the hand of the Lord came upon him" (Ausubel, *The Book of Jewish Knowledge,* Crown Publishers).

Temple music was David's passion. He established among the Levites an order of singers, assisted by instrumentalists. Second Chronicles 5:12 relates that the temple musicians—Levitical leaders Asaph, Heman, and Jeduthun, and their families—sang praises to God accompanied by cymbals, psalteries, and harps with 120 trumpeters.

The Israelites favored the *kinnor,* called "King David's harp." Actually it was a lyre, with ten strings that were plucked with an instrument.

The *nebel* is the biblical psaltery. It was a form of *kinnor,* but was plucked with the fingers. Cymbals were used with frame drums, timbrels, clappers, and rattles to accent the musical instruments (Ausubel). Today, Jews for Jesus' musical gospel teams use the dunbek, a handheld drum.

Nehemiah wrote of the great procession at the dedication of the wall at Jerusalem (Neh. 12:27-47). All the musical instruments described above were present. Nehemiah's description of the praise-filled celebration concludes with the statement, "For in the days of David and Asaph of old there were chief of the singers, and songs of praise and thanksgiving unto God" (vs. 46). The words "of old" are true. The dedication ceremony was scripted by David five hundred years before!

One of the most important duties of the synagogue cantor, or music leader, is the preparation of bar mitzvah boys—and in the case of the liberal Reform movement, bat mitzvah girls—for adult membership. The young people must demonstrate before the congregation the ability to read a portion of the Hebrew Scripture.

In Orthodox and some Conservative synagogues, the preparation includes cantillation, the skill of raising and lowering the singsong voice in the reading of a passage. For centuries this was the requirement for all would-be congregational readers. The Reform movement set it aside some years ago.

Zechariah 14:9 says, "In that day shall there be one Lord, and his name one." Sadly, the Jews omit the first part of the verse, a clear reference to the Messiah: "and the Lord shall be king over all the earth." Only when Jesus is acknowledged as King will we praise Him as we should.

—Lyle P. Murphy.

Guiding the Superintendent

While most people do not rely on receiving compliments, they do enjoy hearing them. It helps boost a person's morale as well as confidence. God does not need anyone to boost His self-esteem, for He is self-sufficient.

In this week's lesson, we will learn more about the importance for all creation to praise God. As we learn, let us commit ourselves to expressing our appreciation to God.

DEVOTIONAL OUTLINE

1. Praise commanded from the heavens (Ps. 148:1-6). Praise is an outward expression of gratitude to God. It can be done in various ways. Music, verbal expressions, and physical expressions such as lifting of hands are some of the methods by which God's people can express praise.

The psalmist emphasized praise in Psalm 148:1. He indicated that this is something we owe God. Since He is the Creator, God deserves to receive glory for His wonderful acts. The psalmist called on the angels to give praise. Within the Bible, we see angels displaying praise through bowing, adoration, and obedience to God (cf. Ps. 103:21).

The psalmist called for the sun, moon, stars, skies, and rain clouds to offer praise to the Lord. In Psalm 148:5-6, the psalmist gave the reasons that they are to praise God. First, by His command they came into existence. Second, He permanently established them. Nothing can defeat God's purpose and eradicate them.

2. Praise commanded from God's creation (Ps. 148:7-10). The psalmist called for the creatures of the sea as well as the oceans to offer praise. All the elements of snow, wind, clouds, mountains, and land are to give adoration to their Creator. Animals, insects, and birds are to be active participants in worship.

3. Praise commanded from humanity (Ps. 148:11-14). Psalm 107:1-2 reminds us that we should express praise to God for all of His redemptive acts. The name of the Lord is to be exalted with adoration. His glorious nature warrants this activity.

Commands to praise are not merely for kings, high-ranking officials, or adults. Children are commanded to praise Him as well. The psalmist understood the significance of children acknowledging God at their young age (cf. Eccles. 12:1).

The saints of God are especially to praise Him. Emphasis is placed on God's chosen people, Israel, rendering thanksgiving to Him.

AGE-GROUP EMPHASES

Children: At an early age, it is important for children to learn proper manners. One important practice throughout life is saying "thank you" when receiving acts of kindness. Help them learn to express gratitude by leading them in praise to God.

Youths: Today's society pushes self-interest as the means for survival. Teens need to be reminded of the importance of thinking of others. Point the young people to directing their interests toward God by showing gratitude and thanksgiving to God. Inform them that God is worthy of it because of His constant care of them.

Adults: Remind adults of the feelings they experience when people compliment them. Encourage them to consistently give homage to God for His wonderful works.

—*Tyrone Keith Carroll, Sr.*

Scripture Lesson Text

GAL. 3:26 For ye are all the children of God by faith in Christ Je'sus.

27 For as many of you as have been baptized into Christ have put on Christ.

28 There is neither Jew nor Greek, there is neither bond nor free, there is neither male nor female: for ye are all one in Christ Je'sus.

29 And if ye *be* Christ's, then are ye A'bra-ham's seed, and heirs according to the promise.

4:1 Now I say, *That* the heir, as long as he is a child, differeth nothing from a servant, though he be lord of all;

2 But is under tutors and governors until the time appointed of the father.

3 Even so we, when we were children, were in bondage under the elements of the world:

4 But when the fulness of the time was come, God sent forth his Son, made of a woman, made under the law,

5 To redeem them that were under the law, that we might receive the adoption of sons.

6 And because ye are sons, God hath sent forth the Spir'it of his Son into your hearts, crying, Ab'ba, Father.

7 Wherefore thou art no more a servant, but a son; and if a son, then an heir of God through Christ.

NOTES

Heirs of the Promise

Lesson: Galatians 3:26—4:7

Read: Galatians 3:26—4:7

TIME: probably A.D. 48   PLACE: from Syrian Antioch

GOLDEN TEXT—"There is neither Jew nor Greek, there is neither bond nor free, there is neither male nor female: for ye are all one in Christ Jesus" (Galatians 3:28).

Introduction

The Jewish world into which Jesus was born was dominated by the Law of Moses. The law was central to the nation's worship as well as daily practice. For the Pharisees, the law, along with their own man-made additions, governed every moment of life in minute detail, and anyone who fell short of keeping it according to their interpretation was subject to rejection and ridicule. Even those Jewish people who were less rigid in their law keeping looked down on Gentiles, who had no concept of God's requirements.

Even a cursory reading of the book of Acts reveals how the newborn Christian church struggled with understanding how believers, especially Gentiles, were to relate to the Law of Moses. Are Christians obligated to observe the Old Testament law? If so, which parts of it? Are believers to ignore the law altogether? Many Christians are still asking those questions. They are confused about the law and what, if any, role it should play in their lives. This continuing confusion makes the book of Galatians as relevant today as when Paul wrote it almost two thousand years ago.

LESSON OUTLINE

I. BENEFITS OF BELIEF—
Gal. 3:26-29

II. TRANSITION IN STATUS—
Gal. 4:1-7

Exposition: Verse by Verse

BENEFITS OF BELIEF

GAL. 3:26 For ye are all the children of God by faith in Christ Jesus.

27 For as many of you as have been baptized into Christ have put on Christ.

28 There is neither Jew nor Greek, there is neither bond nor free, there is neither male nor female: for ye are all one in Christ Jesus.

29 And if ye be Christ's, then are ye Abraham's seed, and heirs according to the promise.

Galatians was probably the first of Paul's epistles to be written. In it, the apostle sought to counter false teachers who were perverting the gospel. These false teachers were seeking to force Gentile converts in the province of Galatia to observe Jewish ceremonies and were promoting the idea that justification and sanctification come through "works of the law" (2:16; cf. 3:2, 5, 10), not merely by faith.

Beginning in Galatians 2:15, Paul gave a lengthy defense of the doctrine of justification by faith—that one is declared righteous before God solely through faith in Christ. What role, then, does the law play? Paul concluded that "the law was our schoolmaster to bring us unto Christ, that we might be justified by faith" (3:24). Once we have come to faith in Christ, "we are no longer under a schoolmaster" (vs. 25). In the verses that follow, the apostle elaborated on what this truth means for believers.

Sonship (Gal. 3:26). Through faith in Jesus Christ, believers have become "the children of God." Such a relationship was not possible through observing the law. Those who are under the law are like children under the authority of a schoolmaster, or tutor. Faith brings one into a family relationship with Christ. "Children of God" is literally "sons of God" and represents mature sons in contrast with children, who are still under a tutor. Those who have faith in Christ are no longer held under bondage to the demands of the law. They have grown up into mature sons of God.

Unity with Christ (Gal. 3:27-28). In verse 26 Paul said that all believers are children of God. This new status comes by faith, not by conforming to Jewish law or practices. Verse 27 essentially restates this truth in different terms, saying, "As many of you as have been baptized into Christ have put on Christ."

The baptism referred to here is the baptism of the Spirit, not water baptism. When a person is saved through faith in Christ, the Holy Spirit at that moment enters the person's life, identifies that person with Christ, and spiritually places him or her into the body of Christ (I Cor. 12:13; cf. Rom. 8:9). As such, the believer puts on Christ; that is, he or she is so united with Christ as to be clothed with Him. Faith both brings one into the family of God and brings about the spiritual baptism that unites one with Christ.

Water baptism is a symbolic act and can effect none of these spiritual realities. Neither can works of the law bring one into union with Christ.

Paul made it very clear to the Galatians that Gentiles did not have to become Jews and follow the law in order to be saved. Justification is by faith alone for both Jews and Gentiles. In fact, although earthly distinctions of race and gender and position remain, "all believers . . . are equally a part of one spiritual entity. They are all 'in Christ Jesus'—in a vital union with Him, whereby they share His life, His perfect righteousness, and the prospect of participating in the promises He will receive as the Messianic Heir" (Kent, *The Freedom of God's Sons,* BMH).

While distinctions will be made in this life—and some are necessary—they have no bearing on one's relationship with Christ. All who come to Christ in faith are united as one in Him.

We do well to remember this truth in our relationships within the church. No one has to conform to some measurable standard in order to join the body of Christ. We have *all* come to Him by faith. Every believer is unique and distinct, but all believers are one in Christ.

Inheritance (Gal. 3:29). All who are in Christ by faith are also "Abraham's seed, and heirs according to the promise." Paul had already stated in verse 16 that Christ is uniquely Abraham's seed. Now he affirmed that those who are in Christ are likewise Abraham's seed and heirs of the promises made to Abraham.

Abraham was given a number of promises (cf. Gen. 12:1-3). Some were intended for him personally and some for the nation that would descend from him (Israel). The Abrahamic promises that all believers inherit are those blessings that were promised to come to "all families of the earth." Through Jesus Christ, Abraham's descendant, believers of all nations receive the blessing of justification and all the blessings that accompany that work of God.

The significance of Paul's argument is this: "These benefits are made possible not by the Mosaic Law, for the law could not make men sons of God, Abraham's seed, nor heirs. They are due solely to God's promise which is received by faith" (Kent).

TRANSITION IN STATUS

4:1 Now I say, That the heir, as long as he is a child, differeth nothing from a servant, though he be lord of all;

2 But is under tutors and governors until the time appointed of the father.

3 Even so we, when we were children, were in bondage under the elements of the world:

4 But when the fulness of the time was come, God sent forth his Son, made of a woman, made under the law,

5 To redeem them that were under the law, that we might receive the adoption of sons.

6 And because ye are sons, God hath sent forth the Spirit of his Son into your hearts, crying, Abba, Father.

7 Wherefore thou art no more a servant, but a son; and if a son, then an heir of God through Christ.

From children and servants (Gal. 4:1-3). The Apostle Paul had listed some of the benefits of belief, particularly the new status believers possess in Christ as sons and heirs. All these benefits come solely through faith in Christ, not through observance of the Mosaic Law. But if the law was given by God and is therefore beneficial, how does it relate to the status believers now enjoy? Paul addressed this issue through an illustration.

The apostle had just spoken of believers as heirs of the Abrahamic promises. Now he spoke of an heir who is still a child. One may be an heir in a household and legally master of the entire estate when his father dies, but as long as he is still a child, he is no different from a servant in that household. In fact, the heir is under the supervision of servants until his father declares him to be an adult (Gal. 4:2). "Tutors" were those who served as guardians of children. "Governors" were household managers. Such positions often were held by slaves.

The illustration seems to come specifically from Roman custom, but Paul applied it to himself and Jewish believers. He said that when they were "children," they "were in bondage under the elements of the world" (Gal. 4:3). "Children" speaks of the spiritual immaturity of Paul and the Galatians before they came to Christ. At that time, they did not have the freedom of full-grown sons and heirs. In fact, they were enslaved.

What were these elements of the world that kept them in bondage? Some think Paul was talking about demonic forces that enslaved the pagan Galatians before their conversion. Others believe he meant religious bondage in general, whether Jewish or pagan. The context, however, points to the Law of Moses, which kept the Jewish believers in bondage and even now threatened to enslave Gentile believers.

In what sense was the law a slavemaster? Before Christ came, the Jewish people stood condemned by the law God had given them. It pointed out their sin but offered no permanent solution for it. Thus, while the law in a sense kept people in the bondage of sin, Paul also accurately described it as a "schoolmaster" that brought people to Christ so that they might be justified, or declared righteous, forever through faith (Gal. 3:19-25).

Like the tutors in a household, the law instructed people and showed them their sin so that when Christ came, they would see their need to trust Him to save them. Sadly, the Judaism of Paul's day saw the law as the means of salvation rather than the means God used to point people to the Saviour.

By redemption (Gal. 4:4-5). The transition from bondage and childhood to freedom and sonship was accomplished through Christ's coming and the redemption He purchased. This occurred in "the fulness of the time." It was exactly in accordance with the prophetic timeline of Daniel 9:24-27 and at a time the world was perfectly prepared for His arrival.

At the perfect time in God's eternal plan, He sent forth His Son to be born of a woman and "under the law" (Gal. 4:4). The One who is fully God is also fully man. By stressing Jesus' humanity and the fact that as a Jew He was under obligation to the Mosaic Law, Paul identified Jesus with His Jewish people. Unlike His fellow Jews, however, Jesus kept the law perfectly (cf. Heb. 4:15), and this is what qualified Him to redeem them.

Redemption "denotes the means by which salvation is achieved, namely, by the payment of a ransom" (Elwell, ed., *Evangelical Dictionary of Theology,* Baker). The price paid for our salvation was the death of Christ. In relation to Jewish believers and the law, Christ's death redeemed those who were under the law and its bondage.

Abraham and those like him who had faith in the Lord were counted as righteous before God (cf. Gen. 15:6). But they could be counted as righteous only on the basis of Christ's death, which actually paid for their sin. In time and according to God's plan, Christ came and died in their place to redeem them, to purchase their freedom from bondage (cf. Gal. 3:13).

In the context of the apostle's argument, the implication is clear: "Since Christ redeemed and set free those who were under the Law, why should Gentile converts now wish to be placed under it?" (Walvoord and Zuck, eds., *The Bible Knowledge Commentary,* Cook). Why would anybody want to trade his freedom for spiritual bondage?

Christ's redemption enables all who believe in Him to receive the "adoption of sons" (Gal. 4:5). The biblical idea of spiritual adoption focuses not on being transferred from one family to another but rather on the conferral of the full rights of sonship. Those who have been born again into the family of God are like heirs who have now reached adulthood and are no longer under a guardian. Again, the implication is that it is utterly unthinkable that God would demand that those He has redeemed and made His sons solely through faith in Him now submit to the bondage of the law, whether they are Jews or Gentiles.

To sons and heirs (Gal. 4:6-7). Believers have been elevated to a new spiritual status through the redemptive work of Christ. They now have a new relationship to God as mature sons. As sons, they enjoy the presence of the Holy Spirit, who resides within them and gives them assurance of their relationship with God (cf. Rom. 8:14-16). This assurance enables them to cry "Abba, Father" (Gal. 4:6).

"Abba" is the Aramaic form of the word "Father." It conveys "intimacy and trust as opposed to the formalism of legalism" (Walvoord and Zuck). We who have trusted in Christ and been redeemed through His death can cry out in joy as sons, addressing our God personally as One we know and love.

In Galatians 4:7 the Apostle Paul summarized his argument. In doing so, he switched from the plural ("ye") to the singular ("thou"), thus applying his point to individual Christians. Each Galatian believer had experienced a transition from being a servant to being a mature son. He was no longer a slave in bondage to the law but free. More than that, he had the privileged position of son.

As Kent pointed out, "This answers the question of why the law is not binding on Christians as it had been on Old Testament saints. The period of the law's guardianship ended with Christ's coming. Full sonship is the present believer's experience."

Furthermore, because he is a son, the believer in Christ is also an heir to everything God has. He inherits the promises to Abraham and his seed (cf. Rom. 8:17). And this inheritance is based not on keeping the law but on faith in Christ.

The good news is that Paul called even the confused Galatians sons and heirs because of their faith in Christ. But the fact that Paul had to set them straight offers a warning to us that even Christians can adopt wrong and destructive ideas.

It is solely through faith in Christ that we have become redeemed sons and heirs of God's promises. We are saved through faith (Eph. 2:8-9), and we are to walk by faith (II Cor. 5:7). To add the law or anything else to faith is to place a heavy and unneeded burden on ourselves. The law has served its purpose by revealing our sin and pointing us to the Saviour. It cannot save us, and it cannot sanctify us.

The gracious work of God has freed us from bondage and made us sons and heirs. There is nothing we can add to that and nothing greater we can attain.

—*Jarl K. Waggoner.*

QUESTIONS

1. What were the false teachers in Galatia promoting?

2. What is justification? How is it received?

3. To what sort of persons does "children of God" in Galatians 3:26 refer?

4. What is the baptism spoken of in verse 27? What does this baptism accomplish?

5. What promises to Abraham do all believers in Christ inherit?

6. What analogy did Paul use to express the believer's relationship to the law?

7. What was the bondage under which Jewish believers had been held?

8. In what sense is the law a slave-master?

9. What is redemption, and how is our redemption accomplished?

10. How did Paul's argument counter the false teaching in Galatia concerning the law?

—*Jarl K. Waggoner.*

Preparing to Teach the Lesson

As a teacher, you must understand and accept the spiritual principles taught in our lesson this week so that you can teach them to others. Study the lesson text carefully. There is a teaching in some Christian circles that asserts that God is finished with the Jews and that Christians are now the "chosen people." This is not correct. It is true that we become children of Abraham through faith in Christ, but God's plans and prophecies for the Jewish people will still be fulfilled at the designated time. Our part is to rejoice in our standing as heirs of the promise of righteousness by faith, just like Abraham.

TODAY'S AIM

Facts: to understand what the promise does for us as contemporary believers.

Principle: to learn to align our thinking with God's revealed promise, which will help us spiritually and mentally.

Application: to understand and appreciate what God has done for us by including us in this promise.

INTRODUCING THE LESSON

Spiritual principles are at work in this world. We can either be under the principles, or elements, of the world or under the spiritual principles of the children of God. We have a choice; God does not force us to obey the righteous spiritual principles. Before we came to faith in Christ, we were under bondage to the elements, or spiritual principles, of the world and did not have a choice. We could not do that which was righteous. We were then children of Adam, not children of God.

However, the promised Holy Spirit comes to indwell us when we are saved. We inherit this promise to Abraham that all the world would be blessed through his "seed," or spiritual children. The primary fulfillment of this is the Lord Jesus Christ. Then all who trust Him and become children of God become spiritual descendants of faithful Abraham.

DEVELOPING THE LESSON

1. Our position in Christ (Gal. 3:26-29). It can be hard to understand our position in Christ as children of God, but it is true. Just as Abraham was justified by faith and made right with God through faith, so are we who believe in Him. This does not depend on our good works to bring us spiritual merit, or on our feelings that may at least momentarily convince us that we are believers. If we truly believe that the Lord Jesus died and rose again on our behalf, then we are children of God. At the time we come to faith, we may be in sin with no apparent way out of it. If God wants to move us out of the sinful situation, He can make a way if we are willing.

Abraham could have continued in unbelief. He could have wondered whether God was real and had a purpose for him. However, Abraham chose to listen to God and obey Him. He left his people and his country and journeyed to find the land God had promised him. He believed God would give him many descendants even though he had no children yet. He believed that God was going to do something special with his life and his descendants. God promised to send a blessing to all the people of the world through Abraham's descendants. This was, of course, the Lord Jesus and His saving work on the cross.

2. Former enslavement to the world and its spiritual principles (Gal. 4:1-3). Paul gave us this detailed explanation, which includes the fact that before we came to Christ in faith, we were locked into the spiritual principles of this world system. This includes not believing in the Lord and many popular spiritual ideas like "God helps those who help themselves." This is useless and makes no sense whatsoever. Of course, God does expect us to do those things we can do. No matter how much we pray and believe God, He will not tie our shoes for us! If we will not tie them, we may trip and fall on our faces.

This world system believes in luck, Mother Nature, or cleverly outsmarting others for dishonest gain. It believes in seeking out advantages and exploiting whatever is needed to get ahead. However, the person of faith who believes in Christ is told, "Seek ye first the kingdom of God, and his righteousness" (Matt. 6:33). He must let God lead and direct his life. God will bring the right circumstances and opportunities so that His child can fulfill his calling.

3. Freedom and inheritance in Christ (Gal. 4:4-7). God's timing is perfect; He is never too early or too late. We may not know all the details of why it was the best time for Christ to be born, live, and die, but it occurred at "the fulness of the time." Despite attempts to change it, all human history is still divided into "before Christ" (B.C.) and "in the year of our Lord" (A.D., or *anno Domini*).

God's timing in the rise and fall of nations and in the lives of His children is flawless. He sent His Son at exactly the right time, and He sends His Spirit to enlighten us, to bring us to salvation, and to bring order to our lives. Through Christ, we have been freed from the necessity to keep the Mosaic Law, since Christ fulfilled all the law. We are drawn by His Spirit to call out to God as our Father. We are His children and heirs. We can relax in His care and know that because of our relationship with Him, all is well for us spiritually, no matter what is going on in our lives economically and socially.

We are heirs of the promise of eternal life in Christ. Because our sins are forgiven, we have a home in heaven. Abraham looked for a city whose builder and maker was God. We look for new heavens and a new earth wherein righteousness dwells. This is promised to us as those who believe God and are heirs of these "great and precious promises" (II Pet. 1:4).

ILLUSTRATING THE LESSON

Our standing in Christ brings us many blessings, including the promise to Abraham.

CONCLUDING THE LESSON

While we do not become Jews as physical descendants of Abraham, we do become spiritual children of Abraham as those who believe God and are committed to following Him. Abraham left his homeland and started out to find God's best for him. We leave behind our attachment to this world and its spiritual principles and start out to find God's best for us.

ANTICIPATING THE NEXT LESSON

Next, we explore our deliverance from bondage to the spiritual principles of this world.

—*Brian D. Doud.*

PRACTICAL POINTS

1. As children in the family of God, we must not go our own way. We need to love the members of God's family (Gal. 3:26).
2. Let Christ be the garment you wear with pride (vs. 27).
3. Christ brings unity to His body. Jews and Gentiles alike are one in Him (vss. 28-29).
4. Just as a child in a family outgrows his tutors, so grace brings about spiritual maturity (4:1-3).
5. God operates on His own timetable. What may appear as a random event is part of His plan (Gal. 4:4-5; cf. Jas. 1:17).
6. As part of God's family, we have the privileges of sons and heirs (Gal. 4:6-7).

—Lendell Sims.

RESEARCH AND DISCUSSION

1. Many people would agree with Galatians 3:26 that we "are all the children of God." Why is the last phrase of the verse critical to a proper understanding?
2. Why is it so difficult to live out the truth of verse 28?
3. "Tutors and governors" (4:2) refers to the law. Since the way of salvation has been made plain in Christ, to what extent is it still necessary to follow the law?
4. Why do you think it is that Jews largely have not comprehended the need for the Saviour from sin?
5. Does working for a reward contradict the reality of receiving an inheritance from God?

—Lendell Sims.

ILLUSTRATED HIGH POINTS

Have put on Christ

We know that believers are positionally and legally "in" Christ (cf. Phil. 3:9). However, in another sense, through public confession, we have "put on" Christ for the world. We are His representatives through which they see Him (cf. II Cor. 3:2-3).

Do you know there are schools and training camps for those who wish to don a big-headed, furry suit and be a team or company mascot? As ambassadors of those they represent, mascots take their work very seriously. We might learn something about representing Christ from the following mascot guidelines:

- Study and learn your character.
- Think and act like the character.
- Wear the complete costume.
- Never let your voice be heard.
- Never let your flesh be seen.
- Let a guide lead and protect you.
- Build endurance—take the heat.

All one in Christ Jesus

We once installed an inflatable, above-ground pool with a feature called "quick set." The soft sides of the pool were supported by the pressure of the water against the interior walls. The pool had to be perfectly level. If one side was higher, all the water would flow out.

It is human nature to inflate ourselves above others. Who is better: a Jew or a Greek, a slave or a free man, a man or a woman? What kind of car do you drive? Which neighborhood are you from?

Paul shows us that the kingdom of God is organized quite differently. Christ alone is lifted on high, while the rest of us stand and serve Him on level ground. As humble, caring members of His body, we can then truly be filled with Living Water that will not escape (cf. Eph. 4:1-5).

—Therese Greenberg.

Golden Text Illuminated

"There is neither Jew nor Greek, there is neither bond nor free, there is neither male nor female: for ye are all one in Christ Jesus" (Galatians 3:28).

As we contemplate the high calling of belonging by faith to the church of the Lord Jesus, we are led into a consideration of some very important concepts, such as inheritance. Inheritance is a rich truth in the Bible, going all the way back to the promise of worldwide blessing given through the patriarch Abraham (Gen. 12:1-3). Believers in Jesus are heirs of this blessing.

The book of Galatians explains that an heir is a son and will come into his inheritance in due time. A son or heir has a superior position to that of a slave or a servant. A believer in the Lord Jesus Christ becomes an heir of salvation through faith in Jesus Christ. He is connected to God and to the church of Jesus Christ, having received the privilege of a rich family inheritance.

Our text outlines the beautiful truth that our position as heirs of God and joint heirs with Christ takes no notice of ordinary human distinctions. Three couplets are marked out for our understanding.

The first couplet is racial (and perhaps religious). Among religious Jews of the first century, the sharpest possible distinction was maintained between themselves as the people of Israel and the other "nations" (Gentiles). Fellowship between religious Jews and Gentiles was not possible on any level. One group was "in" and the other groups were "out"—outside of the covenant of blessing, outside of God's grace, yes, out as far as one can be out. But in Christ, no matter what religious or racial background one has, faith in Christ brings us into the same church, with the same salvation and the same inheritance. The former distinctions no longer count.

The second distinction is class, which of course had powerful implications in the ancient world. There were large numbers in the slave class in the Roman world—estimates range from ten percent of the population to as high as sixty percent.

Slaves were owned by masters and consigned to their lot in life. They had certain occupations and duties, but they could escape their predicament only in certain prescribed ways, which they did not control. The free class had all the power. One group had rights; the other group had no or very limited rights. But when the gospel was preached, slave and free received the same salvation and came into the same church.

This is why we see so much teaching in the New Testament on the relationship between slave and free. It was a big deal for those two populations to mix in the same churches—and mix they did. Jesus Christ takes believers of all classes and makes them equal heirs of salvation.

Finally, the distinction of gender was addressed. Both men and women are invited to drink equally of the mercies of Jesus. All who believe, whether male or female, are privileged to belong to Him as co-heirs. What wonderful unity all the heirs of salvation possess! Let us make sure we live it out. What love should be found in the church! So much of life is about unbiblical restrictions, preferences, obstacles, and prohibitions. The logic of grace destroys these common barriers within the church.

—*Jeff VanGoethem.*

Heart of the Lesson

While we never like to think of our loved ones moving from this world to the heavenly realm, we still need to plan for it. Recently, my parents were working on updating their last will and testament. In the process, they were looking at their possessions and determining which child would receive each item. This is not an easy task, because my parents love each of us equally. It is difficult to ensure that the possessions are divided evenly. My brothers and I have been given a promise of what we will receive after their deaths.

God says that we are His children. He says we are heirs to the kingdom of God. Our promises from God include much more than eternal life!

1. By faith (Gal. 3:26-29). The Apostle Paul reminded the Galatians who they were. He combated a mentality held by the Galatians that brought limitations. Paul said, "There is neither Jew nor Greek, there is neither bond nor free, there is neither male nor female: for ye are all one in Christ Jesus." Since we have become children of God by faith, we are no longer held captive by those things in the law that brought forth division. There is no hierarchy in Christ. It no longer matters if we are Jews or Greeks, men or women, slave or free. We are children of God—part of Abraham's seed.

2. A child heir (Gal. 4:1-2). In this portion of Scripture, the Apostle Paul was trying to illuminate the fact that we are God's children and that therefore we have a right to inherit all that God has promised His children. Nevertheless, we have to understand that even if we have a right to something,

we do not always receive it immediately. If a parent dies an untimely death, a minor child will not be able to access his inheritance until he comes of age. The child is appointed a guardian who will watch over and protect whatever it is that he is destined to inherit. In Paul's day, until the child became an adult in the eyes of the Roman government, he was no different from a slave—even though he was in reality the owner of the estate.

3. Adopted as sons (Gal. 4:3-7). The Apostle Paul was saying that while we were in bondage to the world (our sin nature), we were children. "When the fulness of the time was come, God sent forth his Son, made of a woman, made under the law, to redeem them that were under the law, that we might receive the adoption of sons."

In other words, Jesus Christ came and fulfilled the law through His life, death, and resurrection. Because we are now washed clean and redeemed, we are no longer children of the world but have been adopted into God's eternal family. We know that we are sons and daughters of God because His Spirit within us cries out to God as our Father.

Since we are now sons and daughters of God, we no longer need to live as slaves to the world. We have a guaranteed inheritance waiting for us. We are no longer children in the sense of being under age and unable to access our inheritance; we are adults. We have access to all the promises of God now. We no longer have to wait to receive them. We can stand confidently on His Word as His beloved children and heirs.

—*Kristin Reeg.*

World Missions

I have always admired people who can speak several languages fluently. Blair, a young man I worked with several years ago, was such a person. He was the Spanish teacher in a Christian school. Besides English and Spanish, Blair had mastered French. He practiced his languages during summer missionary trips to Central America and French-speaking African nations.

During the eight years I worked with Blair, I never tired of hearing his stories from his summer trips. As impressed as I was with Blair's enthusiasm for missions, I respected him most for his love for people. One fall I heard Blair tell about his desire to join a missions team in Brazil. He spent the school year studying Portuguese and was fluent before spring break. Blair took every opportunity to expand his ministry to the peoples of the world.

One autumn a new teacher, Kenny, joined our staff. Kenny was a recent retiree from the United States Navy. His job had been to intercept messages and interpret them. He was assigned to translate Russian messages into Japanese. We all knew what languages Blair would seek to learn next. Kenny and Blair became friends quickly. They practiced their languages daily. The joke in the teacher's lunchroom was that we should rename it the United Nations room.

The faculty and staff at our school rarely understood the diverse dialogues between Kenny and Blair. We did, however, understand why they engaged daily in their verbal exchanges. Kenny was teaching, equipping, and preparing Blair for what would become a series of missionary endeavors.

After eight years, Blair launched into full-time ministry as a global missionary. His dream of spreading the gospel throughout the world began to come true. His missionary work continues today. Blair's love for people and his interest in their cultures inspired him to learn many languages and dialects. God blessed him with success and opportunities as he was faithful in sharing the gospel with all people.

"There is neither Jew nor Greek, there is neither bond nor free, there is neither male nor female: for ye are all one in Christ Jesus" (Gal. 3:28). The heart of God is for us all to be one in Jesus, no matter who we are. Blair's life illustrates that he agrees with this verse. In his work he preaches to and teaches people of many cultures, wherever he is sent. Despite barriers of languages, politics, or gender, Blair looks for ways to communicate the good news of Jesus Christ. He has been privileged to bring people to Christ in many corners of the world. Blair offers testimonies of the dramatic conversions he has seen. But even in his exciting reports, he remembers to express his appreciation for the people who help him accomplish his missions. Some give him finances, some pray consistently for him, and others send him encouraging messages. Blair understands and acknowledges that we all are one in Christ and heirs to the promise.

Missionaries tie nations, languages, and cultures into one body through the preaching of the gospel. No matter our role, each of us has a responsibility to support those who carry the glorious message that makes us one family of God.

—*Beverly Medley Jones.*

The Jewish Aspect

Lewis Sperry Chafer quoted Galatians 3:27 in affirming the important truth that Spirit baptism places every believer into Christ, into God's forever family (Gal. 4:5-7) (*Systematic Theology,* Kregel).

The Jews say that Christianity is, so to speak, a daughter religion of Judaism, inasmuch as our Founder was a Jew (Ausubel, *The Book of Jewish Knowledge,* Crown Publishers). The emphasis in our text for today is that the Christian has gladly passed up any worldly identification for oneness in Christ. Judaism has no counterpart to our position in the Lord, despite the Jews' standing as the very special people of God.

Modern Jewish rabbis believe that Israel's real beginnings were at Sinai and not as the children of faithful Abraham. Abraham's covenantal circumcision is as far as they go in loyalty to the patriarch Abraham (Gal. 3:7-9).

Identifying the Jews as a particular people group is a daunting task. As a primary consideration, we must say the Jews are not a race. Neither can it be said they are a nation at this time, for while the State of Israel is a sovereign entity, over half of the world's Jews do not live in the land of their fathers and some are antagonistic towards Israel.

A second step in Jewish identification is simply to define a Jew. I tried out my definition on my Jewish doctor. I suggested that a Jew is one who calls himself a Jew and who is called that by other Jews.

However, this definition immediately falls flat when you consider they adamantly refuse to call Messianic Jews, believers in the Messiah Jesus, Jews. This is the case even if these Messianic Jews have identified their roots in the Jewish faith without a break of any kind. Yet, the Reform synagogue may take twenty Gentiles into their membership and recognize them thereafter as fully Jewish! Ancient Jewish tradition has held that you are of the same faith as your mother. Israeli courts have rejected the pleas of Jews with Gentile wives to have their children declared to be Jews.

A separate problem in identifying the unique position of Jews is the matter of tribal identification. Is Isaac Levin a true Levite? Is David Rabinowitz a descendant of Reuben, the firstborn of Jacob? The Jews say this cannot be known. Still, a Jewish friend bearing the name of Caleb, the faithful spy, claimed direct descent from the hero of the conquest of the Holy Land with Joshua.

It is well to note that God knows the tribe of every Jew. In the last days, God will commission twelve thousand Jews from each of the tribes to present God's plan of salvation (Rev. 7; 14).

We have considered the "evangelistic approach" Jews take to the incorporation of willing Gentiles into Judaism. A rabbi in our community is an active missionary. He uses Jewish history as a source of discovering Jews who were forced to convert to another faith in the Middle Ages. He visits cities and towns where the most violent proselytism of Jews took place and urges those who might have Jewish roots to return to Judaism.

It is never mentioned, but Judaism needs Jewish children born to Jewish mothers in order to continue Jewish history and culture in a form that approximates that of their ancestors. The risk at present is of a people who do not know their native language, have little grasp of the Bible, and, worse, no understanding of the unfolding of God's plan of salvation.

—Lyle P. Murphy.

Guiding the Superintendent

Parents often set up insurance policies as well as write wills. They want to ensure their legacy continues through contributions to future generations.

In this week's lesson, we will learn that God's people are heirs of a greater promise. The promise established by God was accomplished by sending His Son, Jesus Christ, to earth.

DEVOTIONAL OUTLINE

1. Accepted into the family of God (Gal. 3:26-29). Paul's letter to the Galatians was pivotal. The Galatians were Gentile people. The Jews considered the Gentiles to be beneath them, and they did not readily accept them. The Messiah was promised to the Jews. However, many of them rejected Him.

Through the Apostle Paul's ministry, many people were saved. This letter was written to encourage and inform them of their status in Christ.

Becoming a child of God is accomplished by trusting in Jesus Christ as Saviour. Those who place their faith in Christ are baptized into Him. "This is the baptism of (or in) the Holy Spirit, which . . . joins all believers to Christ and unites them within the church, Christ's body" (Walvoord and Zuck, eds., *The Bible Knowledge Commentary,* Cook).

Beyond becoming a part of the body of Christ, there are certain barriers that were eliminated by Christ.

Paul informed the Galatians that in God's eyes they were not second-class citizens. In Christ, there were no ethnic, gender, or slave barriers. They were all one in Christ. Paul informed the Galatian Gentile believers that they were heirs of the kingdom, just like their Jewish counterparts.

2. Enslaved before salvation (Gal. 4:1-3). Paul illustrated the significance of the inheritance of the righteous. A child could not receive his inheritance until he matured. He was subject to his guardians. He was little better than the father's servants in his degree of freedom. Before Christ came, the world was subject to the law. Because of man's sinfulness, the law was at times overbearing and oppressive. However, through Christ grace entered, and sins were washed away.

3. Heirs through Christ (Gal. 4:4-7). At the appropriate time, God sent Jesus to earth. Born of a virgin, Jesus entered the world to fulfill the law (Matt. 5:17). This was done to break the law's bondage. Subsequently, the Lord has adopted all those who receive Him. Because of His sacrifice, all who trust in Jesus can call God Father.

AGE-GROUP EMPHASES

Children: Children need to know that they are special to God. They need to know the extent of God's love for them. Help them understand the importance of trusting Jesus as their Saviour.

Youths: Many teens suffer from peer pressure and self-esteem issues. Lead them to understand the unconditional love of their Saviour. Help them understand that God's acceptance of them far surpasses the rejection of others. Remind them that they are children of the Lord.

Adults: Many people base their value on worldly standards. Inform the adults that their value is not based on possessions, education, economics, ethnicity, or employment status. Share with them that a personal relationship with Christ is their greatest blessing. Inform them that their value is in Christ.

—*Tyrone Keith Carroll, Sr.*

Scripture Lesson Text

GAL. 4:8 Howbeit then, when ye knew not God, ye did service unto them which by nature are no gods.

9 But now, after that ye have known God, or rather are known of God, how turn ye again to the weak and beggarly elements, whereunto ye desire again to be in bondage?

10 Ye observe days, and months, and times, and years.

11 I am afraid of you, lest I have bestowed upon you labour in vain.

12 Brethren, I beseech you, be as I *am*; for I *am* as ye *are*: ye have not injured me at all.

13 Ye know how through infirmity of the flesh I preached the gospel unto you at the first.

14 And my temptation which was in my flesh ye despised not, nor rejected; but received me as an angel of God, *even* as Christ Je'sus.

15 Where is then the blessedness ye spake of? for I bear you record, that, if *it had been* possible, ye would have plucked out your own eyes, and have given them to me.

16 Am I therefore become your enemy, because I tell you the truth?

17 They zealously affect you, *but* not well; yea, they would exclude you, that ye might affect them.

18 But *it is* good to be zealously affected always in *a* good *thing*, and not only when I am present with you.

19 My little children, of whom I travail in birth again until Christ be formed in you,

20 I desire to be present with you now, and to change my voice; for I stand in doubt of you.

NOTES

Delivered from Bondage

Lesson: Galatians 4:8-20

Read: Galatians 4:1-31

TIME: probably A.D. 48   PLACE: from Syrian Antioch

GOLDEN TEXT—"But now, after that ye have known God, or rather are known of God, how turn ye again to the weak and beggarly elements, whereunto ye desire again to be in bondage?" (Galatians 4:9).

Introduction

It was the Apostle Paul who set forth in his writings to Timothy and Titus the qualifications for the church's leaders (I Tim. 3:1-13; Titus 1:5-9). Conspicuously absent from those biblical qualifications are several traits churches today especially seem to prize—qualities such as a dynamic personality, eloquent speaking ability, and even an attractive appearance.

The biblical qualifications for leadership focus on character and faithfulness to God's Word. Paul knew from experience how important these qualities are, for no matter how impressive one presents himself to others, if he does not speak the truth and does not back his message with godly character, there will be no positive, long-lasting results from his ministry.

The Apostle Paul not only proclaimed the truth; he also lived it. That is why he could appeal effectively to the wayward Galatians. He was not the most impressive man, but they knew he spoke the truth, was sincere, and genuinely cared about them—in contrast to those who were leading them astray.

LESSON OUTLINE

I. **THE GALATIANS' PROBLEM**— Gal. 4:8-11

II. **THE APOSTLE'S PLEA**— Gal. 4:12-20

Exposition: Verse by Verse

THE GALATIANS' PROBLEM

GAL. 4:8 Howbeit then, when ye knew not God, ye did service unto them which by nature are no gods.

9 But now, after that ye have known God, or rather are known of God, how turn ye again to the weak and beggarly elements, whereunto ye desire again to be in bondage?

10 Ye observe days, and months,

and times, and years.

11 I am afraid of you, lest I have bestowed upon you labour in vain.

Paul's letter to the Galatians was occasioned by confusion in the churches of this Roman province in Asia Minor (modern-day Turkey). False teachers, known as Judaizers, had introduced the idea that Christians must observe the Mosaic Law, contradicting Paul's teaching. The book of Galatians is Paul's response to this error.

They had forgotten their previous spiritual bondage (Gal. 4:8). At the root of the Galatians' confusion was their failure to grasp their own spiritual history. Here Paul was speaking specifically to the Gentile converts in the Galatian churches. The apostle took them back to the time when they did not know the true God at all. They had worshipped so-called gods that were nothing more than man-made images. In fact, they did "service" to them, meaning they were enslaved to them, forever doing works that could offer no assurance of salvation. Their religion was their own creation, so there was no way they could be sure their worship was right, acceptable, or adequate.

Similarly, the Jewish believers had previously been enslaved to law keeping, having perverted it into the way of salvation in place of faith. Similar too are millions of people today who slavishly follow practices they or others have created in the groundless hope of making themselves acceptable to God.

They were returning to a new form of spiritual bondage (Gal. 4:9-10). Having reminded his readers of their previous enslavement to hopeless rituals, Paul then pointed out that they had been freed from this bondage by coming to know God. To know God is to be born again to eternal life through faith in Christ (cf. John 17:3). This had occurred when the Galatians had responded in faith to the preaching of the gospel.

Paul was quick to elaborate on this, however, stating that their coming to know God was not merely a matter of their effort but a work of God Himself. They were "known of God" (Gal. 4:9). That is, He had chosen them and graciously acted to bring them to faith and salvation.

The sad irony was that these Galatian believers, who had been delivered from the terrible bondage to pagan gods, were now being influenced by false teachers to enslave themselves again to weak and useless principles. The "elements" mentioned in Galatians 4:3 are called "weak and beggarly" here in verse 9. They were weak in that they had "no power to rescue man from condemnation" (Lightfoot, *The Epistle of St. Paul to the Galatians,* Zondervan). These elements were beggarly, or impoverished, and thus unable to provide the spiritual wealth that only Christ can give.

What were these elements to which the Galatians were turning? Our text tells us they involved the observance of days, months, times, and years. These were Jewish celebrations—Sabbaths, feasts, and other special days established by the Law of Moses. It is likely that this list is representative of all the Jewish religious practices the Judaizers were proclaiming as incumbent on followers of Christ.

It was not that merely observing some of Israel's feasts was wrong; rather, it was the idea that such practices were required of believers to gain or maintain their acceptance by God that was wrong. This was replacing faith with legalistic practices.

It is not so much the outward acts that are important but the inward attitudes. If the reason we do certain things is that we think they will gain us some spiritual advantage before God, we are legalists, abandoning God's grace for our own righteousness and abandoning liberty to return to slavery.

They were discounting Paul's teaching and work (Gal. 4:11). Paul's letter to the Galatians turned more personal at this point. He expressed the fear that all his labor among the Galatians would be in vain if they followed the legalistic teaching of the Judaizers.

If those who had come to Christ through faith, whether Jews or Gentiles, continued to observe Jewish ceremonies under the impression that they conferred some spiritual benefit, "Paul's labors to establish churches in Galatia based on the gospel of salvation by faith in Christ would have been for nothing, for the churches would be abandoning the principle of grace and would be turning to a system of righteousness by works which has never saved anyone" (Kent, *The Freedom of God's Sons*, BMH).

THE APOSTLE'S PLEA

12 Brethren, I beseech you, be as I am; for I am as ye are: ye have not injured me at all.

13 Ye know how through infirmity of the flesh I preached the gospel unto you at the first.

14 And my temptation which was in my flesh ye despised not, nor rejected; but received me as an angel of God, even as Christ Jesus.

15 Where is then the blessedness ye spake of? for I bear you record, that, if it had been possible, ye would have plucked out your own eyes, and have given them to me.

16 Am I therefore become your enemy, because I tell you the truth?

17 They zealously affect you, but not well; yea, they would exclude you, that ye might affect them.

18 But it is good to be zealously affected always in a good thing, and not only when I am present with you.

19 My little children, of whom I travail in birth again until Christ be formed in you,

20 I desire to be present with you now, and to change my voice; for I stand in doubt of you.

Based on their previous acceptance of him (Gal. 4:12-15). With the very real danger that the Galatians might fully turn to Jewish legalism, the Apostle Paul pleaded with them to embrace Christ alone and to walk by faith rather than put themselves under the law. The law was a "schoolmaster to bring us unto Christ, that we might be justified by faith" (3:24). The Galatians had been justified by faith, but many "were now 'dropping out' of the school of grace and enrolling in the kindergarten of law!" (Wiersbe, *Be Free,* Cook).

Because Paul was a man of utmost integrity and by God's grace had conducted himself in a pure and upright manner among the Galatians, he could appeal to them on the basis of his past experience with them. He urged them, "Be as I am; for I am as ye are" (Gal. 4:12).

This expression is probably better understood if we translate it literally: "Become like me, for I also became like you." When Paul had come to the Galatians, he had not come as one who was enslaved to Jewish legalism. He had lived like one of them—a Gentile who was not burdened by the law. Now that some of them were being influenced to turn from grace to the law, Paul urged them to be like him: free from the law through faith in Christ and living in the grace and freedom that Christ gives.

Paul reminded the Galatians that they had not harmed or wronged him. When he was among them, the Galatians had found no fault with him for living free from the law and teaching justification by faith.

In fact, when Paul had preached the gospel in Galatia, he had done so while experiencing an "infirmity of the flesh" (Gal. 4:13). Yet the Galatians had welcomed him. They had not yielded to the temptation to despise or reject him but had received him "as an angel of God" (vs. 14). Those who believed his message treated him even as they would have received Christ Himself.

Paul did not say what his infirmity was or why it presented a temptation to the Galatians to reject him. The physical weakness could have been malaria, a serious eye problem, or the continuing effects of persecution. The Greeks in general valued a speaker's appearance and delivery almost as much as the content of his speech. And even when Paul might have been healthier, his "bodily presence" was considered "weak" (II Cor. 10:10). The Galatians, however, were not put off by his appearance.

In view of the Galatians' past acceptance of the apostle, Paul asked where their joy, or sense of being blessed, was now. The joy they had experienced through faith in Christ was no longer evident. They had turned from the grace of God to legalism and, consequently, had turned from the one who had delivered to them the truth of the gospel.

Paul reminded the Galatian believers that they had loved him and rejoiced in the message he brought them so much that they would have plucked out their own eyes if they could have given them to Paul to help him. "Paul apparently had poor eyesight. . . . He often used a secretary to compose his books (Rom. 16:22). When he did write he used large letters in his printing ([Gal.] 6:11)" (Gromacki, *Stand Fast in Liberty,* Kress). This may have been the infirmity Paul wrote of in Galatians 4:13.

The joy of salvation through faith in Christ had caused them to fully accept Paul and made them willing to do anything for him. But that joy now was fading away, as false teaching was bringing them again into sorrowful bondage.

Based on his faithful teaching (Gal. 4:16-18). Paul then asked, "Am I therefore become your enemy, because I tell you the truth?" The false teachers who were pushing their doctrines in Galatia had impugned Paul's integrity. At least by implication, they suggested that he had been insincere and had not taught the truth. Paul had responded to the situation in Galatia by issuing strong condemnations of the false teaching (cf. 1:6-9).

Paul's forceful teaching of the truth, both in the past in delivering the gospel to the Galatians and in the present in countering error, did not make him their enemy as the Judaizers suggested. Indeed, the Galatians had accepted him in the past as their friend, recognizing the truth of his message and the integrity of his character.

Paul had spoken the truth to them, but, sadly, they were now listening to those who told them lies (Gal. 4:17). To "zealously affect" means "to eagerly desire or seek." The expression can be used in either a positive or a negative sense. Here it speaks of the false teachers eagerly seeking "to curry favor with the Galatians, ostensibly being deeply concerned about them" (Hendriksen, *Galatians and Ephesians,* Baker).

The motives of the Judaizers, however, were not honorable. In fact, Paul said their goal was to isolate, or exclude, the Galatians from all other influences—and no doubt Paul in particular. Their hope was that they would gain the trust of the young believers so that they would seek after the Judaizers and adopt their teachings.

Paul was quick to acknowledge that it is good to be eagerly sought out for a good purpose. Paul himself had sought the best interests of the Galatians by preaching the gospel. He wished only that their loyalty to the gospel of grace had continued when he was no longer in their presence.

Sadly, it seemed they not only had turned away from Paul but also were departing from the truth.

Based on his desire for them (Gal. 4:19-20). As Paul concluded this very personal section of Galatians, he addressed the believers as his "little children." He was their spiritual father, but he adopted maternal language in saying he had experienced the pains of their birth into God's family as he preached the gospel. Now he was experiencing similar pain in seeing them falter in their faith and turn from the truth. That pain would continue as he sought to correct them and until Christ was "formed" in them.

The word translated "formed" (Gal. 4:19). refers to an inner transformation to which the outward conduct should correspond. The Galatians were believers, so Christ lived in them (cf. Col. 1:27). "What was needed was a display of the characteristics which their new life in Christ should have been producing. Maturity in the faith, rather than vacillation or toying with legalism, is the form which Christians should display" (Kent). This was Paul's desire for them, and it would come about only when they fully embraced the grace of God and abandoned works of the law as a means of gaining or maintaining their relationship with God.

Paul concluded by expressing his desire to be present with the Galatian Christians again. He frankly acknowledged his doubts about them, for he did not know how much of the Judaizing heresy they really had embraced. He could not know for sure until they responded to his letter or he saw them in person. But his hope was to see them again and be able to speak to them in a different tone of voice because they had heeded his warnings and turned fully to the truth he had preached to them.

This portion of Galatians has important lessons for us today. First, it reminds us of the critical importance of living by faith, not giving in to the perpetual temptation to base our relationship with the Lord on works.

Second, it illustrates how important personal integrity is in serving the Lord. Paul's appeal to the Galatians would have lacked a great deal of weight had he not been able to point to his commitment to preaching the truth out of sincere concern for the Galatians and his selfless desire for their salvation and growth.

Finally, this passage warns us against those who desire and demand our sole allegiance. Godly leaders will gladly point us to others who can also help us grow spiritually. They will not isolate us from others and suggest that they alone possess the truth.

—*Jarl K. Waggoner.*

QUESTIONS

1. What characterized the Galatians' previous religious experience?

2. In what way did the Galatians show a desire to again "be in bondage" (Gal. 4:9)?

3. What was wrong with observing Jewish religious celebrations?

4. What fear did Paul have with regard to the Galatians?

5. How had Paul conducted himself among the Galatians?

6. How had the apostle been received by them?

7. What temptation had the Galatians resisted regarding Paul?

8. How did the false teachers make Paul into the Galatians' enemy?

9. How did the motives of Paul and the Judaizers differ?

10. What was Paul's desire for the believers in Galatia?

—*Jarl K. Waggoner.*

Preparing to Teach the Lesson

To be a slave is to be cheated out of much of one's life and to have one's personality subverted to the will of another. There is still slavery of many kinds throughout the world. The worst form of slavery is spiritual slavery, slavery to wrong spiritual principles instead of freedom in Christ.

If this week's lesson, through God's grace, enables you to help someone enter into the freedom he can have in Christ, you can count yourself—and the person—blessed indeed. You may enter into His freedom more fully as well. We are not free to sin and do that which our Lord does not approve. We are free to unconditionally love others and help them in any positive way we can. We are free to act toward others in the ways the Lord Jesus did in His earthly ministry—helping, healing, loving, and bringing the good news of the gospel to as many as we can.

TODAY'S AIM

Facts: to see clearly our freedom in Christ.

Principle: to realize that we can choose to enter into the freedom Christ has bought for us.

Application: to recognize that when we know, understand, and practice true freedom in Christ, we will be blessed greatly and also be a blessing to others.

INTRODUCING THE LESSON

There is a sense in which everyone is a slave to something or someone. Our text this week points out that before we came to Christ, we were slaves to false beliefs. These might include a whole religious system or the general mores, fears, and opinions of the world. We can be slaves to fear of what others might think or will think if we do something. We might be slaves to the thought that something we do or say may cause bad luck.

However, having trusted Christ, we are freed from many things including keeping all the sacrifices and observances the Jews were commanded to follow. We now have freedom in Christ to be and do anything that answers our conscience as informed by the Word of God and the promptings of the Holy Spirit, which arise from that word. We are delivered from bondage into His freedom.

Some might be afraid of this freedom. They might think it is easier and safer to be told what to do and think, to be told what religious observances will earn us favor with God, and to have carefully drawn patterns of life that our spiritual leaders "know" are best.

DEVELOPING THE LESSON

1. Without Christ, we are slaves to wrong beliefs (Gal. 4:8-11). The Galatian Christians were surrounded by people who believed in numerous gods. You could probably have found a group of people worshipping almost anything you can imagine and a lot of things you cannot imagine! They had religious observances on days, months, seasons, and years! Just as there is the Gregorian New Year, the Jewish New Year, and the Chinese New Year, they had holidays that had to be observed but were totally useless spiritually.

Now that the Galatian Christians had become believers in the Lord Jesus, they should have dropped all those things. They were no longer responsible to observe any other religious practice but were free in Christ from them. It would not hurt their position in Christ to drop all other religious observances, but it could be a distraction to honoring the Lord. It would be something like believing in luck, running our lives by the signs of the zodiac, and being enslaved to those things, when we are really free in Christ from all that.

2. Relationships with others are affected by beliefs (Gal. 4:12-16). When Paul brought the message of Christ to the Galatians, they trusted Christ and were freed from their previous observances and practices. They thought very highly of Paul and would have done anything for him. They were so thankful for the message. They were happy in Christ and in having their sins forgiven. Now they were drifting back into the old ways. Perhaps some of their family members were drawing them back. It would be like going to a heathen ceremony and then to a Christian prayer meeting. They thought they had to do these old things.

By this practice, they had lost their joy in the Lord. This is referred to in Galatians 4:15 as their "blessedness." Anything that robs us of our joy in the Lord is probably a sin and is certainly a spiritual step backward.

3. False teachers are enslavers (Gal. 4:17-20). Many organized or institutionalized religious groups seem to be thinly veiled mechanisms that control and manipulate people, ostensibly "for their own good." Now that Paul was no longer around, teachers of false doctrines and practices were trying to woo the Galatian Christians back into the old ways. Maybe it was like a group of men trying to get a new Christian to come back to the sports bar to watch the game. Not to comply with their wishes could result in ridicule or shaming or at least arguments. It is hard to believe you are really free from all these things when people you once thought were right tell you that you have been misled and your pastor is wrong. A Bible-believing pastor should always want to please the Lord and bring you into God's freedom. He should love you and share your burdens, not enslave you to religious practices.

ILLUSTRATING THE LESSON

The pull of previous practices can be difficult to us as believers.

DELIVERED FROM SIN

SIN

BREAKING THE CHAINS

CONCLUDING THE LESSON

Some people might think that it is restrictive and enslaving to be a really spiritually minded Christian. However, what is really enslaving is to ignore your freedom in Christ and to put yourself back under religious and social observances as though you had to do them to save yourself or keep yourself saved. Doing this may offend the Holy Spirit, who is with you to guide you into all the truth. He wants to guide you into gratefully loving the Lord and people for whom He died, serving the Lord through serving others, and living a life of joy and peace in the Holy Spirit.

We are free in Christ to be and do all that pleases Him. This makes our lives fulfilling and free more than any other way. We are free from thinking that we have to keep certain days or hold certain ceremonies lest God be displeased with us.

ANTICIPATING THE NEXT LESSON

In our next lesson, we dig deeper into the subject of our freedom in Christ.

—*Brian D. Doud.*

PRACTICAL POINTS

1. We should give honor and allegiance only to God (Gal. 4:8).
2. Like the prodigal son, we should realize that our Father has all we need (Gal. 4:9; cf. Luke 15:17).
3. There is a tendency in our fallen human nature to return to those things that held us in bondage (Gal. 4:9-12).
4. Even those who know the truth can get off track in their Christian walk (vss. 13-16).
5. Zealousness, though a good quality, can be misdirected to the wrong ends (vss. 17-18).
6. Spiritual oversight can be a challenging and frustrating task for those called to ministry (vss. 19-20).

—Lendell Sims.

RESEARCH AND DISCUSSION

1. In a conversation with a non-Christian religious person, how might we explain who God is without greatly offending him?
2. Can you identify anything in the church today (a tradition, a cultural practice, etc.) that hampers the proper worship of God and is a stumbling block to faith?
3. When we are honest about unbiblical practices, we make enemies. What does this say about spiritual maturity in the church?
4. Can an apostate denomination, congregation, or Christian organization ever be brought back to the truth of the gospel?

—Lendell Sims.

ILLUSTRATED HIGH POINTS

Desire again to be in bondage?

The Galatians' sin was that of returning to mere religious form and ritual and spurning the gospel of grace.

All sin is bondage (cf. Prov. 5:22; John 8:34), but many people choose sin (with its resulting bondage) over freedom and righteousness. The trend in recent years has been for criminals with drug charges and DUIs (driving under the influence) to refuse probation and force the courts to give them jail time. Why do they choose bondage over freedom? Probation comes with community service, rehabilitation, and strict accountability for up to two years. These defendants prefer prison to healing measures on their behalf. Like the Israelites who wanted to return to their Egyptian captivity (cf. Exod. 16:2-3), the unrighteous find sin's bondage appealing.

Labour in vain

Computers can increase productivity, but they can also be exasperating when a glitch wipes out hours of hard work. Recently, the forums for graphic designers were humming with complaints about a flaw in a popular software program. It seems they were suddenly unable to save their work or undo mistakes, causing them to lose hours of labor.

Both Paul and the prophets feared that their efforts to spread the Word of God would be wasted if their hearers failed to heed their teaching (cf. Neh. 13:14; Phil. 2:16; I Thess. 3:5). If only we, like designers, could hit the Save icon frequently and know that our work was safe. However, we forget that it is not our work to save (cf. Ps. 127:1). We cannot save our work or undo mistakes, but our great Designer can. He saves it all, and it will all bear fruit (cf. Ps. 126:6; Isa. 65:23; I Cor. 15:58).

—Therese Greenberg.

Golden Text Illuminated

"But now, after that ye have known God, or rather are known of God, how turn ye again to the weak and beggarly elements, whereunto ye desire again to be in bondage?" (Galatians 4:9).

The crux of the Galatian problem is revealed in this golden text. The Galatians started well. They responded to the preaching of the gospel. But starting is one thing; persevering and finishing is another. After they received the pure gospel of grace, they were threatened by teaching that demanded they fulfill the law to be saved. As young believers, they were being influenced to not hold firmly to grace. Two points should be made from this text.

First, the Galatians had surely embraced the gospel of Jesus Christ. The first part of Galatians 4:9 is worded in an unusual way. Paul stated that they had come to know God. Then he corrected himself and said that, rather they were *known of* God. The latter is actually more theologically correct. It is not whether we think we have come to God that makes the difference. It is when God has come to us and secures us in His salvation that things are really settled. God saves us. In this sense the Galatians had truly become God's children through faith in Christ.

The point is that no matter how religious a person thinks he is, a relationship with God is secured by the truth that God knows us as His own children. It is not our subjective feelings, our thoughts, or our opinions that matter, but the objective knowledge that God has saved us. This is an important point because it is always tempting to fall into the trap that some kind of religious action can save us. The Galatian believers were known by God. They were His own children, and for them and us, that is true salvation.

A second point to be made from this text is that the Galatians had faltered in their understanding of salvation. They were being lured back to the belief that salvation was based partly in fulfilling the works of the law. This is bondage all over again. Paul called it returning again to the "weak and beggarly elements."

The apostle was referring to the basic elements of human religion, which always involve the bondage of doing good deeds to secure salvation. In the case of the Galatians, they were being told to add Jewish works to salvation. These things are weak and beggarly (powerless and worthless efforts to obtain salvation or growth in holiness). Such elements are of the world (Gal. 4:3, 10) and of the flesh (vs. 23).

Religion that is based on works can define sin but cannot forgive it. It can point to righteousness, but it cannot provide it. Works-based religion comes with something in the hand to offer God. True gospel religion comes with nothing; rather, it pleads for grace and mercy.

True deliverance is the salvation of God, secured solely by the grace and power of God. By this means we are made free from our bondage to human religion. To be ultimately and truly delivered from bondage, we must come by faith alone, in Christ alone, by grace alone. The Galatians received this at first, but they were in danger of failing to persevere in it. Let us resist anything that would pull us away from depending wholly on Christ.

—*Jeff VanGoethem.*

Heart of the Lesson

When reading the book of Galatians, it is important to remember that the Apostle Paul was writing to converted Gentiles. His audience was not Jewish; therefore, they were unfamiliar with the law and the customs of the Jewish people. These Christians had lived their lives in ignorance of the true God, worshipping pagan gods. Now Jewish legalists, though professing to follow Christ, were trying to bind them to Jewish laws.

1. Concern (Gal. 4:8-11). On October 27, 2004, I was visiting Boston, Massachusetts. This just happened to be the same day that their baseball team won the World Series. The city was fanatical with support for their home team. Sadly, I was completely lost in the city. I had clear instructions from the airport to my hotel. I had started out on the right path, but somewhere along the way a fifteen-minute drive turned into three hours. How did that happen? I was following the instructions perfectly until I thought I had found an easier or quicker way. Obviously, I was mistaken.

This happened with the Galatians. No, they did not lose their way in Boston! Nevertheless, Paul had given them clear instructions on how to follow Christ. He had explained to them the freedom Christ gave them because of the cross. So imagine Paul's distress when he learned that these Christians had begun to adopt the law as evidenced by their observing of the Jewish calender. Paul was so distressed by the actions of the Galatians that he feared he may have wasted his time ministering to them.

2. A plea (Gal. 4:12-16). Paul appealed to the Galatians in hopes of reaching their hearts. He stated that he had no quarrels with them. Paul reminded the Galatians of the great affection they had shown toward him when he was sick and preaching the gospel to them. "Ye know how through infirmity of the flesh I preached the gospel unto you at the first."

Paul was perplexed in his letter. It was as though he were asking, "How can these people, who once showed me such great love and who would have done absolutely anything for me, choose to turn a deaf ear toward me?" Paul pointedly asked the Galatians, "Am I therefore become your enemy, because I tell you the truth?" (Gal. 4:16). It is interesting how we may assume that those who are willing to tell us what we do not want to hear do not have good intentions when, in fact, they are really trying to protect us.

3. Zeal (Gal. 4:17-20). In these verses Paul was telling the Galatians that it was good to be passionate; however, one must be passionate about the right things. The Galatians had allowed the zeal of the legalists to sway them toward the law. Paul desired that the Galatians be zealous for the things of the Eternal God. He wanted to be present with them to express his concern about their spiritual growth.

This is why accountability and prayer partners are so important. We need people to encourage us to stay the course. We need people to speak the truth, even when it hurts. We need people to help us when we think we have lost our way. If I had had a travel buddy in Boston, I can assure you that it would not have taken me three hours to find my hotel!

—*Kristin Reeg.*

World Missions

I will always remember Pastor Darrin and Brother Troy. They expanded my knowledge of the variety of ways God uses His missionaries. Through my brief interaction with these men, I also learned to cherish the Christian heritage upon which my country, the United States of America, was founded.

A friend of mine gathered a group to attend a midweek service being held in a school gymnasium in our city. She had few details, but she had heard that foreign missionaries would be featured. I thought it strange that the event was not broadly publicized and that none of the local churches met in that school. But since I have always been inspired by stories of missionaries, I decided to join my friends and attend.

As we entered the tiny gym, we could tell the gathering would be a small one. Fifty chairs in five rows separated in half by a narrow aisle faced a rickety wooden podium. About half the chairs were already filled with groups of people chatting quietly. As we took our seats, we heard drums in the hall getting louder as they approached. Our attention shifted to the doors as two men entered, each playing African drums slung across their bodies. As they walked in cadence, they chanted, "Praise ye the Lord! Praise ye the Lord! Servants of the Most High God, come and give Him glory!"

These gentlemen marched up to the front of the congregation. They welcomed us and introduced themselves. Pastor Darrin and Brother Troy were natives of Liberia, a West African nation. The next line from Pastor Darrin astonished me. These men were missionaries sent from Liberia to evangelize America. Yes, the foreign missions board from their denomination had commissioned these men to help the United States return to the truths upon which it had been built. They explained to us that they were on an outdoor evangelistic tour in several cities. The meeting in our city was to take place in the city commons downtown the following Saturday.

Pastor Darrin and Brother Troy took turns explaining why they were having outreaches in the United States. Through tears, Brother Troy spoke of his love for this country. Two generations before him, the United States had sent missionaries to his city and established a church where his grandparents came to know the Lord. The Christian legacy resulting from those conversions has continued in his family. His gratefulness to America appeared genuine as he went on to explain his intense desire to help bring the gospel back to the forefront of this country.

The encounter with Pastor Darrin and Brother Troy impacted me greatly. I felt convicted for watching my country decline into secularism and moral decay. I was embarrassed that the United States, the home of the greatest number of missionaries on the planet, now needs teams of foreign missionaries to come to our country to help salvage our godly heritage.

The Apostle Paul decried the Galatians' error in returning to works for salvation. Pastor Darrin and Brother Troy noticed a similar pattern in the United States, not in depending on works, but in returning to sin and immorality. Both will lead to widespread bondage. Pray for our nation, and thank God for missionary efforts to bring America back to her Christian roots.

—*Beverly Medley Jones.*

The Jewish Aspect

God's plan of salvation involves our baptism—that is, our placement—into the body of Christ. We are one in Christ and are in the very family of God.

Thinking about our position as Gentiles, we discover we had no standing with God at all. Paul reminded the Ephesian believers (Eph. 2:12) that as Gentiles they had no stake in Christ as the Messiah. He noted Gentiles were aliens from the household of Jacob (Israel), outside the great promises to Abraham of a land and a people. Added to this, we were "without God in the world." Yet by God's grace, we have been saved and brought into Christ's body, where there is no distinction between Jews and Gentiles.

Today's theme is cause for rejoicing. In salvation, we are delivered from bondage. Yet our golden text warns that we can slip back into bondage (Gal. 4:9). How could a person God has delivered want the bondage of the world, the flesh, and the devil?

Sadly, believers can fall prey to myths and statements about the Jewish people that should not be once named among us. Anti-Semitism, making or repeating false or vicious statements about the Jews, should be dealt with as sin.

In my nonreligious home, there was one word for the chosen people: "Dirty-jew." Two words were reduced to one. We were unsaved then, but that was no excuse for maligning a people we did not know. "Dirty" had nothing to do with their bathing habits; it was simply taken as gospel truth that in every way they were unwanted, unwelcome, and a blight on society. They were people no one called friends. No one ever explained to me how the Jews became so bad.

My salvation and consequent growing knowledge of the Jews showed me they were God's unique people and all the false statements made about them were satanic in origin. The wicked one cannot hurt God, so he targets Jews, as well as Christians, as his special enemies.

The charges against the Jews demonstrate how far a lie can travel. Early in the last century, large numbers of Jews lived in European countries. With few exceptions, they were hated, and every effort was made to make life miserable for them. Jewish efforts to assimilate themselves into a foreign culture failed in Germany. The Jews of Russia and eastern Europe endeavored to live free of Gentile influences of every kind. This approach, like the attempts in Germany, was unsuccessful.

Early in the 1900s, a spurious pamphlet called "The Protocols of the Elders of Zion" claimed that the Jews had plans to take over the world through a global financial scheme. One powerful people having a common language would seize the world's assets in order to create a vast, Jewish-controlled empire.

The pamphlet bore no author's name. It was satanically inspired yet had a warm reception all over the world. Why would Satan so boldly suggest such a sinister plan without a shred of evidence to support it? The wicked one needs to attack God's people—the Jews and the born-again Christians. If these two great peoples of God were destroyed, it would facilitate Satan's rebellion.

I have a copy of "The Protocols." The well-worn pamphlet has someone's marginal notes that suggest the former owner believed the ridiculous plot. Were those marginal notes the convictions of a Christian?

Anti-Semitism is fed by the half-truth that the Jews killed Jesus. Acts 4:26-28 spreads responsibility around for that murder. Indeed, I find myself guilty.

—Lyle P. Murphy.

Guiding the Superintendent

Abandoning bad habits is not as easy as acquiring them. Sometimes there is a strong pull through people or surroundings to revert to previous behavior. If one is not careful, habits can bring destructive consequences.

Our lesson this week shows us the impact of God's deliverance. His goal is to get us permanently delivered from bondage.

DEVOTIONAL OUTLINE

1. Paul's appeal to the Galatians (Gal. 4:8-12). In Paul's letter to the Galatians, he discussed their previous sinful lifestyle. The Galatians worshipped idols. The result of their lifestyle was bondage. God delivered them, but they were being tempted now by a legalism that was also of the world. Paul knew worldly behavior was detrimental. However, the Galatians tried to stay in favor with God by maintaining the religious attitudes common to the world.

Paul knew that the mere observance of ceremonies to have a relationship with God was unsatisfactory. Because of their reversion to previous errors, Paul wondered whether perhaps his labor among them had been wasted. Paul encouraged them to follow his example and turn away from legalistic principles.

2. Paul's reprimand to the Galatians (Gal. 4:13-16). Paul reminded the Galatians of his health challenges when he came to them. This demonstrated his sacrifice as well as his love for them. Despite his condition, he commended the Galatians for accepting him. The Galatians were kind to Paul and attended to his needs.

Paul was disturbed by their sudden change of heart. He reprimanded them for changing their behavior. At one point, they would have given their eyes to him. Unfortunately, they had become indifferent. Their attitude caused Paul to think the Galatians viewed him as an enemy.

3. Paul's strong warning to the Galatians (Gal. 4:17-20). Paul told the Galatians about emerging false teachers. The false teachers were attempting to manipulate the Galatians. They tried to dissuade the Galatians from listening to Paul. He had no problem with teachers who had good motives.

Paul felt like a mother enduring birth pains. He believed this would continue until the Galatians matured. Paul's desire was to be with them, but all he could do presently was send letters.

AGE-GROUP EMPHASES

Children: It is never too early to teach children about the consequences of sin. Stress the importance of obedience to God, parents, and Christian leaders. Inform them of the feelings God, parents, or Christian leaders experience when those in their charge are disobedient.

Youths: The world seems swamped by a wave of immorality and vile activity. There are multiple temptations attempting to pull teens away from God. Young people need to know the importance of living pure and holy lives. They need to be reminded that God redeemed them to be a godly example. Help them understand the importance of staying away from sinful activity.

Adults: Accountability can be an issue for some adults. They have freedom to make decisions. However, they need to be reminded that God positions Christian leaders to carry out correction when necessary. Help them understand that leaders are there to foster their growth and assist them in their Christian walk.

—*Tyrone Keith Carroll, Sr.*

Scripture Lesson Text

GAL. 5:1 Stand fast therefore in the liberty wherewith Christ hath made us free, and be not entangled again with the yoke of bondage.

2 Behold, I Paul say unto you, that if ye be circumcised, Christ shall profit you nothing.

3 For I testify again to every man that is circumcised, that he is a debtor to do the whole law.

4 Christ is become of no effect unto you, whosoever of you are justified by the law; ye are fallen from grace.

5 For we through the Spir'it wait for the hope of righteousness by faith.

6 For in Je'sus Christ neither circumcision availeth any thing, nor uncircumcision; but faith which worketh by love.

7 Ye did run well; who did hinder you that ye should not obey the truth?

8 This persuasion *cometh* not of him that calleth you.

9 A little leaven leaveneth the whole lump.

10 I have confidence in you through the Lord, that ye will be none otherwise minded: but he that troubleth you shall bear his judgment, whosoever he be.

11 And I, brethren, if I yet preach circumcision, why do I yet suffer persecution? then is the offence of the cross ceased.

12 I would they were even cut off which trouble you.

13 For, brethren, ye have been called unto liberty; only *use* not liberty for an occasion to the flesh, but by love serve one another.

14 For all the law is fulfilled in one word, *even* in this; Thou shalt love thy neighbour as thyself.

15 But if ye bite and devour one another, take heed that ye be not consumed one of another.

16 *This* I say then, Walk in the Spir'it, and ye shall not fulfil the lust of the flesh.

17 For the flesh lusteth against the Spir'it, and the Spir'it against the flesh: and these are contrary the one to the other: so that ye cannot do the things that ye would.

NOTES

Freedom in Christ

Lesson: Galatians 5:1-17

Read: Galatians 5:1-17

TIME: probably A.D. 48   PLACE: from Syrian Antioch

GOLDEN TEXT—"Brethren, ye have been called unto liberty; only use not liberty for an occasion to the flesh, but by love serve one another" (Galatians 5:13).

Introduction

For some people, freedom is a frightening concept. We might find that difficult to understand, but it is true, especially for those who have never known it.

The Israelites spent more than four hundred years in Egypt. Most of that time they suffered in slavery. But under the leadership of Moses, the Israelites were freed from Egyptian bondage by the mighty hand of God.

Probably over two million people left Egypt, bound for the Land of Promise. Yet only days after leaving the land of slavery, the multitude was complaining that they would have been better off remaining in Egypt. They were free, but when they encountered hardships under God's chosen leader, they longed to return to the bondage they had always known under the Egyptians.

Likewise, those who have known nothing but spiritual bondage often are tempted to return to what is familiar to them rather than fully embrace the responsibilities that accompany freedom in Christ. This is particularly true when there are people present who are teaching that faith in Christ is incomplete without adherence to certain legalistic standards. Paul faced this problem in his day, even as we do today.

LESSON OUTLINE

I. REMAINING IN LIBERTY—
Gal. 5:1-6

II. THE THREAT TO LIBERTY—
Gal. 5:7-12

III. THE PROPER USE OF LIBERTY—Gal. 5:13-17

Exposition: Verse by Verse

REMAINING IN LIBERTY

GAL. 5:1 Stand fast therefore in the liberty wherewith Christ hath made us free, and be not entangled again with the yoke of bondage.

2 Behold, I Paul say unto you, that if ye be circumcised, Christ shall profit you nothing.

3 For I testify again to every man that is circumcised, that he is a debtor to do the whole law.

4 Christ is become of no effect unto you, whosoever of you are justified by the law; ye are fallen from grace.

5 For we through the Spirit wait for the hope of righteousness by faith.

6 For in Jesus Christ neither circumcision availeth any thing, nor uncircumcision; but faith which worketh by love.

A command (Gal. 5:1). Paul's command to the Galatians to "stand fast" in liberty was based on the truth that this was where Christ Himself had placed them. Through faith in Christ, they were freed from their terrible spiritual bondage. Now the apostle was telling them to keep on standing in that liberty they enjoyed—to stay free.

The other half of the command was not to let themselves be burdened down again under a yoke of slavery. Both Jewish and Gentile believers in Galatia had been enslaved by religion before their conversion to Christ. But under the influence of the Judaizers, who were promoting adherence to the Mosaic Law as necessary for Christians, these believers were in danger of becoming entangled in the Jewish law. Although they were free in Christ, they were being told that more was needed for them to be rightly related to God.

A warning (Gal. 5:2-4). Paul issued a very strong warning to those who were thinking of adopting the Mosaic Law as a means of becoming or remaining righteous before God. Clearly, this was directed at Gentile converts who were being pressured by the false teachers to submit to circumcision and all the demands of the law. To seek righteousness by submitting to circumcision was to declare that one was not fully trusting Christ alone.

When works of the law are added to grace, the very concept of grace, God's unmerited favor, is compromised. The Galatians were confused by the Judaizers. Some were thinking that adopting the law, and particularly the law of circumcision, was necessary or at least helpful in "establishing a right relationship with God" (Kent, *The Freedom of God's Sons,* BMH). But Paul warned that to truly seek righteousness through the law meant that Christ would be of no profit. His death and resurrection would have no value.

"Saving faith trusts Christ only and repudiates any attempt of man to produce a meritorious work. Paul warned that if anyone received circumcision as an additional means of salvation he would manifest that he was really an unsaved person" (Gromacki, *Stand Fast in Liberty,* Kress).

Furthermore, if one is required to observe the law of circumcision, he is obligated to keep the whole Law of Moses (cf. Jas. 2:10). The law is a unit. One cannot pick and choose what part of it to obey and what part to ignore. To place oneself under the law is to be required to keep it all and thus be condemned since no one can keep the law (Gal. 3:10).

Paul concluded his warning by repeating that Christ's work is of no value to those who are seeking to be justified by the law (Gal. 5:4). "Are justified" does not suggest that a person could possibly be declared righteous by keeping the law; rather, it indicates an ongoing attempt at gaining righteousness through the law, which is fruitless. One who insists on making such an attempt is "fallen from grace." To fall from grace is to fall into legalism. And "to choose legalism is to relinquish grace as the principle by which one desires to be related to God" (Barker and Kohlenberger, eds., *The Expositor's Bible Commentary, Abridged,* Zondervan).

An affirmation (Gal. 5:5-6). Much confusion was being sown among the Galatians by the false teachers, who were demanding adherence to the law. Paul warned that such an approach to either salvation or the Christian life is completely contrary to the truth that salvation is "by grace . . . through faith" (Eph. 2:8). Thus the apostle affirmed, "We through the Spirit wait for the hope of righteousness by faith" (Gal. 5:5).

Rather than seek approval from God through observance of legalistic standards that offer no assurance, those who have been born again by the Spirit through faith in Christ patiently wait in faith for the certain hope, or expectation, of righteousness. This refers to a future time when God will publicly declare the believer righteous. "Righteousness is already the believer's possession in justification, but its full realization will be experienced at Christ's coming to claim His own. For this the believer waits in faith. No performance of law could ever achieve it" (Kent).

Paul then affirmed that neither the practice nor nonpractice of the rite of circumcision was of any value. He was not opposed to the practice itself but rather to the idea that circumcision—or uncircumcision—had any spiritual value in making one righteous. The only thing that matters is faith that expresses itself in love.

We accept God's gift of salvation by faith (Eph. 2:8-9), and we live our lives by faith in Christ and His promises (II Cor. 5:7). That faith is not a stale, intellectual acknowledgment, however. True faith demonstrates itself in love. Thus, while faith stands contrary to works with regard to one's relationship with God, genuine faith works; that is, it produces spiritual fruit in the believer's life. A person cannot claim to have faith and then live any way he wishes. His life will demonstrate "his loving gratitude for all that Christ has done for him" (Gromacki).

Paul's point was simple, and it is important to remember today when the temptation to replace God's grace and faith in Christ with works is just as great. Works do not produce salvation; rather, works are the evidence and product of true faith.

THE THREAT TO LIBERTY

7 Ye did run well; who did hinder you that ye should not obey the truth?

8 This persuasion cometh not of him that calleth you.

9 A little leaven leaveneth the whole lump.

10 I have confidence in you through the Lord, that ye will be none otherwise minded: but he that troubleth you shall bear his judgment, whosoever he be.

11 And I, brethren, if I yet preach circumcision, why do I yet suffer persecution? then is the offence of the cross ceased.

12 I would they were even cut off which trouble you.

Its source (Gal. 5:7-8). Using the metaphor of a race, Paul said that the Galatians had started out well in their Christian life. However, something was now hindering them, or literally cutting in on them, so that they were no longer obeying the truth. They were not eliminated from the race, but they were getting off course by mixing faith with various Jewish practices (cf. 3:10) and at least entertaining the thought that such practices were necessary for their acceptance before God. Having begun by faith, they were now turning to legalism to finish the race (cf. vs. 3).

Who had caused this hindrance? The answer should have been obvious to the Galatians. The enticement to turn to the law had come from the Judaizers. It certainly had not come from God, the One who had called them, for His gospel of grace was not the gospel the Judaizers taught (cf. 1:6-7).

Its danger (Gal. 5:9). The danger presented by the false gospel of the Judaizers is expressed in the proverbial statement "A little leaven leaveneth the whole lump" (I Cor. 5:6; cf. Matt. 16:6). Like leaven in bread, the false teaching taking root in Galatia would spread and contaminate the whole church if measures were not taken to eliminate it. That is why the Galatians were to stand firm in their liberty and not become entangled in the bondage of legalism. Such a stand would put an end to the leavening process.

Its judgment (Gal. 5:10-12). For all the dangers presented by the legalism being taught in Galatia, Paul was confident that his readers' faith was genuine and that they ultimately would agree with his teaching and not be carried away into error. He was also confident that the one who was teaching the error, whoever he was, would "bear his judgment." This could refer to the leader of the Judaizers, or it could be a general designation for all of them, since the plural is used in verse 12.

The judgment mentioned here is divine judgment. Error may have widespread and profound consequences, but it will not prevail in the end. God will see to that. We need to remember this truth and not be taken in by popular teachings that do not clearly align with the Bible. Error usually presents itself as popular and attractive, but it stands under the judgment of God.

Galatians 5:11 is difficult to interpret, but it is probably best understood as Paul's response to an accusation made against him; namely, that he had preached the necessity of circumcision but now was preaching a different message. Why such a charge would be leveled is unclear, but it was definitely untrue.

Paul pointed out that if he had taught that the rite was necessary for salvation, he would not have experienced such persecution from the Jews. The gospel of grace he preached, however, was centered in the cross—the crucifixion—of Jesus as the payment for sin. This teaching was offensive to the Jews, who promoted works such as circumcision as the means of acceptance by God. Clearly, Paul was consistent and uncompromising in teaching salvation by grace through faith, apart from any works.

Paul was so adamant about the gospel of grace that he could tolerate nothing that would compromise it. He even wished that those who put such confidence in an act of the flesh would mutilate themselves as their pagan neighbors did in their twisted attempts to please God.

Paul's attitude might seem unduly harsh, but he recognized that anything that diminishes the gospel of Christ turns it into a gospel of man. And a man-made gospel is worse than worthless, for it leads people to eternal destruction.

THE PROPER USE OF LIBERTY

13 For, brethren, ye have been called unto liberty; only use not liberty for an occasion to the flesh, but by love serve one another.

14 For all the law is fulfilled in one word, even in this; Thou shalt love thy neighbour as thyself.

15 But if ye bite and devour one another, take heed that ye be not consumed one of another.

16 This I say then, Walk in the Spirit, and ye shall not fulfil the lust of the flesh.

17 For the flesh lusteth against the Spirit, and the Spirit against the flesh: and these are contrary the one to the other: so that ye cannot do the things that ye would.

Freedom to love (Gal. 5:13-15). It is imperative that believers remain grounded in their freedom in Christ, but that freedom is not a license to indulge any and all fleshly desires. The freedom Christ gives is freedom from sin and its power and consequences, as well as freedom from enslavement to a religious system that can offer no hope of victory over sin. Properly understood, liberty in Christ cannot promote sin. Instead, it should lead to loving service to others.

Obedience to the biblical injunction to love one's neighbor as oneself (cf. Lev. 19:18) sums up the whole law. In fact, it fulfills, or completes, the law (Gal. 5:14). Love is the expression of faith (vs. 6), and when one by faith comes to Christ, that faith produces in the person the kind of love for others the law demanded but could not produce.

Galatians 5:15 assumes there was strife within the Galatian churches, whether it was over the teaching about the role of the law or something else. They needed to be reminded to love one another rather than to consume one another. This they had the power to do if they were truly men and women of faith.

The truth is worth fighting to preserve, but it does not give us the freedom to act in harmful and unloving ways.

Freedom to walk in the Spirit (Gal. 5:16-17). The key to avoiding the kind of conflict Paul described in verse 15 is applying our faith by walking, or living, in the Spirit. We who have placed our faith in Christ have the Holy Spirit dwelling within us. We simply must submit to His power and control, trusting Him to give us victory over temptation and to bring us into conformity with God's will.

Walking by the Spirit is allowing Him to determine the course of our daily lives as He illuminates the teaching of Scripture to us. This is not a passive act on our part. "The principle of the Spirit does not make human effort unnecessary, but arouses it and equips it to put all its forces into the service of the Spirit" (Ridderbos, *The Epistle of Paul to the Churches of Galatia,* Eerdmans).

When we walk in the Spirit, we will not fulfill the "lust of the flesh" (Gal. 5:16). We will not give in to ungodly and selfish desires. Verse 17 explains that there is a continuing internal conflict between the indwelling Spirit and the flesh. The flesh is the old disposition to sin that continues even in those who have been born again. That is why believers still struggle with temptation and sin. Thus, while Paul indicated the way to spiritual victory (walking in the Spirit), he acknowledged that believers can fall into sin even though their ultimate desire is to please God.

Freedom in Christ does not mean freedom to live apart from all restraint. True freedom comes from willingly submitting to the control of the Holy Spirit, and God the Spirit does not lead us into sin. To stand fast in the liberty Christ has given us is to be responsible for walking in the Spirit. This is not always easy, but the rewards are great, for we will be empowered to love and we will not be entangled in religious bondage.

—*Jarl K. Waggoner.*

QUESTIONS

1. On what did Paul base his call to the Galatians to stand fast in liberty?
2. What threatened their freedom in Christ?
3. Why did Paul warn Gentile believers against submitting to circumcision?
4. What does it mean to be "fallen from grace" (Gal. 5:4)?
5. What righteousness do we hope for by faith?
6. How is faith related to works?
7. What danger did Paul express through the proverb about leaven?
8. Of what was Paul confident regarding the Galatian believers?
9. How does faith relate to the fact that love fulfills the law?
10. What is walking "in the Spirit" (vs. 16)? What results from it?

—*Jarl K. Waggoner.*

Preparing to Teach the Lesson

As you teach this lesson, be aware that you may have people in your class from very different persuasions. They may have been brought up in a tradition that tries to mix law and grace, or at least works and grace. Some may think we have to keep certain elements of the law or do certain good deeds to really be holy people.

Sabbath observance was pretty carefully prescribed in my home church. We were allowed to talk and go for a leisurely walk on Sunday but not to play a softball game. It was to be a day of rest and a day of religious observance. We were always pressed to witness to unsaved people. There was a lot of talk about doing but not enough about resting in faith in the Lord.

TODAY'S AIM

Facts: to clearly see the contrasts drawn between a life under the law and a life under grace.

Principle: to understand that we are saved by God's grace, not by our works.

Application: to live a life of freedom in the Holy Spirit and love to others.

INTRODUCING THE LESSON

It is clear in Scripture that trusting in the Lord Jesus moves us from being under the law to being under grace. We have a freedom in Christ that we could never have under the law. There was a bondage under the law, a carefully outlined lifestyle that was actually designed to bring its followers to realize that they had to depend on God's gracious gift of salvation in order to be saved. The law was a schoolmaster to bring people to Christ and the salvation God provided instead of people trying to save themselves.

Freedom can be somewhat frightening. If we can do anything, what will we actually do? This was enough of a problem that a large portion of the letter to the Galatians is devoted to it. How much of our salvation is provided by the Lord? Is there a portion we must do to make it effective?

DEVELOPING THE LESSON

1. Freed from the obligation to keep the law (Gal. 5:1-12). In such an important matter as eternal destiny, it is not surprising that some people want to "cover all the bases." If we keep all the law, the behavior God had prescribed, will we not be more pleasing to Him?

Paul addressed the matter of circumcision. Abraham had been given this rite as the seal of the promise God had made to him in response to his faith in God and His promise. All the faithful down through the ages since that time had received circumcision as physical and spiritual descendants of Abraham. It was perhaps very hard for people to refrain from the practice. However, Paul pointed out that if they did this, they were responsible to keep the whole law, which no one could ever do.

Trying to keep the law for our salvation makes us slaves to the law. It stands as a barrier to freedom in Christ. If we are slaves to the law, we have no standing in the grace of God. We cannot mix law and grace; it is either one or the other.

2. Freedom is not license to sin (Gal. 5:13-15). Our freedom is not freedom to sin but to do good apart from any thought of saving merits. We are free to love our brothers and sisters in Christ without relating it to having anything to do with saving us. If the law is fulfilled in loving our neighbors as ourselves, then as long as we have this attitude and follow through with deeds of kindness and love, we are effectually keeping the law.

Just as the Lord Jesus in His earthly ministry said that He was doing what He saw the Father do, so we can cooperate with the Holy Spirit and what He wants us to do for our neighbors. The alternative is to resist the Holy Spirit and fail to do that which is loving and kind. If we are critical and condemning in our relationships, we risk discouraging and crushing the spirits of our neighbors—that is, if we "bite and devour one another" (Gal. 5:15).

3. Freedom in the Holy Spirit, not in the flesh (Gal. 5:16-17). Paul admonishes us to walk in the Spirit. This means that we should respond to the Holy Spirit's promptings as we live our daily lives. He will guide us to do what we can to show love and encouragement to our brothers and sisters in Christ. Our human nature—the flesh—is selfish, greedy, grasping, and usually negative in our relationships. As He dwells within us, the Holy Spirit is just the opposite. He loves and looks out for the well-being of other believers. The Holy Spirit will interest you in the salvation and spiritual growth of others.

It may be a struggle to listen for the Holy Spirit's promptings and put down our old fleshly desires. But the battle is the Lord's, and we can learn to obey the spiritually positive guidance of the Holy Spirit. Whatever your struggle may be, remember that others have gone this way before and that it is far better to persevere.

ILLUSTRATING THE LESSON

We should walk in the Spirit. In this way, we will allow no room in our lives for fleshly desires.

WALK IN THE SPIRIT

HE WILL GUIDE YOUR STEPS

CONCLUDING THE LESSON

It is easy to *say* that we must stand fast in the liberty we have in Christ and walk in the Spirit. It is much harder to *do* it. Remembering to listen for the promptings of the Holy Spirit and walking by them can be both difficult and easy things to do. We may understand the first time we hear His word and do very well right from the start. Or we may have difficulty in understanding and take a lifetime to learn to do right.

It should be the natural state of mind for a Christian to obey the Holy Spirit, but sometimes it also feels natural for a Christian to follow the thought patterns and reactions of the unsaved people around us. We also have old thought patterns. We have choices to make every day as to which way we will go. The Lord Jesus loved you and died for you; it is now your turn to love others and build them up in faith and hope as much as you can. You are free to do this. You have the ability. It is the Holy Spirit within you who empowers you. If you do, you will not fulfill the desires of the flesh.

ANTICIPATING THE NEXT LESSON

In our next lesson, we will explore more of the activities and results of living in the freedom we have in Christ.
—*Brian D. Doud.*

PRACTICAL POINTS

1. The freedom that Christ gives must be guarded so that the old ways do not enslave us again (Gal. 5:1).

2. Tradition, rituals, and customs cannot save us (Gal. 5:2-4; cf. Rom. 10:9).

3. Righteousness is an attribute of God. Our goal is to be like Him (Gal. 5:5; cf. II Tim. 4:8).

4. Love overcomes obstacles, breaks barriers, and creates opportunities. It unifies the body of Christ (Gal. 5:6; cf. I Pet. 4:8; Matt. 22:38-39; II Tim. 1:7).

5. A bad influence can retard spiritual growth (Gal. 5:7-10).

6. Following Christ means a complete break with the past (vss. 11-17).

—Lendell Sims.

RESEARCH AND DISCUSSION

1. Who did the Lord initially instruct regarding circumcision (cf. Gen. 17:9-14)? Why did the Lord command circumcision? Why was Paul now speaking against the custom in Galatians?

2. To the Jews of the day, what was the general feeling about those who were uncircumcised?

3. How can tradition and customs push us away from God? What are some of the things we celebrate that have become more of a tradition than a celebration of God?

4. It is important that we keep our focus on the things of God so that we understand His mind-set. How do we do this?

—Lendell Sims.

ILLUSTRATED HIGH POINTS

Consumed one of another

The military strategy of "bait and bleed" is the practice of pitting enemies against one another. The strategist then simply waits on the sideline as his enemies engage in battle.

Russia's Catherine the Great said, "I am racking my brains in order to push the courts of Vienna and Berlin into French affairs . . . to be kept busy and out of my way." In 1941, United States Senator Harry Truman said, "If we see that Germany is winning we ought to help Russia, and if Russia is winning we ought to help Germany . . . let them kill as many as possible." Upon withdrawing from World War I, Russia's Vladimir Lenin said, "We rid ourselves . . . of both imperialistic groups fighting each other. We can take advantage of their strife . . . and use that period . . . to develop" (Bunyan and Fisher, *The Bolshevik Revolution, 1917-1918,* Stanford University).

The devil is a war strategist. Let us not play into his hands.

Contrary the one to the other

Conflict, climax, and resolution—English teachers will tell you these are the three basic elements of plot development. Conflict is the struggle between opposing forces; climax is the most intense moment; and resolution is the conclusion of the matter.

Our spiritual journeys also contain these classic plot elements. Obviously, our major antagonist is the devil (cf. I Pet. 5:8), yet Paul identified another bitter enemy—our old man, or flesh (cf. Rom. 7:15, 18, 23). Believers fight a conflict not mentioned by English teachers—human flesh versus God's Spirit (cf. Gen. 6:3). The indwelling Holy Spirit brings this ancient conflict right into our hearts (cf. I Tim. 6:12).

—Therese Greenberg.

Golden Text Illuminated

"Brethren, ye have been called unto liberty; only use not liberty for an occasion to the flesh, but by love serve one another" (Galatians 5:13).

In Galatians, Paul was correcting a young church's slide into a false understanding of salvation. The church had been born aright—on the gospel of the Lord Jesus Christ, on salvation by grace through faith—but its spiritual growth had faltered due to unsound doctrine. They were being told to add works to grace. So Paul was emphasizing the great truth of liberty in Christ.

Christian liberty means freedom—freedom from the debt we incur by our failure to live up to God's law. Through faith in Christ, believers are set free from the dominion of the law, that is, from having to try to work their way into God's favor and heaven. The Galatians had lost the precious sense of their standing in Christ. This happened through false teaching that added works to faith. Paul called them to return to and embrace grace, that they might once again live in the realm of liberty. Salvation is by grace through simple faith in Christ.

Once liberty was firmly in place, Paul had two admonitions for pressing on in the Christian faith. The first was not to use freedom in Christ as an opportunity for the flesh.

"Flesh" is a term that refers to our inward sinfulness, the ungodly appetites that lead to sin. If grace is understood in a false way, sinful indulgence can be a real temptation. Someone might think, *If I am saved by grace and not by works, then I can go ahead and do anything I want. It cannot affect my salvation.* Although it is certainly true that a truly regenerated believer cannot come into God's eternal judgment, a life of prevailing sinfulness is an utterly false response to grace.

Indulging in sin fails to acknowledge the inward change that the new birth brings as the Holy Spirit invades the personality of the believer and creates a capacity to walk with God in the Spirit. To live our lives serving the cravings of the flesh is simply to return again to bondage, the exact opposite of what the Lord intends when He saves us. That is unthinkable! That is wrong! Salvation by grace through faith was meant to make us free to serve God, not to make us slaves to the basest part of our natures.

That leads us to Paul's second admonition. Instead of serving the flesh, believers are instructed to serve one another in love. The nature of biblical love is demonstrated in concrete actions. It is a practical love that reflects the great commandment that we should love our neighbor as ourselves. Sincere love for God and others is the sum of the whole law. Love is not merely a feeling; it also involves a firm commitment to do all the good we can do in this world. Every Christian should be a blessing to others.

That is why Paul emphasizes serving. In love we are to become the servants of all. Servanthood expresses love. We have been set free to serve. Far from being a license to serve our flesh and to sin at will, our freedom in Christ is an invitation to glorify God by becoming loving servants. The believer set free in Christ should spend his or her life looking for ways to glorify God through serving others.

—*Jeff VanGoethem.*

Heart of the Lesson

Freedom. Emancipation. Shackles removed. Captives released. This is what the death and resurrection of Jesus Christ did for us. It set us free from the law of sin and death. When we stand before God on Judgment Day, Jesus will stand with us. He took upon Himself the punishment we rightly deserve. This is love.

1. Persevere in freedom (Gal. 5:1-6). We all have heard that bad habits are hard to break. Believe it or not, it is easier to acquire freedom than it is to maintain freedom. For instance, the first day of a diet is always the easiest. Why? Because it is only day one, and we are full of motivation. However, when day three or four arrives, and the boss brings in doughnuts, it is much more difficult to resist the temptation. If we choose to persevere and resist, on day sixty the doughnuts will not even be an issue. We will have overcome our temptation.

In this passage, the Apostle Paul urged the Galatians to stand fast, or persevere, in the freedom that Christ gave them. Paul did not preach circumcision to the Galatians. Other Jewish Christians had convinced these Gentile converts that in order to truly become Christians, they had to follow the law and become circumcised. It was almost as if there were initiation rituals to becoming a Christian among these legalists.

Paul combated this philosophy, saying, "I testify again to every man that is circumcised, that he is a debtor to do the whole law" (Gal. 5:3). In other words, we have a choice. We can try to follow the law and fail, or we can choose to be saved by grace.

2. No freedom in confusion (Gal. 5:7-12). If the truth were told, people are biased. We may not always want to admit it, but we are. When people ask our opinion or advice on an issue, we give it to them based on our knowledge, our experience, and our understanding. We can also base our answers on our emotions, our reactions, and our strengths or weaknesses.

This was why Paul asked the Galatians who it was that was hindering them in their race. Whoever they were, they were misinformed. The information they were providing did not line up with Paul's teaching. What once was clear had become clouded; the grace that had been freely given and freely received now had preconditions. One lie that sounds like the truth can pull us from the faith. This confusion does not originate with God.

3. Final warnings (Gal. 5:13-17). Contrary to some teaching, just because Jesus Christ came to give us freedom does not mean that we are free to do whatever we want. Be careful not to gratify the sin nature. The law is summed up with one simple yet profound command: "Thou shalt love thy neighbour as thyself" (cf. Lev. 19:18; Matt. 5:43). If we fight with one another, then we will ultimately be destroyed by one another. But if we keep in step with the Spirit, then we will be able to silence the cries of our flesh that so easily tempt us. Be aware that there is a constant war raging between our flesh and the Spirit.

Jesus Christ came to set the captive free. Freedom always comes with a price. Jesus paid the debt; now we must sacrifice the will of our flesh to maintain it.

—*Kristin Reeg.*

World Missions

There are numerous excellent articles and books about the incredible story of Eric Liddell, a devout Christian and Olympic champion. Eric was born in China in 1902 to Scottish missionary parents. Eric and his brother were sent to school in Scotland while Eric was a young child.

Eric showed an early interest in running. He received training up to the Olympic level and represented his country in the 1924 Olympics in Paris, France. Because a heat for the 100-meter race was scheduled for a Sunday, Eric refused to run. He did, however, run in the 400-meter race on another day and won the gold medal. He set several Olympic records that year. He also broke Scottish records in the 220- and 100-yard sprints. Eric went on to participate in a relay team that set a world record. Eric became known as the fastest man in Scotland. To this day his nickname remains "The Flying Scotsman."

After his success as an Olympian, Eric returned to China to be a missionary in 1925. Many people in sports and media disagreed with his decision to leave such a successful career in athletics to work on the mission field. In response to one inquirer, Eric said, "It's natural for a chap to think over all that sometimes, but I'm glad I'm at the work I'm engaging in now. A fellow's life counts for more at this than the other" (Keddie, *Running the Race,* Evangelical Press).

Eric's first assignment was teaching children and promoting Christian values. He integrated academic lessons with biblical teaching. He also worked after school with students who wanted to participate in athletics. The school where he started in Tianjin is still in operation. Eric stayed in China, expanding his missionary work and making a lasting impact on China.

In 1941, the Japanese invaded deeper into China. Eric and his brother were working in a rural medical mission. Despite warnings to accept furlough, Eric stayed to help distribute food, medicine, and supplies for the continuous stream of people needing care. In 1943, the Japanese took over the mission station and placed Eric and the other missionaries in an internment camp.

Eric Liddell died in 1945 at the camp. It is believed that a brain tumor, exhaustion, and malnutrition contributed to his death. According to a fellow missionary, Eric's last words were "It's complete surrender," referring to how he had lived his life for God.

Eric Liddell had been called into liberty. Because of his trust in Jesus as his Lord and Saviour, he stepped into the freedom that comes only with Christ. Though his freedom allowed him to pursue many avenues, Eric chose to spend his life serving others. A gifted athlete, Eric left us an example of one who made a higher choice—to answer the missionary call on his life. Such a life will always be remembered. Eric Liddell's daughter celebrated his life by visiting China in 1991 and presenting his school with one of his medals.

Though we may not be confronted with the choice to walk away from promising careers, we will be challenged to bring God into our chosen vocations. As Eric Liddell used his freedom in China, we are called to use ours to serve one another wherever God places us.

—*Beverly Medley Jones.*

The Jewish Aspect

Our theme for today, "Freedom in Christ," sounds the promise of joy for those in whom the Holy Spirit dwells.

Our Jewish friends pride themselves on following the teaching of the early fathers, particularly in respect to their care and concern for others. The Jewish community lives by the summary of the second tablet of the law, that portion dealing with responsibility to love others: commandments 6 through 10.

Jewish charity is seen in the word *tzedakah.* Its first meaning is righteousness, but they argue that it must also mean justice. The sages of Israel reasoned that since God owns the silver and the gold, to give it only to the rich is a violation of natural law. It has to belong to the poor as well. Therefore, to give to the poor is just and righteous (Ausubel, *The Book of Jewish Knowledge,* Crown Publishers).

The Jewish sages felt it was important to make benevolence giving a part of their religion. Rabbi Joshua Ben Korha said, "He that turns his eyes away from the needy worships idols!" (Ausubel).

At the same time, the Jews wisely thought it necessary to bestow some visible honor on the givers. They were careful to screen out those who gave for crass, personal reasons but lauded the righteous for their gifts.

In every synagogue in our city, prominent space is provided to list those who have made a substantial gift to the building of the sanctuary. One can be sure the benevolence giving there is also outstanding.

Rabbi Yechiel Eckstein, an eminent American Jewish religious leader, believed that American Christians might be open to provide humanitarian aid to Israel. Through the organization he founded, 20 to 50 million dollars are given annually for the poor and needy in the State of Israel. None of the funds go to the Israeli military.

Jesus exposed the scandalous giving of the Pharisees. He revealed how they would give a gift to the temple, declare it *corban,* and by that exempt themselves from supporting aged parents (Mark 7:10-13).

No race or group of people has ever outgiven the Jews. Their *tzedakah* is extended to maintenance of the State of Israel. No other nation in the world has ever existed largely on the freewill gifts of her people worldwide!

The Jews tell the delightful story of the *Lamed-vavniks. Lamed-vav* is the number thirty-six, and those who are among the righteous thirty-six in each generation are the *niks* in Yiddish. The fourth-century Talmud teachers held that there were thirty-six men in the world upon whom the Shekinah-glory rested. These men were unsung heroes, who by their righteousness kept the world turning. They did not know they were in such distinguished company, but in times of great need, they arose to deal with the matter. When their work was done, they fled the scene in order not to miss the blessing that God would extend to them (Ausubel).

It is doubtful the Jews would grant Lamed-vavnik status to a Christian Jew, but we have a nominee. Rachmiel Frydland, a Polish Jewish Christian, worked among the Jews of his home country. When Poland was occupied by the Nazis, Brother Rachmiel moved about quietly reaching out to his people, who were in great peril. Jews from all over Europe were enclosed in the Warsaw ghetto. Frydland crept in to minister to those marked for death. He went in again and again, until Gentile Christians turned him in to the Nazis, believing Romans 13 required it.

—*Lyle P. Murphy.*

Guiding the Superintendent

There is a story of a bird that was held captive. It was chained by rope to a wooden stake. All the bird would do was circle the stake. A man observing the bird's dilemma sought its freedom. He paid a large amount for the bird's release. He quickly disconnected the bird from its rope. Sadly, the bird continued circling the stake. Although the bird was free, it failed to take advantage of its freedom.

This week's lesson teaches us that through Christ we are made free. We will discover that nothing can eradicate this reality. Through Him, we are recipients of grace that cancels our former bondage. But living in that freedom can be a challenge.

DEVOTIONAL OUTLINE

1. Freedom in Christ (Gal. 5:1-5). The Apostle Paul called the Galatian church to persevere in its freedom. He admonished the people to no longer be bound by the law.

Regrettably, the Jews tried to impose the old covenant law on the Galatians. They attempted to force circumcision on new believers. Paul admonished the Galatians that attempting to follow the law would never bring them a right relationship with God. A right relationship with God is accomplished only by faith.

2. Misled Galatians (Gal. 5:6-12). Those who trust Christ as Saviour do not need circumcision. God desired the Galatians to have faith that expressed itself in love.

Paul commended the Galatians for their initial faith walk. However, false teachers had misled some of them. God's message of love and grace was being distorted. The false teachers attempted to circumvent the gospel message. Paul stated, "A little leaven leaveneth the whole lump" (Gal. 5:9). This meant a slight twist from the truth could distort the gospel message.

Paul had a strong hope that the Galatians would not accept the false teaching. He declared that the false teachers would be penalized for their evil deeds. Some accused Paul of propagating erroneous doctrine. He asked if that was so, why was he being persecuted by false teachers? Apparently frustrated, he desired castration for the false messengers.

3. Wise use of freedom (Gal. 5:13-17). Although they were free, Paul cautioned the Galatians not to recklessly use their freedom. He directed them to love one another. Doing this was the true fulfillment of the law. They were instructed not to hurt one another. For this to occur, they had to allow the Holy Spirit to guide their lives.

AGE-GROUP EMPHASES

Children: Although they are young, children need to know the benefits of being a believer. Help them understand the importance of allowing Jesus to guide their lives. As they yield to Him, they will exhibit godly behavior.

Youths: Teens need to be properly prepared for their future adult lives. They need to know the importance of not allowing their flesh to control them. Highlight the importance of yielding themselves to the Holy Spirit. Emphasize that He will assist them in living holy lives.

Adults: Adults have free access to many activities. Encourage them to use their freedom wisely. Help them understand the importance of making sound decisions as well as being godly examples.

—*Tyrone Keith Carroll, Sr.*

Scripture Lesson Text

GAL. 5:18 But if ye be led of the Spir'it, ye are not under the law.

19 Now the works of the flesh are manifest, which are *these***; Adultery, fornication, uncleanness, lasciviousness,**

20 Idolatry, witchcraft, hatred, variance, emulations, wrath, strife, seditions, heresies,

21 Envyings, murders, drunkenness, revellings, and such like: of the which I tell you before, as I have also told *you* **in time past, that they which do such things shall not inherit the kingdom of God.**

22 But the fruit of the Spir'it is love, joy, peace, longsuffering, gentleness, goodness, faith,

23 Meekness, temperance: against such there is no law.

24 And they that are Christ's have crucified the flesh with the affections and lusts.

25 If we live in the Spir'it, let us also walk in the Spir'it.

26 Let us not be desirous of vain glory, provoking one another, envying one another.

6:1 Brethren, if a man be overtaken in a fault, ye which are spiritual, restore such an one in the spirit of meekness; considering thyself, lest thou also be tempted.

2 Bear ye one another's burdens, and so fulfil the law of Christ.

3 For if a man think himself to be something, when he is nothing, he deceiveth himself.

4 But let every man prove his own work, and then shall he have rejoicing in himself alone, and not in another.

5 For every man shall bear his own burden.

6 Let him that is taught in the word communicate unto him that teacheth in all good things.

7 Be not deceived; God is not mocked: for whatsoever a man soweth, that shall he also reap.

8 For he that soweth to his flesh shall of the flesh reap corruption; but he that soweth to the Spir'it shall of the Spir'it reap life everlasting.

9 And let us not be weary in well doing: for in due season we shall reap, if we faint not.

10 As we have therefore opportunity, let us do good unto all *men*, especially unto them who are of the household of faith.

NOTES

Holy Living in the Spirit

Lesson: Galatians 5:18—6:10

Read: Galatians 5:18—6:10

TIME: probably A.D. 48   PLACE: from Syrian Antioch

GOLDEN TEXT—"The fruit of the Spirit is love, joy, peace, longsuffering, gentleness, goodness, faith, meekness, temperance: against such there is no law" (Galatians 5:22-23).

Introduction

We have seen it many times. A well-known person is caught saying or doing something that is very embarrassing. A public apology is then offered, along with the assurance "That is not who I am." We may have good reason to be skeptical of such apologies, but it is certainly true that people can sometimes act in ways that are inconsistent with "who they are."

Consider the Apostle Peter. When he first met Jesus, the Lord declared, "Thou shalt be called Cephas" (John 1:42), meaning "stone." Peter's rock-like character and commitment to Jesus were unquestionable, yet pride and fear took control for a brief period and he denied Christ three times. Peter's denials, though painful, did not define or reflect his true character.

Like Peter, our intentions as followers of Christ are commendable, but we are not unblemished. What we do does not always reflect who we really are in Christ. This is why the Bible often reminds us of *who* we are, even as it tells us *what* to do. Because of who we are in the Lord, we have the power to do consistently what the Lord commands.

LESSON OUTLINE

I. **THE CHRISTIAN'S CHARACTER**—Gal. 5:18-24

II. **THE CHRISTIAN'S CONDUCT**—Gal. 5:25—6:10

Exposition: Verse by Verse

THE CHRISTIAN'S CHARACTER

GAL. 5:18 But if ye be led of the Spirit, ye are not under the law.

19 Now the works of the flesh are manifest, which are these; Adultery, fornication, uncleanness, lasciviousness,

20 Idolatry, witchcraft, hatred, variance, emulations, wrath, strife, seditions, heresies,

21 Envyings, murders, drunkenness, revellings, and such like: of the which I tell you before, as I have also told you in time past, that they which

do such things shall not inherit the kingdom of God.

22 But the fruit of the Spirit is love, joy, peace, longsuffering, gentleness, goodness, faith,

23 Meekness, temperance: against such there is no law.

24 And they that are Christ's have crucified the flesh with the affections and lusts.

Led by the Spirit (Gal. 5:18). Our last lesson ended with verse 17, which affirmed that we believers still struggle with sin and do not always do what we should, even though we desire to honor Christ. Paul reiterated, however, that the answer is not to put ourselves under the law. To make obedience to the law obligatory only puts us in bondage. The law does not free us from sin's power; it merely reveals our sin and points us to the One who removes sin and its consequences (3:24).

Christ has freed us from the bondage of the law (Gal. 3:25; 5:1) and given us the Holy Spirit to lead us and empower us to please God. Thus, a Christian can be characterized as one who is "led of the Spirit" and so is "not under the law" (5:18). This is what we are: free in Christ to live in the realm of the Spirit.

Not marked by fleshly works (Gal. 5:19-21). As Christians, our character is also marked by the absence of "works of the flesh." Paul proceeded to list some of the more obvious sins that characterize the "lust of the flesh" (vs. 16). Kent noted that "'works' is an apt designation of these productions of the natural man, for they are the result of natural human activity unaided by the Spirit of God" (*The Freedom of God's Sons,* BMH).

The sins listed in Galatians 5:19 are sexual in nature and cover illicit relations among both married and unmarried people. "Uncleanness" extends to one's immoral thoughts, and "lasciviousness" refers to complete lack of restraint in sexual matters. The next two works of the flesh relate to corrupt religion (vs. 20). "Idolatry" is worshipping images or other things, putting them in the place of God. The word translated "witchcraft" literally refers to the use of drugs, but it came to mean the "preparation and application of magical devices" (Ridderbos, *The Epistle of Paul to the Churches of Galatia,* Eerdmans).

The remaining vices listed in Galatians 5:20-21 are social in nature. "Hatred" gives rise to "variance," which is strife. "Emulations" is misdirected zeal, while "wrath" refers to outbursts of anger. The word translated "strife" seems to indicate selfish displays. "Seditions" refers to divisions that come from conflict, and "heresies" denotes the separate groups that form as a result of divisions. The list ends with "envyings, murders, drunkenness, revellings." The latter refers to drunken parties.

Paul made it clear these sins are representative and not exhaustive. The apostle then stated what he had told his readers before: those who practice such things will never inherit the kingdom of God. These are characterizing marks of those who are unsaved.

This does not mean that such people are beyond hope or that anyone who commits one of these sins is lost. It simply means that anyone whose life is characterized by sins such as these demonstrates that he or she is not a follower of Christ. Christians can sin and can sin quite grievously, but their lives cannot be persistently characterized by works of the flesh.

Marked by spiritual fruit (Gal. 5:22-24). In contrast to the works of the flesh, Paul listed the fruit of the Spirit. This fruit is produced by the indwelling Holy Spirit, not by our effort. This does not mean we have no role, however, for it is only as we submit to Christ and seek His will that the Spirit produces these qualities in us. The singular form of "fruit" in the Greek language emphasizes the "unity and coherence of the life in the Spirit"

(Pfeiffer and Harrison, eds., *The Wycliffe Bible Commentary,* Moody) and may even suggest that these qualities are one fruit consisting of nine elements. They are listed separately, however, and each one should be present and growing in the believer's life.

Christlike love, as Paul explained elsewhere (I Cor. 13), is selfless, unconditional, and unending. It always seeks the good of others. Joy is inner contentment that is unaffected by outward circumstances. Peace is "that inner calmness of emotions and thoughts which rests on the assurance that God is too good to be unkind and too wise to make mistakes" (Gromacki, *Stand Fast in Liberty,* Kress).

Longsuffering is patience, especially in the face of opposition. Gentleness, or kindness, describes one who has a tender regard for the interests and feelings of others. Goodness is very similar to gentleness, though the emphasis seems to be more on generosity. Faith should be understood as faithfulness in following the Lord and being reliable.

Meekness is gentleness in strength. In secular Greek the word was used of taming wild animals (Friedrich, ed., *Theological Dictionary of the New Testament,* Eerdmans). Finally, temperance is self-control.

These Spirit-produced qualities obviously do not need to be restrained by laws, as do the works of the flesh. Those who are Christ's display these qualities in their lives. This is because every true believer has crucified the flesh with its passions and sinful desires. The Christian makes a definitive break with sin when he or she believes in Christ. The believer can still fall into sin on occasion, but sin no longer has power over him or her. Rather, the Christian's life is characterized by godly fruit.

THE CHRISTIAN'S CONDUCT

25 If we live in the Spirit, let us also walk in the Spirit.

26 Let us not be desirous of vain glory, provoking one another, envying one another.

6:1 Brethren, if a man be overtaken in a fault, ye which are spiritual, restore such an one in the spirit of meekness; considering thyself, lest thou also be tempted.

2 Bear ye one another's burdens, and so fulfil the law of Christ.

3 For if a man think himself to be something, when he is nothing, he deceiveth himself.

4 But let every man prove his own work, and then shall he have rejoicing in himself alone, and not in another.

5 For every man shall bear his own burden.

6 Let him that is taught in the word communicate unto him that teacheth in all good things.

7 Be not deceived; God is not mocked: for whatsoever a man soweth, that shall he also reap.

8 For he that soweth to his flesh shall of the flesh reap corruption; but he that soweth to the Spirit shall of the Spirit reap life everlasting.

9 And let us not be weary in well doing: for in due season we shall reap, if we faint not.

10 As we have therefore opportunity, let us do good unto all men, especially unto them who are of the household of faith.

Selfless in service (Gal. 5:25-26). Having presented what a Christian is and is not through the lists of works of the flesh and fruit of the Spirit, the apostle now began to issue directives for what Christians are to do. At this point, Paul shifted from an emphasis on doctrinal truth to the application of that truth in daily life. First, if (or since) we "live in the Spirit," we must also "walk in the Spirit." In other words, we are to conform our conduct to this new life we entered when we were saved. Among other things, this means we are to serve God and others selflessly.

We are not to proudly seek glory for ourselves. We are not to provoke others with a selfish attitude. And we are not to envy those who might be more honored than we are. There is no place for self-centeredness among those who belong to Christ.

Compassion for the needy (Gal. 6:1-3). Instead of being focused on ourselves, we are to help those in need. "Overtaken in a fault" can mean either that the one overtaken was surprised by the fault itself and did not mean to fall into sin, or it can mean the person was surprised when someone discovered his sin. In either case, the offender is a Christian whom his fellow Christians are to restore.

The word for "restore" in Galatians 6:1 was used of mending nets (cf. Matt. 4:21; Mark 1:19). What is envisioned here are more mature, or spiritual, believers restoring a sinning brother or sister to usefulness in the church. This affirms that Christians do, in fact, fall into sin at times. It also tells us that although all believers should exhibit the fruit of the Spirit, there are various levels of fruitfulness among Christians simply because the Christian life is a continuing process of growth and development of Christlike character.

Those who are more mature in the faith are to look out for those who are struggling with sin, and they are to restore them. They are to do so in a spirit of humility or meekness. The same word is used for one fruit of the Spirit and emphasizes that the restorers must be exhibiting that fruit. The one who restores needs to take heed to himself, being mindful of his (or her) own potential for falling into sin.

The principle stated in Galatians 6:2 may have many applications, but in this context it refers to restoring a sinning brother or sister, relieving that one of the heavy burden he or she bears. When we do this, we demonstrate Christlike love and "so fulfil the law of Christ." "'The law of Christ' is: 'Love one another' (John 13:34; 15:12). Paul has already discussed the 'law of love' (Gal. 5:13-15), and now he is applying it" (Wiersbe, *Be Free,* Victor).

Galatians 6:3 is a warning against pride. Pride or conceit can interfere with Christians acting in a compassionate way to bear the burdens of fellow believers. When they think so highly of themselves that they refuse to help the lowly person trapped in sin, they are deceiving themselves, for they are no better than the sinning brother or sister. In fact, "measured by God's standards, no one amounts to anything" (Barker and Kohlenberger, eds., *The Expositor's Bible Commentary, Abridged,* Zondervan).

Reflective and responsible (Gal. 6:4-5). "Let every man prove his own work" is an implied warning against comparing ourselves to others. We each have our own work to do, and we must "prove," or test, the quality of our work by God's standards, not man's. We are not to take pride in achieving or exceeding the expectations of people. Rather, we are to examine ourselves to see if we are accomplishing what God wants us to do, for that is the only legitimate grounds for rejoicing.

At first, the call for everyone to "bear his own burden" (Gal. 6:5) seems to conflict with verse 2. Paul used a different word for burden here, however, probably to distinguish this statement from the previous one. Here the burden is not sin or its consequences but the work of verse 4, or the "normal duty which falls upon every man" (Ridderbos). Each person is responsible for his own work before God.

Supportive of leaders (Gal. 6:6-9). Another duty of Christians is to "communicate" with those who faithfully teach them. The word for "communicate" here means "to share with." This refers to financial support. Those in the church who devote themselves to instructing the saints are worthy of support, as Paul repeatedly stated (cf. I Cor. 9:14; Phil. 4:15-18; I Tim. 5:17-18).

In the context of all that Paul had previously said in Galatians, the statement in 6:7, "Be not deceived; God is not mocked," probably contained a final warning against honoring the false teachers who were deceiving them while treating faithful teachers of the Word with disdain. To do this was to treat God with contempt. The universal principle that one reaps what he sows is applicable here (cf. I Cor. 9:10-11; II Cor. 9:6). If the Galatians did not generously support honest, faithful teachers, they would reap emptiness and even hardship in their lives.

The principle is restated in Galatians 6:8, where the apostle gives it much wider application; namely, that sowing to the flesh reaps "corruption," and sowing to the Spirit reaps "life everlasting." One who consistently directs his life toward pleasing the flesh will reap corruption, or moral decay. His self-centered life proves he is not a Christian. A Christian should consistently be sowing to the Spirit; that is, he should be directing his life toward the things of God. Such a person proves by the life he lives that he is a follower of Christ and will reap eternal life.

Again, a believer can sin, as we have seen, but he cannot continue in such a lifestyle if he is truly born again. It is important that the Christian make daily choices to sow to the Spirit so that his life reflects who he truly is in Christ.

The reward of godly living is not always immediately evident, so there is the temptation to grow weary of the commitment to do good. Paul urged his readers to remain diligent in this, realizing that the basic principle of sowing and reaping is unalterable and that the harvest of divine blessing will come in God's good time.

Doing good to all (Gal. 6:10). The good we do—and the good we reap as a result—is not limited to our treatment of godly teachers. We are obligated to do good to all people as we have the opportunity. Paul added, however, that our first priority is to our own family, the "household of faith." Our loving concern is to be expressed for all people, but our special concern is our fellow Christians.

If we are being led by the Spirit (Gal. 5:18), the Spirit will be producing in us Christlike character (vss. 22-23). Such character will be evident in selfless service to others, and we will reap God's blessing both in this life and in the life to come.

—*Jarl K. Waggoner.*

QUESTIONS

1. How does being led by the Spirit differ from being under the law?
2. What did Paul say about Christians and the "works of the flesh" (Gal. 5:19)?
3. How is the fruit of the Spirit produced in Christians?
4. What might be suggested by the fact that the fruit of the Spirit is singular (vs. 22)?
5. What is added by the idea of walking in the Spirit (vs. 25)?
6. What is our duty to Christians "overtaken in a fault" (6:1)?
7. With what attitude should we approach those who are in sin?
8. How does bearing our own burden (vs. 5) differ from bearing one another's burdens (vs. 2)?
9. What is our obligation to those who teach us the Word?
10. How does the law of sowing and reaping relate to not growing weary in doing good?

—*Jarl K. Waggoner.*

Preparing to Teach the Lesson

As you may be well aware, there is a lot of false and misleading talk about spiritual life. Some gurus and teachers in the world have a totally false idea of what is spiritual and what is carnal, or fleshly, the fruit of a fallen human nature. Part of your responsibility as a teacher is to correct any misunderstandings your students may have about this and to educate them as to what real spiritual life is.

TODAY'S AIM

Facts: to see clearly the elements of refusing the works of the flesh and living in the Spirit.

Principle: to learn to walk in the Spirit each day of our lives.

Application: to daily refuse to do the deeds of the flesh and to obey the promptings of the Holy Spirit.

INTRODUCING THE LESSON

As a class, we need to be so aware of true spiritual life and so used to practicing our walk in the Spirit that we can help and encourage one another in its pursuit. The world at large teaches what it calls "spiritual" things. They are really emotional things.

The Scripture is clear that before we trust Christ and are born again, our spirits are fatally flawed. We are "dead in trespasses and sins" (Eph. 2:1). We have emotions and aspirations, even a hunger for spiritual things, but our spirits are dead without Christ. That is the reason so many false religions and philosophies are spawned. We have a hunger for answers, and if we do not get the light of Scripture and the right answers, we invent answers. Inventions from flawed hearts and minds are always sinful and anti-God. We must study the Word of God to receive correct spiritual information. We must respond to that information positively in order to walk in true spiritual life instead of spiritual death.

DEVELOPING THE LESSON

1. Free from the law but not free to sin (Gal. 5:18-21). Notice that it is only when we are "led of the Spirit" that we are free from the law. When the Holy Spirit, resident within us through faith in the Lord Jesus Christ, prompts us to godly activities and thoughts, we do not have to even think about keeping any kind of law or regulation. That does not mean we can violate any of them; it means the Holy Spirit does not lead us to act in any way that God does not approve of. Even though we are saved, we still have a fallen human nature, and it is flawed in such a way that we can still take part in sin. The sins listed in these verses are indicative, not exclusive. The scriptural pronouncement is clear. Those "[who] do such things shall not inherit the kingdom of God."

2. What to expect when walking in the Spirit (Gal. 5:22-26). Notice that the "works of the flesh" (vs. 19) section is in the plural and the "fruit of the Spirit" (vs. 22) section is in the singular. Although nine results of walking in the Spirit are given, it is referred to as the fruit (singular) of the Spirit. When walking in the Spirit, there is a unified way of thinking and feeling with a resultant way of doing what is truly spiritual. When we have crucified the flesh with its affections and lusts, we are dead to them. They can no longer have any place in our lives.

3. What to do as a Spirit-led believer (Gal. 6:1-6). Sometimes believers behave like unbelievers and violate the rule of the Lord over them. They fall into sin. If you and I are walking in the Spirit and are not in sin ourselves, we are to gently and humbly attempt to help people see their error and repent of it and return to Christ's lordship over them. This may be the hardest thing for any of us to do, but it is essential to the body of Christ, the church. Most of the time, we see Christians criticizing sinning brothers or sisters. Condemning others is a sin, and it certainly does not help solve the problem.

4. In for the long haul (Gal. 6:7-10). We are told not to be deceived; that is, we should not kid ourselves! We should never think that we can somehow get away with sin just because we prayed about it and the temptation to do it did not go away. God expects us to obey the promptings of the Holy Spirit. He will not do for us that which we refuse to do or neglect to do. God will not tie our shoelaces. If we trip and fall because we did not tie them, it is our responsibility, not God's. We will reap what we sow. We will reap later, and we will reap it multiplied, some thirtyfold, some sixtyfold, and some a hundredfold as Jesus mentioned in His parables.

In God's perfect timing, we will reap a harvest of blessing if we walk in the Spirit. We have no idea what that will be like, but it is a merciful and loving God who is preparing it. He wants to graciously and lavishly bless His children. We will have plentiful opportunities to do good to "all men, especially unto them who are of the household of faith." And Paul encourages us to never give up or get tired of doing good.

ILLUSTRATING THE LESSON

Blessings to others result from walking in the Spirit.

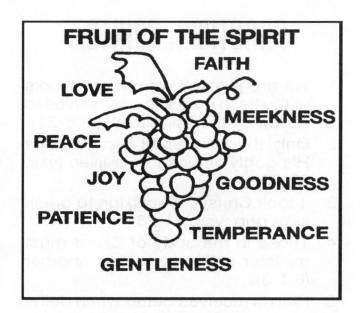

CONCLUDING THE LESSON

It is impossible to overstate the importance of this week's theme. The whole point of the Christian life is encompassed here. As we yield our own wills to the prompting of the Lord through His Holy Spirit, we will be living a holy and blessed life free from sin and the negative works of the flesh. This is part of that for which Christ died. Being saved and going to heaven when we die is wonderful, but so is a life on earth filled with the presence and power of the Lord. This is a life lived for others, not self, just as Christ lived.

There is no higher calling. The humblest Christian can walk in the Spirit just as effectively as the most powerful saint. There are no required qualifications except trusting Christ and obeying His Holy Spirit. No one and nothing can stop any one of us from doing it. All of heaven's resources are behind the one who walks in the Spirit and does not fulfill the lusts of the flesh.

ANTICIPATING THE NEXT LESSON

In our next quarter of study, we will examine the various facets of God's love.

—*Brian D. Doud.*

PRACTICAL POINTS

1. We are protected from the works of the flesh if we allow ourselves to be led by the Spirit (Gal. 5:18-21).

2. Only the Holy Spirit can produce His godly virtues in our lives (vss. 22-23).

3. It took Christ's crucifixion to break sin's grip (vss. 24-26).

4. Those in the body of Christ must minister selflessly to one another (6:1-3).

5. Help is received better when delivered with love. We should always act in humility (vss. 4-5).

6. We all are in the same race and should not compete with but help one another to the finish (Gal. 6:6-10; cf. Rom. 12:5).

—Lendell Sims.

RESEARCH AND DISCUSSION

1. The world's population is divided into numerous cultures. Is there any difference from one culture to another in the manifestation of the works of the flesh? Are certain cultures more prone to works of the flesh than others?

2. How can the fruit of the Spirit negate the works of the flesh?

3. Romans 12:2 instructs us to "be not conformed to this world." How can we evangelize those we are supposed to be separated from?

4. How do we see the law of reaping and sowing played out in our own culture?

5. When evangelizing, how do we know whether we are the one planting or watering?

—Lendell Sims.

ILLUSTRATED HIGH POINTS

And such like: . . . against such

Paul did not limit fleshly works or spiritual fruit to the items he listed in Galatians 5:19-23. This is indicated by the phrases "and such like" and "against such."

A unicyclist rode his unique vehicle on a Coney Island sidewalk, leading the police to give him a ticket. He then filed a three million-dollar lawsuit, pointing out that the law prohibits bicycles and defines "bicycle" as a "two- or three-wheeled device propelled by human power" ("Letter of the Law, Spirit of the Law," www.brooklynspoke.com). Since his vehicle had only one wheel, he reasoned he was not in error.

There are tens of thousands of laws on the books simply because we duck, dodge, and fly through loopholes with the greatest of ease. We could, however, put aside the law volumes if we understood the law of love written on our hearts (cf. Rom. 2:29; I Thess. 4:9).

Ye which are spiritual, restore

In a news interview, a Christian mother spoke of her family's grief after the death of their eighteen-month-old son in a hot car. Her husband drove to work and forgot that it was his turn to drop the child off at daycare. Through their pain, the family has pulled together and is even endeavoring to help others. Sadly, a portion of the public has been cruelly judgmental.

This mother understands their reaction and identifies it as a "fundamental attribution error." This psychological term basically means that we tend to blame the person when something like this happens to someone else but the circumstances when it happens to us. Let us lean more toward kindness and forgiveness than faultfinding.

—Therese Greenberg.

Golden Text Illuminated

"The fruit of the Spirit is love, joy, peace, longsuffering, gentleness, goodness, faith, meekness, temperance: against such there is no law" (Galatians 5:22-23).

Everything about salvation in Christ shouts to us of living a holy life through the power of the Holy Spirit. The church was born for this. There can be no confusion. As believers we must realize that God has saved us to be holy, and He has provided His Spirit to create the capacity to live a holy, godly, God-pleasing life. What is such a life all about? This text gives us two things to think about.

The first is that a holy life has a manifold expression—it is a multiplicity of virtues. We note that the term "fruit" is singular, but that one fruit has an abundance of expressions in the life of the Christian. All of these expressions should emerge in our lives in a unity. We should see a "fruit cluster," a ninefold expression of the sacred presence of the Spirit in our lives.

The fruit of the Spirit is in contrast to the works of the flesh, each of which is a singular expression of sinful activity. Our sinful nature has many potential expressions of sin. But when the Holy Spirit is in control of our lives, we will see a fullness, a completeness, to our character in Christ.

We should manifest love, the capacity to act in the best interests of others. We should manifest joy, an inner happiness in God that transcends our trials and troubles. We should manifest peace, an abiding tranquillity present in our minds and hearts. We should manifest longsuffering, a patience that is able to endure difficulty without a response of the flesh.

We should also personify such things as gentleness and goodness, a kindly generosity of spirit toward others. We should show forth faith, or faithfulness—the ability to be steady, committed, and strong throughout all the seasons and challenges of life. And we should exhibit meekness, a humbleness of spirit that is willing to yield to others. Last but not least, we should display temperance, or self-control, diligently putting into practice what we are learning from God's Word in a disciplined way.

Do you see this "fruit cluster" emerging in your life? As we yield to the Holy Spirit hour by hour and minute by minute, these expressions of holy living will emerge in the life of the true Christian, to the glory of God. It is a wonderful and manifold statement of the difference Christ makes in our lives. These are not standards we achieve by human effort, but rather the fruit of the Holy Spirit's presence in our lives.

The second thing to think about from the golden text is that a holy life yields not only this beautiful, manifold expression of fruit; it also constitutes a powerful force. Paul states the firm truth that against this kind of life there is no law. Nothing can be erected to stop it. If the Holy Spirit is producing this fruit, then it does not matter what the enemies of the Christian life do. It does not matter what the world does. This fruit will come. It is intrinsically powerful because it is of God; it comes from the presence of the Spirit. Let us do all we can to nurture the presence of the Holy Spirit within us, that His manifold and powerful fruit may emerge in our lives.

—Jeff VanGoethem.

Heart of the Lesson

What does it mean to live holy lives in the Spirit? First, let us broaden our concept of the word "holy." Holiness is often equated with purity, but it also can be defined as "set apart." God wants us to be holy. He desires that we are literally set apart. In other words, do our words, our actions, and our attitudes differ from those who have not been redeemed by the blood of the Lamb? Sinners are going to act like sinners. It is confusing when the saints are more adept at behaving the way sinners do than they are at behaving the way children of God should.

1. The flesh and the Spirit (Gal. 5:18-26). When we fulfill the desires of the flesh, we find that our hunger for them grows. The more we feed the flesh, the more we learn that we are never able to satisfy the lusts of the flesh. Instead, our moral compass keeps being pushed beyond its limits until one day we have lost our moral perspective completely.

The Apostle Paul provides us with a list of the works of the flesh. This is not an all-inclusive list but rather a summary. If we are able to steer clear of the things Paul spoke about, chances are that we will not succumb to other temptations.

Just as there are works of the flesh, there is fruit of the Spirit to enable us to overcome temptation. "The fruit of the Spirit is love, joy, peace, longsuffering, gentleness, goodness, faith, meekness, temperance: against such there is no law" (Gal. 5:22). We can indulge in the fruit of God's Spirit without measure. As we partake of the fruit of the Spirit, we are able to live in the Spirit. As we live in the Spirit, we are also able to walk in the Spirit.

2. Watch (Gal. 6:1-6). If someone falls into sin and begins to walk in his flesh rather than his spirit, we are to restore him gently. Why? What if we were tempted by the same issue? What if we fell? Would we not want to be restored? We all need a spiritual realignment now and then. Sometimes we fall into temptation by choice; sometimes we fall into sin through ignorance. Either way, we need to repent and turn away from that sin.

Sometimes we need other people to show us the error of our ways. This can be done by a spiritual leader or by a trusted, godly friend. It is what Paul meant when he said, "Bear ye one another's burdens, and so fulfil the law of Christ" (Gal. 6:2). We are to help our brothers and sisters in Christ overcome the works of the flesh and encourage them to walk in the Spirit.

3. Warning and promise (Gal. 6:7-10). "Be not deceived; God is not mocked: for whatsoever a man soweth, that shall he also reap." There are two ways to look at verse 7: as a warning and as a promise. If we live our lives based solely on our desires, with no regard for anyone else, this verse is a warning. However, if we seek God and walk in His Spirit, this verse is a promise. This is why Paul urges us not to get weary in doing good toward others. It is going to pay off!

If we believe that the Bible is true, then we can be assured that God keeps tabs on how we treat one another. God is not mocked. As we strive to be a blessing to others, we will be blessed!

—*Kristin Reeg.*

World Missions

Our God is a God of excellence, lining up every detail of His Word in perfect order. The list of fruit of the Spirit is deliberately sequenced according to how God works in our lives. For example, without a foundation of love, no life will produce fruit. And temperance, or self-control, may appear last because once a person loses it, there may be nothing else to do but to start over with love. God has made this fruit available to us to combat the works of the flesh and to demonstrate His overcoming power in our lives.

Belinda came to a Reach & Rescue Ministries' homeless shelter on the day she was released from prison. Our group was there to provide the weekly chapel service. I brought a rousing message; at least I thought so. Many of the women were moved. Several came up for prayer for salvation, healing, and other issues. Belinda did not budge. Her face was like stone as she stared forward, waiting for the dismissal prayer.

At "amen," she stumbled across a row of stragglers, dashing for the exit. I trotted after her but missed her. She became the object of many of my prayers for the next week. I was determined to make contact with her on the subsequent visit. When I saw Belinda enter the next week, I stopped her at the door, introduced myself, and thanked her for coming. She blandly responded, "They said I had to."

Again Belinda sat through our service, scrambling out the door as soon as we finished. Again, I felt the need to target her in my prayers. The third week, I met her again at the chapel door. This time I obeyed the words that had been echoing in my head all day: "Love her." God was letting me know that He would soften her with love. I planned to say hello, but out of my mouth came, "Would it be all right if I hug you?"

Belinda stared at me for a few seconds, appearing to be stunned. "I guess," she said. As the service began, I noticed tears coming from Belinda's eyes. At the conclusion, Belinda came up to me for what I thought would be prayer. She pulled me over to the side and told me about some of the childhood abuse and abandonment she had suffered from her parents and the violence and perverted lifestyle that had resulted from such turmoil in her life.

Then she revealed the shocker. She confessed that because she lived an openly sinful lifestyle, her son's friends would call him names and tease him. At twelve years old, her son could take no more and shot himself in the head. Belinda said she could not forgive herself for his death, but reading the Bible and coming to chapel were helping her feel the love of God. She admitted that her life had been a whirlwind and she had no self-control.

The demonstration of God's love prepared Belinda to be open to the gospel. She became progressively softer to accepting love from the Father and gestures of love from the Christians around her. Belinda surrendered her life to Christ several months later. She rejected her former lifestyle and has been growing in Christ. She is an example of how the Holy Spirit starts with love and develops the fruit that eventually leads to self-control.

Holy living is not ours to accomplish alone. Like Belinda, as we allow the Holy Spirit to bear His fruit in us, He will help us live for Him.

—Beverly Medley Jones.

The Jewish Aspect

In Galatians 5, Paul contrasted the works of the flesh with the fruit of the Spirit. Neither the Jewish people of Paul's day nor Jewish people today who have any allegiance to Judaism would disagree that such acts as adultery, murder, and drunkenness are evils. Their problem, like that of so many morally minded people, is not identifying evil but rather avoiding it.

Christians, of course, should recognize that the key to godly living is found in the blessings of the new covenant. The Spirit writes God's law upon the hearts of believers. The history of Jewish family life over the last two thousand years, illustrates the uphill struggles of trying to live morally without the Spirit's empowerment.

In 1215, the Fourth Lateran Council decreed quarantine of Jews in every city in what was called the ghetto. Ghettos were locked up each night and closely guarded. In one sense, this was a blessing for the Jews, for it kept families together and reduced the sinful temptations of the Gentiles from contaminating the Jews. Divorce was virtually nonexistent. Man and wife were required to get along. Rabbis said that the chief ingredients of marriage were mutual respect, devotion, chaste conduct, and kindness (Ausubel, *The Book of Jewish Knowledge,* Crown Publishers).

In our Jewish community, a young, unmarried woman came from Eastern Europe and took up residence. She was extremely attractive, and Jewish wives began to complain that she was too flirtatious with their husbands. As a body they complained to the rabbi about the young woman. He threatened to put her out of the community, but she repented and was restored to the community. She eventually married and won general acceptance among the Jews.

Judaism has always placed great value on marriage and families. Much of the law relates to family life, and Israel's history has reinforced the danger of outside influence and intermarriage with Gentiles.

European Jews always feared for their children, but it was not so in ghetto communities. Mothers were charged with the spiritual formation of children until they could read. Then fathers took over, imbuing them with the tenets of Deuteronomy 6:4-6. The father was released from responsibility when the child reached age thirteen (Ausubel).

After World War II, immigrants swelled the synagogue congregations in most American communities. The Jewish sense of freedom was not without cost, however. It opened the sacred marriage customs of the Jews to be easily ignored. Marriage outside of Judaism has always been a feared consequence of living close to profligate Gentiles. The result has been that 52 percent of Jewish marriages in America are contracted with non-Jews. While Reform Jews seem unconcerned, the Orthodox still seek to maintain their Jewish identity and customs and live upright lives.

What our Jewish friends fail to understand is something many Christians also do not seem to grasp. All the effort in the world to avoid evil can never produce a morally upright life. We might avoid the worst influences from outside, but we cannot escape our own sinful human nature. Thus, no one can live a holy life apart from the work of the Holy Spirit, who indwells only followers of Christ and produces in them the spiritual fruit Paul described. Sadly, Judaism offers no personal Holy Spirit who permanently indwells God's people and empowers them to live holy lives.

—*Lyle P. Murphy.*

Guiding the Superintendent

"Do as I say and not as I do" is a familiar old expression used by some leaders and parents. One of the things this might imply is that authority figures should be unconditionally followed, even though they frequently are not walking according to their words. The fact is that people sometimes give orders or advice without setting a consistent example.

In this week's lesson, we will receive instruction concerning living a holy lifestyle. We will also learn about the works of the flesh.

DEVOTIONAL OUTLINE

1. Living by the sinful nature (Gal. 5:18-21). Paul told the Galatians about the works of the flesh. He listed the sexual sins of adultery, fornication, uncleanness, and lasciviousness. Sins against God such as idolatry and witchcraft display a lack of godly reverence. Paul also denounced hatred, discord, jealousy, wrath, strife, division, and factions.

Paul indicated to the Galatians that a life characterized by participation in fleshly activity would result in not partaking of the kingdom of God. They would not receive God's blessings.

2. Fruit of the Spirit-filled life (Gal. 5:22-26). Shifting toward living in the Spirit, Paul provided a listing of attributes connected to a Spirit-filled life. Love is the anchor of the fruit of the Spirit. Joy and peace reflect contentment.

Longsuffering, gentleness, and goodness are proper traits for believers to show in their interactions with others. Faithfulness reflects the tenacity to stay consistent in the Christian walk. Meekness and temperance demonstrate restraint.

Paul called upon those who trust in Christ to put to death evil passions and lusts. Paul further warned the church to refrain from conceit, jealousy, and provoking one another.

3. Living the Spirit-filled life (Gal. 6:1-10). Paul addressed the Galatian church on how to treat fallen believers. Paul cautioned them not to be demeaning. They were to restore believers with mercy.

Paul wanted the church to display love. The way that could be expressed was by sharing and not becoming conceited. They were not to resort to self-serving comparisons.

Paul next moved the discussion to giving. Paul informed the Galatians that it was their responsibility to share their resources with their teachers. He used the term "communicate" to illustrate his point. Failing to financially support their teachers would result in missing blessings from the Spirit.

Paul encouraged his readers not to allow discouragement to impede their thinking. They would be the beneficiaries of God's blessings if they did not quit. Finally, they were called to do good to all people, especially Christian believers.

AGE-GROUP EMPHASES

Children: It is never too early for children to learn the distinction between right and wrong. Help them aspire to live in a holy manner at all times. Affirm the necessity of listening to God's voice.

Youths: Teens are often tempted to take part in sinful activities. This has a negative impact. Guide the young people to develop ears to hear God's voice. Relate to them the dangers of allowing their flesh to dictate their lives.

Adults: Years ago, "What would Jesus do?" was a popular slogan. When tempted, many believers quoted it. Adults need to be reminded of God's expectations. Teach them the significance of holy living and the power God supplies to accomplish it.

—Tyrone Keith Carroll, Sr.

kingdom as described by the prophets, He was rejected by His own people and eventually crucified. This rejection brought a partial hardening of the nation of Israel and a delay in God's program as described by the prophets.

After Christ rose from the dead, ascended to the Father's right hand, and poured out the Spirit at Pentecost, Peter again called on Israel to repent (Acts 2:22-39). Although three thousand were saved that day (vs. 41), the nation as a whole did not heed Peter's words. Instead, the Jewish leadership persecuted those who followed this new way (8:1; 9:2).

Because of Israel's rejection of their Messiah, a new entity called the church was born at Pentecost. Christ had spoken of building such an assembly even before His crucifixion (Matt. 16:18). Initially consisting primarily of Jews, the church would eventually become predominantly Gentile. This new entity was not known in the Old Testament and would require new revelation from God to explain its existence. The Apostle Paul would be the primary recipient and recorder of this new revelation.

Paul was the perfect choice for this role. He grew up under the Mosaic economy and was educated at the feet of a well-known teacher, Gamaliel. In his own words, Paul was a "Hebrew of the Hebrews; as touching the law, a Pharisee; concerning zeal, persecuting the church; touching the righteousness which is in the law, blameless" (Phil. 3:5-6).

But all that changed when Paul was dramatically converted on the road to Damascus. He was commissioned as the apostle to the Gentiles and sent to them to proclaim salvation by faith in Christ. Like Israel, the church will exist to bring glory to God. They will simply be known as sons of God. In Him there is no Jew or Gentile (Gal. 3:26-29).

Jesus, the Long-Awaited Messiah

FRANK PASS

The promise of One who would conquer Satan and overcome the effects of man's fall into sin appears very early in Scripture. In pronouncing His curse upon the serpent, God said, "And I will put enmity between thee and the woman, and between thy seed and her seed; it shall bruise thy head, and thou shalt bruise his heel" (Gen. 3:15).

In accordance with the Abrahamic covenant, God multiplied the descendants of Abraham and made from him a great nation. That covenant also included the promise that kings would come from Abraham (Gen. 17:6). This initial promise is subsequently picked up and developed in the Davidic covenant. The essence of that covenant is that David, Israel's second king, would never lack a descendant to sit on the throne of Israel (II Sam. 7:16; Jer. 33:17).

Solomon was the first of David's descendants to rule from the throne of Israel. Because of his sin, the kingdom divided into a northern kingdom known as Israel and a southern kingdom known as Judah. The Davidic succession was maintained through the southern kingdom.

A series of twenty kings followed

Solomon. Twelve of these were bad and eight were good, in the sense of walking in the ways of their father David and keeping covenant with God (cf. II Kings 16:2; 18:3). Yet even the good kings were unsuccessful in restoring the nation to covenant faithfulness. As a result, and like the northern kingdom before it, Judah was taken into exile by a foreign power and there was no longer a throne in Israel.

But the temporary suspension of the Davidic throne did not mean a nullification of God's covenant with David. Even as the nation went into exile, God's prophets began to announce the coming of the King whose character and rule would surpass all those who preceded Him. Isaiah wrote about this King, "For unto us a child is born, unto us a son is given: and the government shall be upon his shoulder: and his name shall be called Wonderful, Counsellor, The mighty God, The everlasting Father, The Prince of Peace. Of the increase of his government and peace there shall be no end, upon the throne of David, and upon his kingdom, to order it, and to establish it with judgment and with justice from henceforth even for ever. The zeal of the Lord of hosts will perform this" (Isa. 9:6-7).

Concerning the nation's restoration and its future King, Ezekiel wrote, "And say unto them, Thus saith the Lord God; Behold, I will take the children of Israel from among the heathen, whither they be gone, and will gather them on every side, and bring them into their own land: and I will make them one nation in the land upon the mountains of Israel; and one king shall be king to them all: and they shall be no more two nations, neither shall they be divided into two kingdoms any more at all. Neither shall they defile themselves any more with their idols, nor with their detestable things, nor with any of their transgressions: but I will save them out of all their dwelling-places, wherein they have sinned, and

will cleanse them: so shall they be my people, and I will be their God. And David my servant shall be king over them; and they all shall have one shepherd: they shall also walk in my judgments, and observe my statutes, and do them" (Ezek. 37:21-24).

Malachi, the last of the latter prophets, closed the Old Testament canon with a prediction of the Messiah's forerunner, the one who would prepare the way before Him (Mal. 4:5-6; cf. Isa. 40:3).

After four hundred years of silence by God and anticipation by Israel, the Angel Gabriel appeared to Zacharias, a priest in Israel. Though he and his wife were past the normal age of childbearing, they would be the parents of the Messiah's forerunner (Luke 1:13-17). After John was born, Zacharias praised God that He had "raised up an horn of salvation for us in the house of his servant David" (vs. 69).

Gabriel subsequently appeared to a young girl named Mary with an even more amazing announcement. Although she was still a virgin, she would conceive by the work of the Holy Spirit and give birth to the Messiah Himself! Gabriel's announcement also included a clear connection to the throne of David: "He shall be great, and shall be called the Son of the Highest: and the Lord God shall give unto him the throne of his father David: and he shall reign over the house of Jacob for ever; and of his kingdom there shall be no end" (Luke 1:32-33). The Gospels make clear that Jesus of Nazareth fulfilled the promise of the long-awaited Messiah and the ultimate Davidic Ruler.

The initial proclamation of John the Baptist as forerunner—of Jesus in His own ministry, and of Jesus' apostles— was "Repent ye: for the kingdom of heaven is at hand" (Matt. 3:2; cf. 4:17; 10:5-7). The kingdom was "at hand" because the King was at hand. Jesus taught with authority and did many miracles to back up His claims that He was the Messiah. But the nation's leaders rejected Him as King, even attributing His ability to cast out demons to the ruler of the demons (12:24).

Their animosity toward Jesus not only prevented the fulfillment of the kingdom prophecies in their generation but also led to His death on a cross. This too was in accordance with the plan and foreknowledge of God, for the Old Testament prophets had predicted that the Messiah would suffer before He would reign (Acts 3:18; I Pet. 1:10-11).

After His resurrection, Jesus ascended to the right hand of God in heaven, where He is now seated with His Father upon the throne (Rev. 3:21). But a day is coming when He will return in great power and glory to sit on His own throne (Matt. 25:31). In that day the kingdoms of the world will become "the kingdoms of our Lord, and of his Christ; and he shall reign for ever and ever" (Rev. 11:15).

TOPICS FOR NEXT QUARTER

PARAGRAPHS ON PLACES AND PEOPLE

SYRIA

The land of Syria has undergone tremendous change throughout the millennia of its existence. A number of ancient peoples inhabited and ruled this region, including the Babylonians, the Hittites, the Egyptians, the Philistines, the Assyrians, the Greeks, and the Romans.

Syria has a varied topography, featuring steppes, mountains, river valleys, and a coastal plain. Along the coast and mountains, rainfall averages 30 to 50 inches. In the steppes, it can be 10 to 20 inches.

At the time of Jesus' birth, Cyrenius was the governor of Syria and enforced a census declared by Caesar Augustus. Nazareth was under Cyrenius's jurisdiction, so Joseph was compelled to travel to his hometown of Bethlehem, as recorded in Luke 2.

GALATIA

We know that Paul wrote an epistle to the Galatians, but where exactly did these early believers live? Galatia was unique as the recipient of an apostolic letter in that it was not a city but a province. There is some question as to exactly which city or town Paul wrote to, but it was somewhere within the province, which lay in Asia Minor (modern Turkey).

In the centuries before Paul's missionary journeys, Galatia had been settled by the Gauls of western Europe. It was eventually overtaken by the Roman Empire. Various Roman rulers changed the boundaries of the province, so it is difficult to determine its precise location.

Since Galatia was not a metropolitan area, its inhabitants resided in smaller towns and the open country. This is in stark contrast to other sojourns of Paul's missionary journeys, such as Athens and Corinth.

ELISABETH

Jesus' mother, Mary, was not the only woman who was part of fulfilled prophecy at the advent of the Messiah. Mary's relative Elisabeth also had a special role as the mother of John the Baptist.

God miraculously intervened in the lives of Zacharias and Elisabeth, granting them a child long after they had given up hope of having a baby. Before Elisabeth gave birth to John, she praised the Lord and said, "Thus hath the Lord dealt with me . . . to take away my reproach among men" (Luke 1:25).

Elisabeth was not to be alone in her rejoicing, however. Mary visited her, prompting Elisabeth to announce that Mary was pregnant with Israel's promised Messiah. Elisabeth "was filled with the Holy Ghost: and she spake out with a loud voice, and said, Blessed art thou among women, and blessed is the fruit of thy womb" (Luke 1:41-42).

JOHN THE BAPTIST

John the Baptist also played a special role in the events surrounding the birth of Christ. His connection to Christ began even while in the womb: "When Elisabeth heard the salutation of Mary, the babe leaped in her womb" (Luke 1:41). Alluding to prophecies in Isaiah and Malachi, Gabriel announced that John would "go before him in the spirit and power of Elias, to turn the hearts of the fathers to the children, . . . to make ready a people prepared for the Lord" (vs. 17). Indeed, God was working out John's life even before he was born.

—J.A. Littler.

Daily Bible Readings for Home Study and Worship

(Readings are for the week previous to the lesson topics.)

1. December 4.   The Promise of a Saviour

M.—A Son Is Given. Isa. 9:2-7.
T.—Hannah's Prayer for a Son. I Sam. 1:1-11.
W.—Hannah's Prayer Answered. I Sam. 1:15-20.
T.—A Son Promised to Sarah. Gen. 18:9-15.
F.—Of Whom the Prophets Wrote. John 1:43-46.
S.—The Prophecy of Immanuel. Isa. 7:10-14.
S.—The Birth of Jesus Announced. Luke 1:26-38.

2. December 11.   The Promise Affirmed

M.—Holy and Awesome Is His Name. Ps. 111:1-10.
T.—Make Known His Faithfulness. Ps. 89:1-6, 14.
W.—God's Covenant with Abraham. Gen. 17:1-8.
T.—Surely I Will Be with You. Judg. 6:12-18.
F.—Hannah's Praise for a Son. I Sam. 2:1-10.
S.—The Promised House for David. II Sam. 7:11-17.
S.—Praise from Elisabeth and Mary. Luke 1:39-56.

3. December 18.   The Forerunner of the Saviour

M.—The Priesthood of Aaron. Exod. 40:12-25.
T.—Tending the Altar of Incense. Exod. 30:1-10.
W.—The Lord's Messenger. Mal. 3:1-6.
T.—A Godly but Childless Couple. Luke 1:5-7.
F.—His Name Is John. Luke 1:57-66.
S.—The Testimony of John the Baptist. John 1:19-23.
S.—The Announcement of John's Birth. Luke 1:8-20.

4. December 25.   The Saviour's Birth (Christmas)

M.—The Prophecy of Bethlehem. Mic. 5:1-5.
T.—The Birth of Jesus. Matt. 1:18-25.
W.—The Visit of the Wise Men. Matt. 2:1-12.
T.—The Escape to Egypt. Matt. 2:13-15.
F.—Joseph and Mary's Journey to Bethlehem. Luke 2:1-4.
S.—No Room in the Inn. Luke 2:5-7.
S.—The Shepherds and the Angels. Luke 2:8-20.

5. January 1.   Praising God the Creator

M.—Praise, Worship, and Trust. Ps. 146:1-4.
T.—Our Hope Is in the Lord. Ps. 146:5-10.
W.—The Counsel of the Lord. Ps. 33:10-17.
T.—Hope in God's Mercy. Ps. 33:18-22.
F.—God's Power Seen in Creation. Rom. 1:16-20.
S.—What the Lord Requires. Mic. 6:6-8.
S.—God's Greatness and Goodness. Ps. 33:1-9.

6. January 8.   All Creation Joins in Praise

M.—Sing to the Lord. I Chron. 16:23-34.
T.—Worship the Lord. Ps. 96:7-9.
W.—Justice Will Be Established. Isa. 42:1-4.
T.—Salvation to the Ends of the Earth. Isa. 49:1-7.
F.—Gentiles Will Trust in Him. Rom. 15:7-13.
S.—Worthy Is the Lamb. Rev. 5:11-14.
S.—The Lord Reigns Supreme. Ps. 96:1-6, 10-13.

7. January 15.   Praise God the Provider

M.—Blessing in All Our Increase. Deut. 16:13-15.
T.—The Hope of All the Earth. Ps. 65:3-8.
W.—Come See the Works of God. Ps. 66:1-5.
T.—Come Hear What He Has Done. Ps. 66:6-16.

F.—All Flesh Will Worship. Isa. 66:18-23.
S.—Sharing All Things in Common. Acts 2:37-47.
S.—The Lord's Abundant Blessings. Ps. 65:1-2, 9-13.

8. January 22.   Praise for the Creator's Wisdom

M.—God Laid the Earth's Foundations. Ps. 104:5-9.
T.—God Gives Drink to the Earth. Ps. 104:10-18.
W.—God Set the Times and Seasons. Ps. 104:19-23.
T.—God Will Rejoice in His Works. Ps. 104:31-35.
F.—God Crowned Man with Honor. Ps. 8:1-9.
S.—Trust God to Provide. Matt. 6:25-34.
S.—In Wisdom He Has Made Them All. Ps. 104:1-4, 24-30.

9. January 29.   All Creation Praises the Lord

M.—Praise the Lord! Ps. 150:1-6.
T.—The Morning Stars Sang Together. Job 38:1-7.
W.—Wisdom Present at Creation. Prov. 8:22-31.
T.—Praise from the Mountains. Isa. 55:6-13.
F.—Remember What You Were Delivered From!
    Deut. 24:17-22.
S.—God's Gracious Ways. Ps. 145:13-21.
S.—Let All Creation Praise the Lord! Ps. 148:1-14.

10. February 5.   Heirs of the Promise

M.—In the Spirit by Faith. Gal. 3:1-5.
T.—In Abraham All Are Blessed. Gen. 22:15-18.
W.—The Promise to Abraham. Gal. 3:15-18.
T.—Baptized into One Body. I Cor. 12:12-18.
F.—Children of God by His Grace. I John 2:28—3:3.
S.—Do All in the Name of Christ. Col. 3:12-17.
S.—Heirs of God Through Christ. Gal. 3:26—4:7.

11. February 12.   Delivered from Bondage

M.—Set Free by the Truth. John 8:31-36.
T.—Walk Before Him in Truth. I Kings 2:1-4.
W.—God's Power Shown Through Weakness.
    II Cor. 12:7-10.
T.—The Cost of Discipleship. Luke 9:23-27, 57-62.
F.—New Life in the Spirit. Rom. 8:1-11.
S.—Led by the Spirit. Rom. 8:12-17.
S.—Do Not Return to Bondage! Gal. 4:8-20.

12. February 19.   Freedom in Christ

M.—The Preaching of the Cross. I Cor. 1:18-25.
T.—His Words in Your Heart. Deut. 6:4-9.
W.—You Shall Love Your Neighbor. Lev. 19:13-18.
T.—Delivered from the Law of Sin. Rom. 7:15-25.
F.—Purge Out the Old. I Cor. 5:1-2, 6-9.
S.—Walk as Children of Light. Eph. 5:1-8.
S.—Stand Fast in His Liberty. Gal. 5:1-17.

13. February 26.   Holy Living in the Spirit

M.—Walk in Newness of Life. Rom. 6:1-11.
T.—The Sower and the Seed. Luke 8:4-15.
W.—An Incorruptible Inheritance. I Pet. 1:3-9.
T.—Confession and Prayer. Jas. 5:13-20.
F.—Discipline, Repentance, Forgiveness. Matt. 18:15-20.
S.—Supporting Christ's Ministers. I Cor. 9:3-12.
S.—Walk by the Spirit. Gal. 5:18—6:10.

REVIEW

What have you learned this quarter?
Can you answer these questions?

Creation and Salvation
UNIT I: The Saviour Is Born

December 4
The Promise of a Saviour

1. What indicates the lowly status of both Nazareth and Mary?
2. Was Mary's godly character the key to God's choosing her? Explain.
3. What is meant by the title "Son of the Highest" (Luke 1:32)?
4. What were Mary's first words in response to the angel's announcement? What was her concern?
5. Why is the virginal conception of Jesus necessary doctrinally?

December 11
The Promise Affirmed

1. On what was Mary's blessedness based?
2. What do Mary's words of praise reveal about her?
3. What in Mary's words point to Jesus' deity?
4. What proves that Mary, though a godly person, was not sinless?
5. How does God demonstrate His great strength?

December 18
The Forerunner of the Saviour

1. What made burning incense in the temple the pinnacle of Zacharias's priestly work?
2. How did the angel express John's greatness? How did Jesus later reaffirm this?
3. What evidence would point to the unique ministry of John in God's plan?
4. What would John's ministry entail?
5. To what Old Testament prophet did the angel liken John? Why?

December 25
The Saviour's Birth (Christmas)

1. What did the angel say would result from the news he delivered?
2. What titles did the angel use to describe the newborn Jesus?
3. What is meant by the expression "glory to God in the highest" (Luke 2:14)?
4. To whom did the angels say that God's peace is given?
5. What did the shepherds do as soon as the angels departed?

UNIT II: All Creation Praises God

January 1
Praising God the Creator

1. For what purpose was Psalm 33 designed?
2. In what ways is God's faithfulness seen?
3. What attribute of God fills the whole earth? In what sense is this the case?
4. By what means did God create the universe?
5. What revelation has God given to all humanity?

January 8
All Creation Joins in Praise

1. What is God's glory, and how do we declare His glory among the peoples of the world?
2. Why is the Lord to be greatly praised (Ps. 96:4)?
3. In what sense are all the "gods" of the nations idols?

4. How is the greatness of God contrasted with the gods of the nations?

5. What will characterize the rule of Christ on the earth?

January 15

Praise God the Provider

1. In what sense can worship be silent?

2. What does the Bible mean when it says God hears our prayers?

3. What promise did God give to Israel regarding rainfall?

4. What does the term "fatness" often signify in the Bible?

January 22

Praise for the Creator's Wisdom

1. How does Psalm 104 relate to Genesis 1?

2. What royal imagery is used to picture the greatness of God?

3. What is the one man-made thing the psalmist mentioned? Why did he do so?

4. How does the providence of God relate to our lives?

January 29

All Creation Praises the Lord

1. Why were the sun, the moon, and the stars created?

2. What is personification? How is it used in Psalm 148?

3. How do natural forces on the earth fulfill the word of the Lord (vs. 8)?

4. What earthly leaders did the psalmist list as owing praise to the Lord?

UNIT III: The Church Is Born

February 5

Heirs of the Promise

1. What is justification? How is it received?

2. What analogy did Paul use to express the believer's relationship to the law?

3. What was the bondage under which Jewish believers had been held?

4. In what sense is the law a slave-master?

February 12

Delivered from Bondage

1. In what way did the Galatians show a desire to again "be in bondage" (Gal. 4:9)?

2. What was wrong with observing Jewish religious celebrations?

3. What fear did Paul have with regard to the Galatians?

4. How did the motives of Paul and the Judaizers differ?

February 19

Freedom in Christ

1. On what did Paul base his call to the Galatians to stand fast in liberty?

2. Why did Paul warn Gentile believers against submitting to circumcision?

3. What does it mean to be "fallen from grace" (Gal. 5:4)?

4. What danger did Paul express through the proverb about leaven?

February 26

Holy Living in the Spirit

1. How is the fruit of the Spirit produced in Christians?

2. What is our duty to Christians "overtaken in a fault" (Gal. 6:1)?

3. How does bearing our own burden (vs. 5) differ from bearing one another's burdens (vs. 2)?

4. What is our obligation to those who teach us the Word?